ROUTLEDGE LIBRARY EDITIONS: TRANSPORT ECONOMICS

Volume 19

TRAFFIC AND TRANSPORT

TRAFFIC AND TRANSPORT

An Economic History of Pickfords

GERARD L. TURNBULL

Routledge
Taylor & Francis Group

LONDON AND NEW YORK

First published in 1979 by George Allen & Unwin Ltd

This edition first published in 2017
by Routledge
2 Park Square, Milton Park, Abingdon, Oxon OX14 4RN

and by Routledge
711 Third Avenue, New York, NY 10017

Routledge is an imprint of the Taylor & Francis Group, an informa business

British Library Cataloguing in Publication Data
A catalogue record for this book is available from the British Library

ISBN: 978-0-415-78484-9 (Set)
ISBN: 978-1-315-20175-7 (Set) (ebk)
ISBN: 978-1-138-63791-7 (Volume 19) (hbk)
ISBN: 978-1-138-63794-8 (Volume 19) (pbk)

Publisher's Note
The publisher has gone to great lengths to ensure the quality of this reprint but points out that some imperfections in the original copies may be apparent.

Disclaimer
The publisher has made every effort to trace copyright holders and would welcome correspondence from those they have been unable to trace.

Traffic and Transport

An Economic History of Pickfords

GERARD L. TURNBULL

London
GEORGE ALLEN & UNWIN
Boston   Sydney

First published in 1979

This book is copyright under the Berne Convention. All
rights are reserved. Apart from any fair dealing for the
purpose of private study, research, criticism or review, as
permitted under the Copyright Act, 1956, no part of this
publication may be reproduced, stored in a retrieval system,
or transmitted, in any form or by any means, electronic,
electrical, chemical, mechanical, optical, photocopying,
recording or otherwise, without the prior permission of the
copyright owner. Enquiries should be sent to the publishers
at the undermentioned address:

GEORGE ALLEN & UNWIN LTD
40 Museum Street, London WC1A 1LU

© Gerard L. Turnbull, 1979

British Library Cataloguing in Publication Data

Turnbull, Gerard L
   Traffic and transport.
   1. Transportation – Great Britain – History
   380.5'0941   HE243   79–40678

   ISBN 0–04–300080–0

Typeset in 10 on 11 point Plantin by Bedford Typesetters Limited
and printed in Great Britain
by Unwin Brothers Ltd, Old Woking, Surrey

Acknowledgments

It is a pleasure to record my thanks to the numerous people whose help and encouragement have been important to me. Special thanks go to Harold Elliott, George Skelton and Steve Dunford, all formerly of Pickfords, who encouraged my work and allowed me free access to the records remaining with the firm. My colleagues Forrest Capie, John Chartres, Terence Gourvish and George Rainnie contributed positive criticism of ideas and earlier drafts, which reduced the ambiguities and confusions; those remaining are my own. My thanks are due to the editor of the *Railway Gazette* for permission to use the chart which appears as Figure 7. Finally, I also owe special thanks to Audrey Speak for prompt and accurate typing, and my wife Susan for help and support along the way.

Contents

List of Tables, Figures and Maps

*To
My Mother
and the Memory of
My Father*

Introduction

Most people in Britain must have heard of Pickfords. For some it will
be no more than as a name, perhaps that of the owners of the familiar
red and blue furniture vans which frequent our towns and highways.
Others will have employed the firm to move house, or enjoyed a holiday
organised by its travel service. Many motorists will associate the name
with long, frustrating crawls behind one of the firm's heavy haulage
units. Today Pickfords' operations cover the length and breadth of the
country. Its offices and depositories are to be found in all major towns.
Its name is widely known and instantly recognised.

Pickfords has been part of the inland transport industry for a long
time. For that reason its name is equally familiar to those interested in
the history of transport. Accounts of road transport in the eighteenth
century, canals and railways in the nineteenth and motor transport in
the present century invariably include at some stage reference to the
activities of Pickfords. Its history is part and parcel of the development
of inland transport. For the last 180 years Pickfords has been a prominent, and at times dominant, member of the industry, while its
origins stretch a good way further back. The firm's wagons were
travelling the road between London and Manchester before Richard
Arkwright had perfected the art of mechanised spinning or James Watt
had patented the separate condenser. It is indeed the only transport
firm to have survived from pre-industrial days, a uniqueness which
invites interest and explanation.

No firm can survive for long unless it responds to changing conditions and probably also enjoys a few slices of luck. This has been as
true in transport during the last couple of centuries as in any other
industry. It has been transformed several times, by canals, by railways
and by motors. On each occasion new interests and new firms have
arisen to challenge those already in the field. Sometimes it has been
possible for existing firms to take up the new mode of transport, but
at other times not. From the 1780s road haulage firms could freely
expand into canal conveyance if they so chose, but in the next century
none could contemplate building its own railway in order to preserve
its trade. To have survived several fundamental breaks in the technology
of transport is not the least of Pickfords' achievements.

A study of Pickfords has, therefore, a special contribution to make.
As an old established firm it has a certain claim to attention. Its particular value, however, is that an examination of how Pickfords coped,

by design or accident, with successive revolutions in the technology of transport provides revealing insights into a large area of the history of inland transport.

I

The Background:
The Road Carrying Trade

'The carriage of goods in England,' said Defoe, 'is chiefly managed by horses and waggons; the number of which is not to be guessed at, and is equal, in my opinion, to the whole trade of some nations . . . Our river navigation is not to be named for carriage, with the vast bulk by pack-horse, and by waggons.'[1] Defoe's view of the position of land carriage in the transport system of the early eighteenth century contrasts sharply with that which has been taken by many historians. Until recently the inland trade has been generally regarded as being of only minor importance. Consequently the likely volume of traffic was presumed to have been small, and also any traffic which proceeded more than a few miles invariably to have travelled by water. River and coastal shipping were taken to have formed the heart of the country's transport system. Because of its great expense, road transport was assumed to have been very constrained, confined to a limited range of valuable goods which could absorb the high cost of carriage. To prefer Defoe's opinion and to argue that by his time of writing, the 1720s, there already existed an extensive and well-organised road haulage industry which covered the whole country and catered for a very varied and considerable volume of traffic is directly to challenge entrenched beliefs.[2]

The nature of the conflict is clear. If the received wisdom were correct a road carrying business like that operated by James Pickford in the mid-eighteenth century could not have existed. The fact that it did and that there were plenty of other similar enterprises throughout the country fundamentally weakens the traditional view. The mistake was made not because the existence of such people was deliberately ignored, but rather because historians allowed themselves to be misled by the constant flow of complaints by contemporaries about the state of the country's roads. Travellers like Arthur Young castigated certain stretches of road in highly quotable prose, and what he damned in particular was interpreted as the reality in general by the clinching argument that the record of turnpike trusts returning to Parliament for extensions of their powers was an unbroken catalogue of admitted failure to carry out their appointed task. Roads were considered to have been in such an appalling state that anything but the most limited and primitive provision of road transport was inconceivable. Some writers took a different line and indeed demonstrated the pitfalls of the literary evidence, but little notice was taken of them.[3]

Recent research has vindicated this minority view.[4] The Webbs' belief, which so many writers slavishly followed, that turnpikes were 'scattered' and 'unconnected', and of little importance until towards the end of the eighteenth century, has been entirely discredited. In fact there was a discernible, logical pattern to their development from the start, one which closely followed the transport needs of the contemporary economy. Turnpikes were set up because a growing volume of traffic was causing such destruction to the roads that the normal means of repair could no longer cope. Historians have been right to emphasise the poor condition of England's roads in the eighteenth century and before; the error was to miss the cause and therefore draw the wrong inference. Improvement was undoubtedly slow. Complaints continued, as expenditure on road renewal inevitably lagged behind the pressure of traffic. But the central assumption from which the neglect of road transport has stemmed was clearly wrong.

Having cleared that obstacle it is possible to concentrate on the road transport industry itself. The typical supplier of road transport services was the common carrier. He, too, has been neglected, partly because of preconceived ideas, perhaps more because the available records from which his trade might be studied are very sparse indeed. He appears as an incidental figure in many places, but there is little of substance. However, as the road carrying trade forms the background to this study it is necessary to try and pull the threads together.

GROWTH AND ORGANISATION OF THE ROAD CARRYING TRADE

It is worth recalling that cartage services were part of the manorial obligations. The impression frequently given that there was little or no demand for road transport from the mediaeval economy and society is certainly misleading. The manorial surplus had to be gathered in. The Crown, the courts, barons, bishops and scholars all had occasion to travel and transport their households with them. Baggage trains accompanied civil as well as war-time manoeuvres.[5] More important, the growth of towns, trade and industry depended on adequate transport. Imported produce and industrial raw materials had to be distributed inland, the output of the wool and woollen cloth industries conveyed to London and other ports, towns and cities supplied with their various needs. Most traffic went by water. Of that which passed by road, the majority was local, conveyed by whatever horses and carts were available. But where road traffic was sufficiently extensive and drawn from sufficiently long distances, more than casual provision was required. It was here that the full-time professionals, the common carriers, appeared.

There were several strands to the development of the road carrying trade, and reference to Thomas Censor of Cat Street, Oxford, so far the first man to have been identified as a common carrier, illustrates one of them. In the 1390s Censor provided regular carriage between Oxford and London, Winchester and Newcastle.[6] No doubt it was his good fortune to be mentioned in records which have happened to survive, but the university colleges of Oxford and Cambridge, drawing scholars, pupils and supplies from all over the country, were in any case likely to require regular provision of transport services.

Other carriers served industry and trade. Brief case studies of the trade of Bristol and Southampton in the fifteenth century illustrate their role.[7] Both places were major centres of overseas trade, drawing exportable goods from their hinterland and distributing imports through it. Both were also in touch, by road, with places far distant. In the 1440s Southampton exchanged traffic with London, chiefly by water, but goods were also regularly dispatched by road. Traffic also went by road to Bristol, Gloucester and Coventry, and even as far north as Kendal. Indeed later on in the century a well-organised trade in cloth existed between Kendal and Southampton, despite the enormous distance, as packhorse men travelled south with the famous 'Kendal greens' for export. In like fashion Bristol supported a steady flow of road traffic with London and also drew in supplies from Buckingham, Coventry and Shrewsbury. By the end of the fifteenth century, the economy was sufficiently diverse and industry sufficiently dispersed for the exchange of products across long distances to be a normal occurrence. Perhaps Bristol and Southampton, among the leading ports after London, might be regarded as having been in the way of special cases, but the frequent testamentary bequests during that period for the upkeep of highways and bridges is clear evidence of the importance attached to good roads by the merchant community.[8]

The strongest flows of road traffic from Bristol and Southampton were to London. This was likely to have been the case generally. As capital city and principal port, London dominated the rest of the country. It was the largest centre of population, income and consumption and to it were sucked in great quantities of foodstuffs and manufactures from all parts. As its influence strengthened and widened from the mid-sixteenth century, the movement of goods to London became the most prominent flow of traffic in the country.[9] Again much went by water, but a lot arrived by land, borne by carriers' wagons and horses. The London carrier became an increasingly familiar sight travelling the

country's roads. His services had become sufficiently important by the
early seventeenth century for John Taylor, the so-called water poet, to
draw up a guide to them. His *Carriers Cosmographie*, published in 1637,
contains the first systematic survey of road carrying and provides the
starting point for any close examination of the trade.

It is a deceptively simple source. Taylor lists the places served by the
carriers, the inns they used, the frequency of service and sometimes the
carrier's name. The entry for Gloucester, for example, reads as follows:

> The Carriers of Glocester doe come to the Saracens head without
> Newgate, on fridaies. The Carriers of Gloster doe lodge at the
> Saracens head in carter lane, they come on fridaies. Clothiers doe
> come every weeke out of divers parts of Glocestershire to the
> Saracens head in friday street. The Waines or Waggons doe come
> every weeke from sundry places in Glocestershire, and are to bee
> had at the Swan neere holborne Bridge. There are Carriers of some
> places in Glocestershire that doe lodge at the mer-maide in Carterlane.

How is such evidence to be employed? In particular can it be pressed,
though doubtless Taylor would have been horrified at the prospect,
to yield some sort of statistic which might be used to measure the
dimensions of the trade? Various approaches have been tried. Some
have counted the number of places or number of carriers mentioned,
but the most successful is that which attempts to estimate the level of
services implicit in the data.[10] By plotting the carrier routes and their
operators, it is possible to eliminate duplicate entries and so isolate
place-specific services. The quoted example for Gloucester, a count of
one if place names were recorded, yields a total of four carrier services
per week to the city and the county, five if the clothiers are included.
Should any of these appear to be also recorded for some intermediate
place they could not, of course, be included again. Treating all the
entries in this way it is possible to build up a cumulative measure for
the whole London-based trade and ultimately, by analysing successive
similar lists, an index of the growth of the trade over time.

In 1637 there were about 270 road carrier services per week from
London. The majority, about 55 per cent, were concentrated within
the counties ringing London, but others penetrated far from the
capital. Only seven counties, Cornwall, Cumberland, Durham, Middlesex, Northumberland, Rutland and Westmorland, were deficient in
recorded carrier services, but of these both Middlesex and Rutland
were crossed by carriers to other counties. Middlesex was in any case
well enough provided for by water. The subsequent trend of services
is reasonably clear, at least in outline. The output of services in the
London trade had more than doubled by the beginning of the eighteenth
century and more than doubled again by the early years of the nine-

teenth.[11] It broadly kept in step with the expansion of the economy, but tended to run ahead when the outbreak of war threatened coastal shipping and drove traffic inland for security. The construction of canals weakened this influence, but the vigorous expansion of the economy from the last couple of decades of the eighteenth century combined with the great duration of the wars against France enabled the trade to hold its place. By then, of course, the arms of the London carrying trade reached out to all parts of the country.

The London carriers took the limelight, but beneath them was a supporting cast of local and provincial carriers. Taylor had indicated that the services he described rested on similar operators for local deliveries but did not spell out any of the details. It becomes possible to do this only from about the mid-eighteenth century with the publication of local newspapers and directories. Carriers frequently advertised their services in the columns of the provincial press and compilers of directories usually included as comprehensive a list as they could obtain of the local carrier services. These sources reveal a fuller picture of the carrying trade. The London carriers still emerge as the most important single group but their share of total services in any one place was quite small, rarely more than 10 per cent. Most services were local, terminating within a radius of 25 to 30 miles, while a smaller group catered for more distant traffic, to major provincial centres. The whole trade, therefore, fell into a broadly threefold structure of London, or national, provincial and local layers of carrier services.[12]

Did these three groups remain distinct or did they link up to form a recognisably integrated transport system? If so, how? And how did a potential customer with a parcel to send actually proceed? Carriers were generally identified with particular routes and particular inns. As in the coaching trade, road goods transport was organised in close association with inns and innkeepers. Inns provided feed and stabling for the horses, a place to park the wagon while loading and unloading, even a warehouse in the inn courtyard in which to store goods; the innkeeper provided information about the carrier's movements, kept an eye on parcels left for the carrier to collect and an account of payments made, and performed various other duties. A visit to the carrying inns would, therefore, elicit the required information as to the appropriate carrier to employ and his day of departure. In the provinces several inns might have had to be visited before the right one was found but in London the carrying inns were already highly specialised by the early eighteenth century. Carriers from a particular region tended to patronise the same group of inns, usually located closely together, say, in the Strand or Holborn or Cheapside, so that in the absence of a carrier guide, information about particular services could be quickly obtained by a visit to the appropriate part of the city.[13]

Inns were also the points of contact between carriers, the places at which traffic was exchanged. This was where the different groups of carrier services came together. London carriers stopped off at various inns on their journey and there picked up traffic brought in from outlying districts, or from provincial routes. Northampton was a frequent point of interchange for traffic directed to scholars at Oxford and brought south by the Kendal carriers to London. Provincial and local services tended to be more detached, but there was always a handful of carriers whose services tied the pieces together. In the 1750s the Wigan-based carrier Ralph Jolly travelled between Liverpool and Leeds, and at the latter place handed goods on to the York carriers. James Lea, on the other hand, travelled only between Liverpool and Warrington, but at Warrington he exchanged traffic with a number of carriers from other parts of Cheshire, Lancashire, Yorkshire and the midlands.[14] The same pattern was repeated in all major provincial centres. As a result traffic could be passed on, stage by stage, from village to London carrier or through the provincial system. A parcel from a Devonshire village, say, for Newcastle-upon-Tyne might be taken to Exeter and either sent on in several stages by way of Bristol, Birmingham and Leeds, or, probably more likely, be conveyed in two stages by London carriers. If any obstacle interposed, it would be one of price rather than distance.

There is no doubt that there was by the mid-eighteenth century a well-organised and effective network of carrier services. Of course traffic went astray sometimes, as it still does. And bad weather interfered with advertised service schedules, especially in winter, again as it still does. But, remembering what happens when a touch of frost jams a few railway points or the occasional bizarre adventures of airline baggage, neither of these should be exaggerated. Business correspondence of the mid- and later eighteenth century make it quite clear that the belief that road transport at the time was at best precarious and gave up entirely in winter is misconceived.[15] Journeys took longer in winter and prices were increased, but the carrier's wagons kept moving. His service was not cheap, nor was it swift, even by the so-called 'flying' wagons, but it could be relied on. The carrying system rested on two great strengths, its regularity and the fact that it could reach into most parts of the country.

Any town or village could, therefore, 'plug into' the nationwide carrier network, although not all local connections were necessarily made exclusively by carriers. Plenty of other traders had reason to own horses and carts and in addition to supplying their own needs did not pass up the chance of earning some extra income by engaging in a bit of private carriage on the side. Nor was such activity confined to purely local traffic. In the early eighteenth century some Liverpool cheese merchants took their produce to London by wagon expecting to be able to offset part of the cost by bringing back articles for sale at Chester Fair,[16] and it was common for farmers at slack seasons to invade the London routes even over quite long distances from the capital. These all had a part to play in the supply of road transport services, but they did not diminish the carrier's position. They lacked the professional's skilled expertise, a fact recognised by Lord Fitzwilliam writing from London to his agent in Norfolk. 'If I had goods ready to send downe,' he wrote, 'I should chuse rather to send them by the Carrier, than any Country Waggon, for they know how to packe up Goods safe to deliver them carefully, than any country man can.'[17]

Apart from the skills and experience of the professional, what distinguished the carrier from those who engaged casually in the supply of road transport services? In many cases the answer would probably be, not very much. The majority of carriers travelled no more than 20 to 30 miles, roughly a day's journey. With no more than a single wagon and team of horses and a minimum of organisation, the carrier was in business. He set off from his inn one day, stayed overnight at another inn at his destination, and returned the following day. He needed some capital, for wagons and horses were not cheap, but no fixed premises and no assistance beyond the usual services of an innkeeper. This applied as much to the majority of London carriers as to local carriers in the provinces. Although the character of the London trade was far more significant, many London carriers travelled no greater distances. Their scale and basis of operations were, therefore, much the same. Abraham Voll, a Colchester-to-London carrier in the early eighteenth century, drove his own wagon and travelled a round trip to and from London every two days. His personal wealth at his death, other than his wagon and horses, was only £120. Although not many such men have been identified, he was probably reasonably typical of this category of London carrier, ranked, in social status, alongside the artisan or husbandman.[18]

The major provincial carriers to London were in a separate class altogether. In carrying, scale of organisation and capital needs were determined by two factors, distance and frequency of service. The greater the distance, the more wagons were required to maintain a given level of service. Over distances of 100 miles or more, several wagons were required to provide, say, a weekly service. To set up such a service was, therefore, a lot more costly than for short-haul routes, and, of course, potentially raised much greater difficulties of control and organisation. One solution, which preserved the small-scale operations typical of most carriers, was for several individuals, each of whom worked his own wagon, to co-ordinate their activities so that together they provided a more regular and more frequent service than each could have done alone. It follows that when an individual carrier, or a couple in partnership, ran an equivalent provincial service, owning and operating several wagons and employing men to work them, these were considerably larger business concerns. The men behind such enterprises, therefore, and there were quite a lot of them, rank as the foremost members of the carrying trade, to be compared in the social hierarchy with middle-order urban tradesmen or landlords of the larger provincial inns.[19]

Such men were also marked out by the physical size of the stock they employed. Their horses were bigger and stronger than ordinary farm carthorses, able to haul much heavier loads than those occasional interlopers. Their wagons, too, were heftier and more capacious, even before the broad-wheel wagon was adopted by the carriers as their standard vehicle. Contemporary portrayals of carriers' wagons leave an impression of vast, lumbering objects, creaking under the strain of immense loads. The stratagem of Abraham Walker of Leeds may serve as an illustration. He was offered a haystack containing eight common cart-loads at a knock-down price of £2 provided that he removed it immediately and employed no more than three horses in doing so. If he could not meet these terms, the price would be £20. Walker confounded his challenger, and won the bargain, by calling in the assistance of the London carrier Jackson, three of whose horses harnessed to a broad-wheel wagon easily dealt with the load, 'tho it seemed like a moving Mountain'. Walker thus outwitted 'the Knowing Ones, who had Bet Two to One against him'.[20]

Presumably the resources needed by the leading provincial carriers were somewhat larger than those of their lesser colleagues, but by how much is not clear. William Bass, later of brewing fame, is said to have got his start as a carrier between Derby and London on the strength of a £500 lottery prize. Another carrier, 'poor Mr. Tooley', managed to lose his fortune of £800, being driven into bankruptcy by a more wealthy carrier. These were substantial sums of money; were they of the scale necessary in order to enter the carrying trade? The evidence is so slender it is difficult to be sure. John Lowden left £60 in his will, dated November 1618, to assist the six poorest carriers between Kendal and Wakefield, and London, provided none were 'Lancashire men', but how the gesture is to be interpreted is far from clear.[21] The high entry and death rate of carrying firms implies that capital was not a prohibitive obstacle, but clearly the majority who tried to break into the trade shared Tooley's fate. It seems, though, that the successful provincial carriers could be quite wealthy men.

CONTROL AND REGULATION

The title 'common carrier' denoted a particular status in law.[22] Carriers were included among the so-called common trades, in which the condition of accepting the custom of all-comers was obligatory. The classification was important. Casual or private carriers were left free to set their own terms. The common carriers were bound by strict requirements. All goods offered for towns to which they professed to carry had to be conveyed, and at 'reasonable' rates. They were fully liable in respect of damage or loss, including theft. The only admissible exceptions were acts either of God or of the king's enemies. They were, moreover, denied the normal protection of the law: in any dispute, the carrier was guilty until he proved his innocence. Carriers tried to limit their burden by demanding special rates for valuable items, but customers preferred to hide their valuables in barrels of soap or trunks of clothing in the sure knowledge that should they disappear the carrier had to pay up even though he had known nothing about them. Why such severe obligations were imposed is not really clear. The usual explanation, that otherwise customers would lack the confidence to entrust their goods to the carriers and that ultimately the country's commerce would be threatened, is not very convincing.

The carrier had, indeed, good cause to cast a wary eye at the civil authorities, several of whom sought him out for attention or snared him when looking for poachers elsewhere. All the central aspects of his business, the price he charged, the amount he carried, the vehicle and number of horses he employed, came in for some degree of regulation over and above that imposed by the law of common trades.

Control of the carrier started at the local level. Whoever possessed the crucial transport link with London enjoyed a position of considerable potential power and to protect itself from exploitation the merchant community of several towns treated the office as a regulated monopoly. The carriership of Southampton was awarded in 1608 to John Broadwaye on payment of an entry fine of £10, to be renewed each year, and a promise that any adjustment to his price had to be discussed with and confirmed by the burgesses.[23] They were expressing in practice, in other words, the obligation to carry at 'reasonable rates', thus attaching social constraints to the London carrier's market power. When at the end of the seventeenth century the Justices of the Peace were instructed[24] to settle each year appropriate rates of carriage to London and the major towns in their areas they were only carrying out at a higher level of authority a degree of price control which had long been practised locally. They were not asked, however, to exercise any control over the London carrier's movements which the local authorities had done from time to time, especially to prevent the introduction of plague from the capital.

However, the most pervasive and injurious form of regulation arose out of the flow of legislation from the late seventeenth century which sought to preserve the nation's highways by controlling the traffic which passed over them. The carriers' complaint was not so much against the imposition of maximum weights which they could load on their wagons but about the confused manner in which this objective was approached. To some extent the carriers brought trouble on their own heads since they were adept at devising means of frustrating the intentions of the legislature. In consequence, although at times actual weight limits were imposed, the carriers' tactics resulted in more indirect means of control being adopted. And added to this was a further layer of confusion arising from contrary views of how the basic objective of road preservation should be tackled. As a result just about every conceivable device was tried – the number of horses allowed and their position in the draught, the width of wheels, the alignment of front and rear wheels, flat or rounded rims, the thickness of tyres and the shape of nails by which they were to be fixed to the wheel; followed later by the chopping and changing as to whether broad-wheel wagons should pay toll or not. The upshot was a situation of sheer confusion for those expected to implement Parliament's latest shift of tactics.

But one group gained from the ill wind, the self-appointed posse of informers on which the policing of the legislation rested.[25] They declared open season on carriers confident that, as one of the more notorious of the profession claimed, it was virtually impossible for a wagoner to travel the road without breaking some law. Some read the small print of the Statutes carefully. One Act, 5 Geo. 1, c.12, required tyres to be no less than $2\frac{1}{2}$ inches 'when worn'. Did this refer to a new tyre, as the carriers argued, or a worn-out tyre? Informers, supported by the courts, decided the latter interpretation was the correct one, and promptly reached for their calipers. The carrier Thomas Filkin complained bitterly of having to pay £20 to redeem three horses seized by an informer because just one wheel, the rear nearside wheel which took the heaviest pounding, had been found deficient, though it 'wanted scarce the breadth of a barley-corn of its full breadth'. Others ignored the law entirely and openly engaged in a straightforward protection racket. The two leading gangsters, Richard Feilder and John Littlehale, behaved in true mobster fashion, one taking the western and the other the northern road into London and, under the guise of deputy surveyors of the highways, invited 'contribution money' from the passing carriers to purchase freedom from harassment. Littlehale was twice ordered to be arrested by investigating committees of the House of Commons, but apparently on both occasions he disappeared before the Serjeant-at-Arms caught up with him.

On other occasions carriers were innocent victims, or so they claimed, of regulations aimed at other targets. Attempts by aulnagers to insist on their rights of search and fine often resulted in raids on carriers' wagons in the belief that merchants with whom they were in conflict were trying to sneak out unstamped cloth in this way.[26] And then there were the commissioners to prevent the export of wool. To stop the illegal export of wool, and hence to protect the native woollen cloth industry, the movement of wool was prohibited during the hours of darkness, and officials were appointed to police the ban. Carriers delayed by a breakdown and getting home after dark were liable to have any wool they were carrying seized, or again simply invited to buy protection from such seizures.[27] Confused by Parliament, harassed by informers and robbed by footpads, it is not surprising that carriers showed a marked tendency to combination between themselves, a reaction as much of self-defence as the pursuit of narrow self-interest of which they were frequently accused.

THE CARRIERS' ROLE

Finally, where did the carrier fit into the contemporary transport scene? Who bought his services and what sort of traffic did he typically convey? Only a brief sketch can be given here, sufficient to place the carrier in his proper setting, the wider context of road transport being discussed more fully below (Chapter 4). For the immediate purpose carrier services may be categorised as being of two main kinds, as a support to passenger travel or as the chosen means of conveyance for a wide range of traffic – agricultural, industrial and personal.

The carrier's wagon was the first step up in convenience from walking, although Smollett's account of Roderick Random's journey from Newcastle to London by this means makes it plain that the degree of comfort provided was pretty limited.[28] Passengers had to find what vantage point they could among the bales and boxes and otherwise generally fend for themselves. Travellers more frequently employed the carrier's wagon to carry their heavy baggage while they themselves travelled by coach or horseback. Lord Irwin and family, for example, journeyed from Leeds to London in November 1740 in their private carriage, while the luggage and some of the servants were dispatched on a wagon specially hired from one of the local carriers.[29] Some carriers would also perform a few favours, take a riding horse down for someone returning from London or keep an avuncular eye on a young gent going off to a fashionable school or university.

After London, the universities of Oxford and Cambridge were probably the most frequented centres of travel, requiring special provision and a special quality of service. University carriers in fact formed a distinct branch of the trade. In Oxford they were official appointees (*tabellarii*), and received a monopoly to and from the districts for which they were licensed. The first recorded appointment, in 1553, was that of Robert Towe, as carrier to London. By the 1640s quite a number of the counties of England were similarly provided, especially those to the west and south-west, but also the counties of Lincoln, Rutland, Nottingham and Leicester, and the distant counties of Cumberland and Westmorland.[30] The sons of Daniel Fleming of Rydal Hall, near Kendal, were for many years shepherded to Queens College, Oxford, by successive members of a family of university carriers by the name of Burnyeats. They carried the boys' trunks and boxes of books, and on their regular subsequent visits brought money from their father and a constant flow of letters in each direction. This particular relationship became very close. They were sometimes referred to as 'the carrier', or 'Burnyeats', but more frequently as Peter, Richard or Tom and at times by such fancy titles as 'the trusty Trojan', 'our Cumberland and Westmorland Envoy', or 'His Excellency the Northern Ambassador'.[31] These suggest a degree of familiarity well beyond that of just carrier and customer.

Other carriers provided a continuing, personalised service to a certain clientele, usually customers who could afford to indulge fairly expensive tastes in London and have their purchases brought to them. A second category of goods which the carrier's passengers clambered over included, for example, the game pies, sweetmeats, spices, clothing and a hundred other items transported by several carriers between London and Bolton for the Shuttleworth family from the 1580s to the 1620s. Here, again, the carrier became a family assistant, not just an agent of conveyance. The Purefoy family of Shalstone, near Buckingham, employed several London carriers, and had a special contract with one of them, William Eagles. He especially, but the others as well, were expected to do the family shopping in London, pay bills, arrange for the repair of clocks and rings, and get razors sharpened as well as convey goods to and fro.[32]

In the long run, however, the carrier's third role was by far his most important: the conveyance of produce and manufactures between the provinces and London, as well as to and from provincial and local markets. Again the variety of his traffic was infinite, matching that carried by coaster and recorded in the Port Books, but one commodity stands out above all – cloth. All the major textile areas sent cloth to Blackwell Hall in London, to be sold and redistributed internally and exported overseas, and although it is impossible to be exact about the proportions it is quite clear that a good deal was brought in by road, especially in the sixteenth and seventeenth centuries, partly by carriers, partly by clothiers themselves or other agents. Other goods included silks, lace, linens, stockings, light leather products and small metalware, the output, that is, of that group of light consumer goods industries which formed such a basic part of England's early industrialisation. In that phase of economic development, the carrier's wagon was of considerable importance.

The Pickfords were common carriers between Manchester and London. The foregoing sketch of the carrying trade to about the middle of the eighteenth century provides a context for their activities even before any personal details are known. The business is immediately placed in the most important segment of the carrying trade, the long-distance trade between London and a major provincial centre. Whether it ranked among the leaders would depend on whether or not it was conducted in partnership with others. It could be expected to trade from inns, transport passengers and goods, work in harmony with fellow carriers, and soon disappear into obscurity. How the business actually fared and how the inland carrying trade developed subsequently form the substance of the chapters which follow.

REFERENCES: CHAPTER I

1 D. Defoe, *The Complete English Tradesman* (1726–7; 4th edn, London: Rivington, 1738), Vol. I, pp. 339–41.
2 For the most recent interpretation see T. C. Barker and C. I. Savage, *An Economic History of Transport in Britain* (London: Hutchinson, 1974); J. A. Chartres, *Internal Trade in England 1500–1700* (London: Macmillan, 1977); T. S. Willan, *The Inland Trade. Studies in English Internal Trade in the Sixteenth and Seventeenth Centuries* (Manchester: Manchester University Press, 1976).
3 E. F. Gay, 'Arthur Young on English roads', *Quarterly Journal of Economics*, vol. XLI (1927), pp. 545–51; H. L. Beales, 'Travel and communications', in A. S. Turbeville (ed.), *Johnson's England* (Oxford: Clarendon Press, 1933), Vol. I, pp. 125–59.
4 W. Albert, *The Turnpike Road System in England 1663–1840* (Cambridge: Cambridge University Press, 1972); E. Pawson, *Transport and Economy: The Turnpike Roads of Eighteenth Century Britain* (London: Academic Press, 1977).
5 G. H. Martin, 'Road travel in the Middle Ages', *Journal of Transport History*, new series, vol. III (1976), pp. 159–78; J. F. Willard, 'The use of carts in the fourteenth century', *History*, new series, vol. XVII (1932), pp. 246–50.
6 J. E. T. Rogers, *A History of Agriculture and Prices in England* (Oxford: Clarendon Press, 1902), Vol. I, pp. 95, 660.
7 E. M. Carus Wilson, 'The overseas trade of Bristol', in E. Power and M. M. Postan (eds), *Studies in English Trade in the Fifteenth Century* (London: Routledge, 1933), pp. 183–91; O. Coleman (ed.), *The Brokage Book of Southampton, 1443–1444*, (Southampton, Southampton Records Series, 1960), Vol. I, p. xxii; B. C. Jones, 'Westmorland packhorse men in Southampton', *Transactions of the Cumberland and Westmorland Antiquarian and Archaeological Society*, new series, vol. LIX (1959), pp. 65–84.
8 B. McClenaghan, *The Springs of Lavenham and the Suffolk Cloth Trade in the XV and XVI Centuries* (Ipswich: W. E. Harrison, [1924]), pp. 46 ff.
9 F. J. Fisher, 'The development of the London food market, 1540–1640', *Economic History Review*, vol. V (1934–5), pp. 46–64. E. A. Wrigley, 'A simple model of London's importance in changing English society and economy 1650–1750', *Past and Present*, vol. 37 (1967), pp. 44–70.
10 For an analysis of the use of Taylor and similar later sources see J. A. Chartres, 'Road carrying in England in the seventeenth century: myth and reality', *Economic History Review*, 2nd series, vol. XXX (1977), pp. 73–94.

11 Combining Chartres's findings with a similar count from Critchett and Woods, *Post Office Annual Directory for 1815* (London: Maiden, 1815).

12 G. L. Turnbull, 'Provincial road carrying in England in the eighteenth century', *Journal of Transport History*, new series, vol. IV (1977), pp. 17–39. Current research by Dr Chartres and myself will provide a more extensive analysis of the growth and structure of the road carrying trade than it is possible to give here. What follows draws on that work.

13 J. A. Chartres, 'The capital's provincial eyes: London's inns at the beginning of the eighteenth century', *London Journal*, vol. III (1977), pp. 24–39.

14 *The Liverpool Memorandum Book or Gentleman's Merchant's and Tradesman's Daily Pocket Journal for 1753* (?Liverpool: Williamson, 1753).

15 J. de L. Mann (ed.), *Documents Illustrating the Wiltshire Textile Trades in the Eighteenth Century* (Wiltshire Archaeological and Natural History Society, Records Branch, vol. XIX, 1963); G. Unwin (ed.), *Samuel Oldknow and the Arkwrights* (Manchester: Manchester University Press, 1924); T. S. Willan, *An Eighteenth Century Shop-keeper: Abraham Dent of Kirkby Stephen* (Manchester, Manchester University Press, 1970); out letter books, 1754 onwards, John Wilson & Sons, linen merchants, Leeds City Archives.

16 Cholmondeley Correspondence, c.1709, Cheshire Record Office.

17 Fitzwilliam Correspondence, Fitzwilliam to Guybon, 1703, Northants. Record Office.

18 K. H. Burley, 'The economic development of Essex in the later seventeenth and early eighteenth centuries' (unpublished PhD thesis, London, 1957), pp. 189, 215–16.

19 J. A. Chartres, 'The place of inns in the commercial life of London and western England, 1660–1760' (unpublished D.Phil. thesis, Oxford, 1973).

20 *Leeds Intelligencer*, 12 August 1760.

21 H. S. Twells, 'Mr Drewry and the Derby wagons', *Derbyshire Archaeological and Natural History Society Journal*, vol. 63 (1942), p. 75; G. Eland (ed.), *The Purefoy Letters* (London: Sidgwick & Jackson, 1931), p. 290; HMC 13: 10th R IV: *Corporation of Kendal*, p. 317.

22 A. M. Milne and A. Laing, *The Obligation to Carry* (London: Institute of Transport, 1956).

23 J. W. Horrocks (ed.), *The Assembly Books of Southampton* (Southampton Record Society, 1907–24), vol. I, pp. 70, 94, 101; vol. III, pp. 35, 49, 60.

24 3 William & Mary, c. 12.

25 The following is based on *House of Commons Journal*, January–March 1695(6), vol. XI, pp. 397, 434, 511; March–May 1699, vol. XII, pp. 604, 682–3; February 1707(8), vol. XV, pp. 531, 551, 562–3; December 1719–December 1721, vol. XIX, pp. 210–11, 233, 680, 685, 689.

26 For one of many examples see H. Heaton, *The Yorkshire Woollen and Worsted Industry* (Oxford: Clarendon Press, 1920), p. 198.

27 *House of Commons Journal*, May 1701–March 1702, esp. pp. 501, 570, 703, 783–4.

28 T. Smollett, *The Adventures of Roderick Random* (1748; 1824 edn, London: Rivington).

29 Temple Newsam Collection, TN/EA 12/15, Leeds City Archives.

30 A. Clark (ed.), *Register of the University of Oxford* (Oxford Historical Society, vol. X, 1887), pp. 315–20.

31 J. R. Magrath (ed.), *The Flemings in Oxford* (Oxford Historical Society, vols XLIV, LXII, LXXIX, 1903–24). I owe this reference to Professor T. S. Willan.

32 J. Harland (ed.), *The Shuttleworth House and Farm Accounts* (Chetham Society, vols XXXV, XLI, XLIII, XLVI, 1856–8); Eland, *Purefoy Letters*.

2

The Business Established

Pickfords' origins are obscure. The earliest hard evidence is an advertisement in the *Manchester Mercury*, in August 1756, through which James Pickford, 'the London and Manchester Waggoner', advised 'all Gentlemen, Tradesmen, and Others' that he had moved the London terminus of his wagons from the Blossom's Inn, Lawrence Lane, to The Bell Inn, Wood Street. James Pickford was manifestly already in trade, but how long the business had been established is uncertain. By long tradition within the firm, it is of seventeenth-century origin. Brief accounts of Pickfords written in the early 1900s stress the seventeenth-century tradition, although the evidence alluded to in them no longer survives, and they are supported by the directors' decision, in 1908, to approve 'the idea of stating "Established 300 Years"' in some of the firm's advertisements. There is, moreover, mention of a carrier of the same name, a Will Pickford, who in about 1630 took several items for the Leghs of Lyme Hall to Oxford. Lyme Hall is not far from James Pickford's home territory, grounds, perhaps, for speculating on a family relationship. However, the certain written record now available to the historian breaks with James Pickford and that constrains the context of this study.[1]

Relatively little is known about the family who originally owned the business which still bears its name. The Pickfords were a Cheshire family, living first in Adlington, a village in the parish of Prestbury, a few miles south of Manchester, and later in Poynton, in the same parish. The name was sufficiently common in that part of north-east Cheshire, as so many gravestones in the churchyard of St Peter's, Prestbury, testify, to provide no help in identifying members of this particular family. The record scarcely extends beyond the bare statistics of births, marriages and deaths, and even some of these have to be guessed.

The personal history of James Pickford is sparse. His death in May 1768,[2] at the age of 59, is one of the few facts known about him. He must have been born in 1708/9. The christening of his eldest son

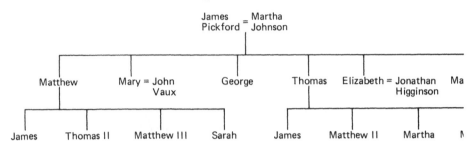

Fig. 1   *Pickford family pedigree*

Matthew in July 1741 implies he was in his early thirties when he married Martha Johnson. They had six children, three boys and three girls. Two of the boys followed their father in the family carrying business, but whether James Pickford had himself similarly inherited a carrying business is unknown. James Pickford died intestate, causing a break in the family genealogy, and although circumstantial evidence points to a certain Matthew Pickford the Elder (1652–1741), of Adlington, as being his father, it is impossible to be certain. If this supposition were correct the absence of any reference to a carrying business in this Matthew Pickford's will[3] might be grounds for believing that James Pickford was the first member of the family to enter the carrying trade, but the evidence does not supply an incontrovertible conclusion.

The few details contained in James Pickford's advertisement are sufficient for a reasonable outline of his business and mode of operations to be worked out. As a Manchester-to-London wagoner, he is immediately identified as belonging to the select band of carrying firms, those who traded between the capital and a major provincial centre. And the fact that he traded on his own rather than, as was usual, in partnership with others, is also significant. Presumably the large capital needed in this branch of the carrying trade came out of his own resources.

James Pickford's capital requirements can be looked at in physical terms first of all. His advertised service was by wagon, twice a week, Wednesdays and Saturdays, from London and Manchester. How many wagons were needed to perform it? The question can be approached in two ways. It can be demonstrated, by a process of estimation which relates frequency and distance to standardised journey times,[4] that the minimum requirement was five wagons. That minimum, however, takes no account of one important feature of James Pickford's service, that the departures were scheduled for certain days of the week. The second approach, therefore, is to consider an appropriate substitute example. Another firm, Mills & Birchenough, advertised the identical service and also published the journey times of its wagons, nine days from Manchester to London, one day less for the return, three weeks for the round trip.[5] Reconstruction of their implicit operating schedule demonstrates that a sixth vehicle was necessary in order to perform it. There is every reason to suppose that James Pickford's wagons worked to the same timetable, and even evidence to confirm it. A second advertisement a year later recorded his stock as precisely six wagons.[6]

What did this mean in money terms? Again it has to be acknowledged that the evidence is pretty slender. It is possible to draw some broad, impressionistic comparisons with agricultural equivalents, but the available price data from which to estimate capital employed are confined to a handful of figures. This is especially true for wagons. The typical vehicle employed in the long-distance carrying trade from the 1750s was the broad-wheel wagon, apparently initially adopted because of its exemption from toll on turnpike roads but retained even after that concession had been withdrawn. Its tare weight was roughly 35 hundredweight and it was mounted on wheels the rims of which measured 9 inches across – evidently something considerably more substantial than the biggest farm wagons which Arthur Young valued, in the 1760s, at about £20 each. The price of a broad-wheel wagon was quoted in 1763 at between £30 and £35. There is no way of checking this figure but it is broadly in line, allowing for changes in the price level, with the £56 asked in 1803 by John Rood of Portsmouth for his 'Hampshire Patent Waggon', a conversion kit whereby a cart could, by bonding another on to it, be converted into a wagon, and the 100 guineas quoted in 1806 by Robert Russell, the famous Exeter carrier, as the price of his extra sturdy, 2-ton wagons.[7] The data leave a lot to be desired, in quality and quantity, but taking £30 as the lower order estimate, James Pickford's six wagons would be valued at £180.

The information concerning wagon horses is rather better, at least in the sense that a little is known about the supply and quality of such horses.[8] Commentaries on the breeding of horses usually include the carrier with the London brewers and draymen as the purchasers of the largest and most powerful draught horses in the country. They were usually mature animals. Many farmers reared or bought in colts, Suffolk punches or the black carthorse breed of Yorkshire and the midlands, broke them in, hardened them slowly to the draught and then sold them off in prime condition at the age of 5 or 6. Without such careful preparation young animals were quickly destroyed by the rigours of London cartage. The carrier's wagon horse was not, therefore, any old nag, like the canal horses of later days, but a carefully finished product which commanded a good price. Quoted prices of carthorses are few, and are in any case more common for the 1790s and early 1800s, in the various county reports to the Board of Agri-

culture, than for the mid-eighteenth century. John Holt in his report
on Lancashire, the edge of Pickford country, quoted £10 as the price
of a good carthorse in 1761 and scattered prices of mature carthorses
recorded in various estate accounts suggest a similar price level in the
1750s.[9] Brewers' and carriers' wagon horses would have been more
expensive but if, to avoid overstatement, that price is adopted, the
estimated value of James Pickford's stock of fifty-four horses was £540.

At this stage in the development of the carrying trade, wagons and
horses formed the great bulk of the carrier's fixed capital. At £120–150
each, the units of capital employed in the trade, a wagon and horse
team, usually nine horses to a team, eight in draught and one resting
or ridden by the wagoner, were large. Since he employed six wagons
James Pickford's total stock, in excess of £700, was very considerable,
and an exceptionally large sum at that time for an individual to sub-
scribe. Comparison with the allied trade of urban innkeeping provides
some perspective on the scale of capital involved. In the first half of
the eighteenth century prospective innkeepers in the west of England
could expect to pay up to £300, by way of purchase price and stock in
trade, for a large urban inn. When The Spread Eagle, Salford, was put
up for sale in March 1756, just four months before James Pickford
first appears on the scene, the asking price was £600, including furniture and stock.[10] Of course, what James Pickford's real burden was
cannot be said. It depends on whether he inherited his business, set it
up from nothing, or bought second-hand one of the several carrying
businesses offered for sale at the time. But wagons had to be maintained and replaced, fresh horses bought in, wear and tear generally
made good. Horses had to be fed, wages paid, possibly claims for
expensive losses met under the obligation of unlimited liability.
Considerable working capital was therefore also required. However
much these notional estimates are scaled down to allow for the deficien-
cies of the data, it remains clear that a carrying business conducted on
the terms and scale of that operated by James Pickford is to be regarded as very substantial, ranking among the foremost of urban
trades.

How likely was James Pickford to have commanded resources of
commensurate scale? Again the financial condition of the Pickford
family can only be guessed at, but there is some evidence which
points to land holding on a significant scale. James Pickford himself
was initially designated a 'yeoman', a status which strictly required the
ownership of land, although by this time it had been stretched to
include leasehold and virtually become an alternative title to 'farmer'.[11]
But whether or not the family owned land it certainly leased, then and
subsequently, a considerable acreage. A tenancy renewed in 1788 was
for a property in Poynton, leased from Sir George Warren, which had
originally been acquired by James Pickford in 1747. The total acreage

was not given, but the terms of the contract suggest a sizeable farm. The lease of another block of land in Poynton, some 60 acres, was offered for sale at a later date by James Pickford's widow, and his younger son Thomas stated on a later occasion that in the 1770s he had 'held' a farm of 300 acres.[12] The Pickfords' family background, therefore, appears to have been that of the small farmer, as appropriate for the long-distance carrier.

James Pickford came from Adlington and presumably moved to Poynton in 1747 to take up the tenancy leased from Sir George Warren. Poynton remained the carrying business's base for many years to come. Whether the move marked an initial or merely a greater commitment to carrying is not known. James himself was still styled as yeoman or farmer in the tenancy documents, and is only referred to as a 'wagoner' at the end of his life. Farming would have provided excellent back-up facilities for a carrying business and was indeed frequently combined with it. Were James Pickford at this point dealing in more than one trade, becoming more of a specialist carrier later on, his action would have been in no way exceptional.

Poynton lies about twelve miles to the south of Manchester. Why choose a base there rather than in Manchester itself? Presumably the farmland was an attraction but, as already explained, carriers did not in fact have to have a fixed base in the terminal towns they served. Many did rent warehouse space in innyards of the town to which they carried, but it was perfectly feasible to operate without it. Turn-round times could be very short, in and out in the course of a morning. A short hop from base to terminus and back again at the commencement or the end of a trip could be easily accomplished within a day. Many carriers worked in this way. Thomas Hulse and Jonathan Higginson, partners in another Manchester-to-London carrying business, were stationed at Knutsford on an alternative road out from Manchester. Elsewhere, Jane Astlett, a wagoner between Southampton and London, worked from her stables in Alresford, a small village close to Winchester.[13] Reference to the various provincial directories of the mid- to later eighteenth century demonstrates that very many carrier services were organised from a base in a town or village along the route rather than from either of the terminal towns.

On further consideration, Poynton turns out to have been an adroit choice. It lay on the carriers' traditional route from the west midlands and the south into Manchester. Tracing the route in the reverse direction, James Pickford's wagons travelled an excellent road from Manchester to Stockport, turnpiked in 1724, and on to Bullock Smithy, the present Hazel Grove. Then instead of staying on the turnpike to Buxton, the wagons turned off through Poynton, Macclesfield and Congleton, and joined the main Holyhead and Carlisle road at Talke o' the Hill on the Cheshire–Staffordshire border. Talke, although only

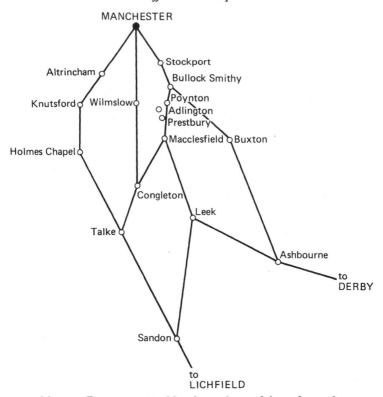

Map 1 *Entry routes to Manchester by road from the south*

a small village, was evidently an ideal stop-over for weary wagoners. Among its unusually large number of inns was The Plume of Feathers, described in the 1730s as 'a great waggoners' inn [where] I have seen above twenty teams of a night'.[14] From Talke the wagons passed through Newcastle-under-Lyme, Stone, Lichfield and Dunstable to London, travelling most of the way on turnpike roads.

Of the several southbound routes out of Manchester, that from Bullock Smithy to Talke had other merits than that of passing through Poynton. Other routes lay through Buxton or through Holmes Chapel by way of Altrincham, Knutsford and Cranage. Both had been turnpiked for all or most of the way and might on that account be expected to have been preferred routes. The Poynton road, however, had certain advantages. Its surface was perhaps not much inferior, at least in the view of those who argued that as it was 'mostly upon gravel', it could easily be kept in good repair and did not need to be turnpiked. More particularly, it was flatter than the Buxton road through the

Pennine Hills, acknowledged to be very tough on horses, and more direct than that through Knutsford. And after the road had been turnpiked,[15] for the opposition failed, Poynton's position was enhanced. The turnpike followed the old line as far as Macclesfield, but was then routed through Leek to Ashbourne and Sandon. Instead of going through Congleton and Talke, Pickfords' wagons were diverted by way of Leek and travelled on to London through Ashbourne, Derby, Loughborough, Leicester and Northampton. For as long as Pickfords

Map 2 *Pickfords' road routes between Manchester and London*

carried by road that route was maintained. The firm's wagons continued to trundle through Poynton, and could be monitored as they passed.

Some flesh can, therefore, be built on to the bare bones of James Pickford's operations as revealed in his original advertisement. A second advertisement a year later nearly brought the story to an abrupt end. In June 1757 he put his business up for sale. Why is not known, but as others also tried to sell the answer probably lay in general trading conditions. As a derived demand, transport is acutely sensitive to the health of the economy. At the national level economic conditions were in fact favourable to road haulage. The downturn caused by the outbreak of war the previous year had given way to recovery, if as yet a little uncertainly. But local circumstances were very different. In 1757 Manchester was facing the second year of severe food shortage and diminishing trade. The peak of the local depression coincided with James Pickford's attempt to sell.[16]

Either there were no buyers or James changed his mind for, whatever the reason, he carried on. However almost nothing is known about him between then and his death eleven years later. He appears in the record only twice more, as a joint signatory of two notices announcing increases in the rates of carriage to London.[17] On each occasion prices were being adjusted for increases in costs, more expensive feed, higher prices for horses, increased tolls on broad-wheel wagons. Two features of them are worth noting. First, they illustrate the carriers' tendency to adjust rates collectively. Secondly, on both occasions James Pickford's name appears at the head of the list. Is it being excessively partial to read a hint of local leadership into this? James Pickford died at Poynton on 10 May 1768, and was buried at Prestbury two days later.

He was survived by his wife Martha, and for four years the business was conducted in her name. She obviously leant heavily on the support of her eldest son Matthew, who had now joined the business, and indeed recorded in her will her thanks for 'the aid and service he has afforded in and about the said business'. There was one small but significant change during her stewardship. The use of two inns in London had led to confusion, with some customers going to the wrong inn to collect their goods. The simple expedient adopted was to concentrate both wagons at the one inn, The White Bear in Basinghall Street.[18] Martha's death ended the first phase of Pickfords' history. The firm had survived its first crisis, and been safely handed on to the next generation.

Matthew Pickford succeeded his mother in 1772 and retained control of the family concern for twenty-seven eventful years.[19] These were critical years during which the road haulage industry progressed rapidly. As investment funds poured into turnpikes, and the pressure of demand rose, the provision and quality of road transport services improved enormously. Fresh routes were opened up, additional services supplied on existing routes, speeds accelerated, improved vehicles introduced and new carrying businesses established. Conditions favoured expansion. If an existing firm had any cause for concern, it was whether it could withstand the new forces of competition which arose.

Road carrying flourished, but that does not mean that all doubts and difficulties were removed. The pressure of demand which underpinned developments in road transport also brought forward a major threat to it, in the form of canals. Some canals were already carrying traffic when Matthew Pickford took over. As yet they were confined to certain limited areas in south Lancashire and around Birmingham, but the construction of a continuous water route from Manchester through the midlands to London had been actively canvassed and a good part of it actually built. Several questions were posed. Would canal conveyance destroy road transport, especially over long distances? Would the organisation of canal services be open to or shut off from existing public carriers? And, even if they were not excluded, how would the organisation of the carrying trade be affected? It was not long before the answers were forthcoming, but in the meantime there must have been an element of uncertainty. Matthew Pickford's primary achievement was to guide the business successfully through these transitional years and in the process take it to a position of national prominence.

Matthew Pickford was 32 years of age when he took over. His record at the helm suggests a man of considerable entrepreneurial ability but, again, very little personal detail is known about him. He had joined his father in the business some time before the latter's death,[20] and the fact that he was able to assist his mother so well suggests that he was by then fairly experienced. The chances are that he had learnt the business the hard way, by travelling with the wagons on the road. At least this seems a plausible explanation of how he met his wife Hannah Taylor, who came from Talke o' the Hill, the wagoners' overnight stopping place. Moreover in addition to his own years of practical experience there were others to whom he could turn for advice. There were contacts with Joseph Hulse and Jonathan Higginson, who also engaged, as partners, in the Manchester-to-London carrying trade. Both attended his wedding in 1776. Higginson was, in fact, already his brother-in-law, married to his sister Elizabeth, and also stood sponsor at the christening of Matthew's older surviving son, Thomas. He had more than his own experience to rely on.

Like his father, Matthew Pickford was accorded a certain pride of place in the Manchester-to-London carrying trade. In the first Manchester directory, published in 1772, he was placed ahead of his six rivals, who appeared in alphabetical order, even though his business, measured by the number of wagons employed, was likely to have been no bigger than at least three of the others.[21] Perhaps he paid better rates for copy. Whatever the meaning then, Matthew subsequently conceded nothing to his competitors. He equalled and eventually exceeded all his rivals in the range and quality of his services. When others accelerated their wagons in the 1780s, halving the journey time to London, he followed suit. He matched them in frequency of service. In 1777 his services were raised from two to three per week, and by 1788 his wagons departed each day from Monday to Saturday, the equivalent of a daily service in the absence of Sunday travel. Matthew

Pickford stole a march on his competitors by taking part in the coaching trade to London, thus gaining direct access to the speediest form of transport. He began to outdistance them decisively when, from the 1780s, he turned to canal conveyance. New challengers arose in Manchester, but none managed to dislodge him.

Manchester's transport system, by road and by water, was apparently developing very rapidly in the last quarter of the eighteenth century, due largely to the city's equally rapid economic growth during those years.[22] The economic growth of Manchester and its hinterland was typified by the rise to dominance of the steam-powered cotton-spinning industry, but traditional craft industries were equally stimulated. It was accompanied by a marked extension in the specialisation of economic activities. Manchester's metropolitan role was also strengthened, as the industrialising textile towns of south Lancashire and north-east Cheshire, Bolton, Bury, Oldham, Stalybridge and Stockport, were drawn ever more firmly into its orbit. The more these towns became linked in a complex system for the manufacture and merchanting of cotton textiles, the more they depended on efficient means of transport.

For similar reasons there were strong ties with London; distance from the capital did not remove the pull of its market. The output of most specialised provincial trades which in the mid-eighteenth century attained a national sale, Lancashire calicoes, Cheshire silks, Manchester wares, was largely consigned to London, and many indeed were actively organised from there. The London warehouseman was still a prominent figure, providing credit, cash and commercial information as well as sales outlets. These influences weakened over time, but London still retained its ascendancy of the cotton product market at the end of the eighteenth century and had only recently been superseded by Liverpool as the primary port of entry for raw cotton. The organisation of banking services and the whole credit system upon which all trade depended ultimately rested upon London. Economic development in Manchester inevitably meant close trading relationships with London, which in turn could only strengthen the demand for transport services.

To indicate the main features of Manchester's economic expansion during the last twenty-five years or so of the eighteenth century is one thing, to put any measure of scale upon them quite another. Crude indicators are a trebling of the population of the townships of Manchester and Salford, compared with an increase of only one-third during the third quarter of the century, and a programme of building which about doubled the size of the town.[23] No direct measures of output exist, but some sense of the potential growth of traffic in the area can be gained from the statistic that between 1775 and 1800 Britain's import of raw cotton increased more than sevenfold, to over

50,000 million pounds weight. A good part of this total must have been consumed in the industrial region centred on Manchester. It is nor surprising, then, to find an equally rapid growth in the construction of productive capacity in the town, from only two cotton-spinning mills in the early 1780s to fifty-two at the turn of the century.[24] The assembly of raw materials and the manufacture and marketing of cotton goods needed extensive transport facilities. Economic growth and the development of transport went hand in hand, a relationship recognised by Aikin who explained the canal promotions of the 1790s from Manchester to Bolton and Bury, to Huddersfield and to Rochdale, as a consequence of 'the vast extension of the Manchester manufactures after the peace of 1783'.[25]

The provision of carrier services in Manchester in the later eighteenth century reflected the buoyancy of demand. According to the five trade directories published between 1772 and 1797 the supply of carrier services increased more than threefold. In 1772, 45 carrying firms operated a total of 101 services. There were 10 services a week to London but the majority were local, 75 per cent falling within a 35-mile radius of Manchester. Twenty-five years later the number of firms had risen to 65, and the total number of services to over 340. Although local services remained dominant the number to London had almost doubled. Much of the increase occurred in the 1790s, perhaps in part because the outbreak of war with France had driven some traffic inland, but local economic growth must have played its part.

The state of the London carrying trade was, therefore, a good deal more challenging for Matthew Pickford than it had been for his father. As his unchanged level of service would suggest, James Pickford probably faced fairly stable conditions of demand, though it bears repeating that in no circumstances was success easily achieved in the carrying trade. Matthew Pickford had to cope with more dynamic conditions, to judge when to move ahead while ensuring he was not left behind. Errors in either direction would have been equally damaging, but these he managed to avoid. He was able to judge the pace of change correctly. While raising the firm's level of service more than threefold, he achieved a larger share of the London trade. Eighteen different carrying firms traded from Manchester to London between 1750 and 1800, but few of them matched Pickfords' staying power. As firms dropped out, services came to be concentrated in fewer hands. Of six carrying firms trading to London in 1772, only two, Pickfords and Higginson, Twiss & Co. were still active twenty-five years later. Over the same period Pickfords' share of services to London rose from a fifth to a third. New firms came along, but found it hard to get established. Thomas Sleath & Co. acquired the business of Messrs Bass & Morris in 1796, and mounted a vigorous challenge. It quickly built up from two to six services per week, provided swift delivery in four days, quoted keen prices and insured with the Phoenix office for goods in transit. Two years later it had gone.[26] Amidst a shifting profession, Pickfords attained a rock-like permanence.

Extra traffic encouraged specialisation. From the later eighteenth century, carriers no longer advertise for 'passengers and goods'. Poor people could still hitch a lift on a carrier's wagon, for a small charge, but their custom was no more than incidental to the main business of goods traffic. The division of road transport into separate categories of passengers and goods, each with a distinctive pattern of organisation and development, had already progressed a long way. During the last years of the century, the major London and provincial carriers increasingly broke away from the traditional form of the trade. What had been one role among several, the conveyance of manufactured goods, now predominated and dictated the shape of future developments. One effect was to persuade some of them to extend into canal conveyance. But within road haulage itself, there was a general move out of the innyard to specialist premises close to the central business district. The industry had reached maturity and become a key element in the industrialisation of the economy.

Pickfords' history bears out these trends, but before the final break was made Matthew Pickford enjoyed a brief, if intense, flirtation with coaching. In 1775, he joined a partnership of innkeepers which ran a coach service to London. Until 1781 that was the limit of his ambition, when he launched into a vigorous programme of promotions, alone and with others. His name appeared in connection with coaches serving Bath, Birmingham, Blackpool, Edinburgh, Glasgow, Leeds, Liverpool and Preston. He left coaching almost as abruptly four years later. His only subsequent, minor contact was horsing the Royal Mail between Macclesfield and Manchester.[27] It is not clear how, if at all, this episode fitted in with Matthew Pickford's main interest in goods traffic. Perhaps it was the small parcels traffic carried by coach which appealed, or just an outlet for surplus energy. There is no point in probing further. It does, however, seem more than a coincidence that he abandoned coaching just as a new career, in canal transport, began to unfold.

Pickfords' development during the 1780s and 1790s reflected the changes in the carrying trade which were then taking place. The Manchester-to-London haul remained the primary strand of the business, but several new road services were also introduced. One, which departed from London for Manchester on four days a week, might have been an auxiliary to the daily wagon, but perhaps taking in a wider area of Derbyshire and Cheshire. A second wagon served Leek, Macclesfield and Stockport three times a week, a grouping of towns which suggests that silk was its major traffic. And later on a third vehicle was added, which served Ashbourne, Buxton and Derby,[28] again suggesting a connection with silk. As well as sharing a common industry, whose product was ideally suited to road transport, they also shared a common location in the hill country of north Derbyshire and north-east Cheshire. Pickfords had by then begun to use canals for its London traffic and they soon became the predominant mode of conveyance on that route. But there were plenty of places in the hilly north midlands, important centres of manufacturing, which were a lot more accessible by road than by water. So although in these years the focus of Pickfords' business began to switch towards canals, as the demand and supply pattern of transport services began to change, it is important to remember that there were sources and categories of traffic which road transport remained best able to exploit.

The provision of new services by road and especially by canal changed Pickfords' scale and organisation. Growth in the size of the firm can be indicated only in a very general way. It is unlikely that any increase was needed on James Pickford's initial fleet of six wagons before the late 1780s. Additional services were achieved by employing the same stock more intensively. The daily service in force from 1788, however, could not have been accomplished with less than ten wagons and most probably required twelve. Pickfords' complement of wagons and horses would at that point have doubled. The extra road services through Derbyshire commenced in the 1790s presumably required additional vehicles. And the adoption of canal conveyance demanded a fleet of boats. Ten were registered in 1795,[29] and others acquired thereafter.

Table 2.1 *Estimated Growth of Pickfords' Working Stock, 1756–1803*

Date	ROAD						CANAL
	Services per Week			*Wagons*		*Horses*	*Barges*
	Manchester to London	*Other*	*Total*	*Additional*	*Total*		
1756	2		2		6	54	
1776	3		3		6	54	
1780	4		4	2	8	72	
1788	6		6	4	12	108	
1790s	6	8	14	16	28	252	
1795							10
1802				16*	44	388	
1803					50	400	28

Source: For sources of the data see text. Total services (column 3) are converted into estimated numbers of wagons and horses (columns 5 and 6) on the basis of nine horses per wagon.
* Two were narrow-wheel wagons; the rest are taken as broad-wheel wagons.

The available scraps of data are summarised in Table 2.1 as a crude guide to the growth of the firm under the first two generations of the Pickford family. James Pickford's stock in 1756 is a known fixed point. The conversion of road services into numbers of wagons and horses is reasonable to 1788 but no more than guesswork for the 1790s. The other main fixed point is the firm's offer of 400 horses, 50 wagons and 28 boats to the government when Napoleon's invasion threatened in 1803.[30] If stock acquired by the purchase in the intervening years of a Leicester haulage firm is allowed for, the real figures and the estimated figures are not too far apart. On this basis, the physical capital employed in the business grew between four- and fivefold, and had reached a scale for Matthew Pickford to be ranked at his death, in 1799, 'one of the most extensive proprietors of the carrying business in the kingdom'.[31]

Extra stock and services were presumably necessary because the volume of traffic had increased. This, together with a greater proportion of industrial traffic, pushed the carrying trade towards the provision of more specialised facilities and individual firms towards the acquisition of self-contained premises from which they could conduct more efficiently the management of their businesses. For Pickfords, the first move in this direction came when Matthew Pickford moved his London base to The Swan with Two Necks in Lad Lane. There he stayed for almost twenty years and eventually took over the whole of its available space. The step from exclusive occupation to ownership of an inn was a small one, both in idea and in practice. When the lease of The Castle Inn, Wood Street, next door to The Swan, fell vacant in 1794, it was bought for the business by Matthew Pickford's younger brother, Thomas. Thomas Pickford took up membership of the Innholders' Company,[32] but The Castle was turned over to the needs of a carrying concern. The building was modified and on occasion extensively reconstructed, and continued to serve as Pickfords' head office in London until the lease ran out in 1918.

The chain of events in Manchester is less clear. Various inns along Market Street/Lane (now Market Street) were used as departure points. Several of them had carriers' warehouses attached which other London carriers employed, but not Pickfords. Working from Poynton nearby, it had less need. Indeed not until about 1780 was a base in Manchester engaged, a warehouse belonging to The Higher Swan in Market Street. Later, in the 1790s, premises were taken at 54 Fountain Street, in the centre of Manchester, and a small warehouse leased at Castle Quay, the terminus of the Bridgewater canal.[33]

The warehouse at Castle Quay emphasises the shift then taking place in the long-distance carrying trade, not only away from inns or transforming them into carriers' premises, but especially away from roads entirely and towards canals. Although the termini and catchment areas of Pickfords' business remained the same, the alignment of the corridors of conveyance between them was substantially changed. Traffic followed a different route, was assembled and trans-shipped in different places and consequently demanded its own complement of premises in locations removed from those dictated by road haulage. In addition to Castle Quay, therefore, Matthew Pickford leased wharf and warehouse premises at Polesworth and Coventry on the Coventry canal, at Braunston on the Oxford canal, and at Blisworth on the Grand Junction canal. Occupation of a large depot at Paddington, the London terminus of the Grand Junction extension canal, was agreed before his death. By then canals had become the dominant force shaping the development of the firm.

When Matthew Pickford died, the family business had become a substantially different concern from that which he had inherited. More capital was employed and there was a greater range of services, employing both road and canal conveyance. It was also a more complex unit. The simple structure of services from a single base in Poynton to an inn in London had been replaced by one which rested on major depots at each end and several others scattered across the country. The organisation of the business was no longer concentrated and increasingly demanded the ability to manage effectively and from a distance elements which were widely dispersed. If the condition of success had once been, as in manufacturing, access to capital and credit, it was now coming to rest on the possession of management skills.

Supervision of the firm was divided between Matthew Pickford and his younger brother Thomas, probably in partnership. While Matthew stayed in Poynton, Thomas went, after his wife's death in 1780, to look after things in London. Since, over time, the real centre of the business slowly gravitated towards London, his active interest in the firm was of some importance. It seems, however, that Thomas' heart was really in farming; he preferred hogs to horses. The wagon horses were a useful source of dung for his 500-acre farm in Market Street, Hertfordshire, but his pride and joy was his herd of 300 pigs. He was in fact a noted agriculturist. His varied farming pursuits, which also included 250 sheep, a brewery (worked in with the pigs) and an extensive area of arable land, can have left him little time for road haulage. Since he had acquired at least part of this estate by 1790, his subsequent contribution to the business could not have been very great. Indeed a long-serving employee later recalled that 'Mr Pickford from Market Street would frequently drive up, but seldom stayed long'.[34]

Had Pickfords depended on Thomas, the story must surely have been very different. Ownership, however, rested with Matthew Pickford. The limited information available identifies him as the dominant influence, although it has to be recognised that this conclusion relies more on negative than positive evidence. But some points can be made. The business was conducted in Matthew's name; all notices were issued over his signature, usually from Poynton. The decision to adopt canal conveyance seems to have been his. Certainly all negotiations with canal companies were conducted by him. What qualities he possessed can only be inferred from his record, but clearly energy and foresight were among them. His coaching career suggests a man of vigour, and he was quick to recognise the potential of canal conveyance. Beyond that he can only be judged on his performance. While rivals declined, Pickfords became a top-rank carrying firm of national reputation.

How profitable the business was is unknown. Matthew and his brother appear to have enjoyed modest wealth, but how far it was derived from the business or other sources there is no way of knowing. Thomas owned land and gained an income from farming. He was able to pay £2,400 for his estate, settle a marriage portion of £5,000 on his eldest son, and leave bequests in his will totalling £15,000.[35] There is even less detail about Matthew's financial condition, but it is unlikely to have been inferior to his brother's. One implicit sign of substance is that the family home at Poynton came to be included with other 'gentlemen's seats' in contemporary road gazetteers. And when he subscribed to John Aikin's *Description of . . . Manchester*, included among his fellow sponsors were representatives from the best local county and urban circles, Sir George Warren, Peter Drinkwater, Thomas Percival, John Gladstone and William Roscoe.[36] Matthew Pickford's career can be summarised in two words. Born a 'yeoman', he died a 'gentleman'.

REFERENCES: CHAPTER 2

1 *The Commercial Motor*, vol. 1, 16 March 1905; *The World's Carriers and Contractors Review*, vol. 1, 15 October 1904; minutes, directors' committee, 8 January 1908, PRO/BTHR Rail 1133/14; E. Legh, *The House of Lyme from its Foundation to the End of the Eighteenth Century* (London: William Heinemann, 1917), p. 130.

2 Parish Register Transcripts, EDB 172 Prestbury, Cheshire Record Office, Chester.

3 Transcript, Pickford papers KS/3/1, from the original in the Cheshire Record Office.

4 Chartres, 'Road carrying in England', pp. 84–6, for the details.

5 *Manchester Mercury*, 26 June 1759.

6 *Manchester Mercury*, 7 June 1757.

7 A. Young, *A Six Months' Tour Through the North of England*, 2nd edn (London: Strahan, Nicoll, 1771), and *A Farmer's Tour Through the East of England* (London: Strahan, Nicoll, 1771); *House of Commons Journal*, vol. XXIX, p. 519; *Annals of Agriculture*, vol. 40 (1803), p. 635; *Select Committee* (SC) *on the Use of Broad Wheels*, Parliamentary Papers (PP), 1806, vol. II, appendix 2.

8 The following is based on W. Marshall, *The Rural Economy of the Midland*

Counties, 2nd edn (London: Nicol, Robinson & Debrett, 1796), Vol. I,
pp. 99 ff., 256 ff., and *The Rural Economy of Yorkshire*, 2nd edn (London:
Nicol, Robinson & Debrett, 1796), pp. 249–50; and among Board of Agriculture reports, Murray on Warwickshire (1813), Vancouver on Cambridge-
shire (1794), Davis on Wiltshire (1794) and Billingsley on Somerset (1798).

9 J. Holt, *General View of the Agriculture of the County of Lancaster* (1795;
Newton Abbot: David & Charles, 1969), pp. 180–1; also abstracts of estates
accounts kindly made available by Dr J. Chartres.

10 Chartres, 'Place of inns', pp. 144 ff.; *Manchester Mercury*, 16 March 1756.

11 P. Laslett, *The World We Have Lost* (London: Methuen, 1965), p. 43.

12 Various leases, Pickford papers, CHP/1, 3, 5; *Annals of Agriculture*, vol. 42
(1804), p. 385.

13 *Bailey's British Directory*, 1784, Vol. 3, entry for Knutsford; J. Sadler,
Hampshire Directory, 1784 (Winchester), p. 48.

14 R. Parrott, 'An accountt who hath enjoyed the severall estates in the parish
of Audley and hamlett of Talk in the county of Stafford for 200 years last
past', *Collections for a History of Staffordshire for 1944* (1947), p. 63.

15 *House of Commons Journal*, vol. XXIX, 20 January 1762, p. 107; generally,
W. Harrison, 'The development of the turnpike system in Lancashire and
Cheshire', *Lancashire and Cheshire Antiquarian Society*, vol. 4 (1886), pp.
80–92.

16 *Manchester Mercury*, 7 June 1757; T. S. Ashton, *Economic Fluctuations in
England 1700–1800* (Oxford: Clarendon Press, 1959), pp. 20–1, 59, 172–3;
A. P. Wadsworth and J. de L. Mann, *The Cotton Trade and Industrial
Lancashire 1600–1780* (Manchester: Manchester University Press, 1965),
pp. 356–61.

17 *Manchester Mercury*, 24 September 1765, 1 December 1767.

18 *Manchester Journal*, 30 November 1771.

19 To set the context in which the firm developed some aspects which are
treated fully in subsequent chapters have to be briefly mentioned in this
section.

20 In February 1768 the manorial constables of Manchester paid him £1 3s 4d
for fetching water-buckets from London. J. P. Earwaker (ed.), *The Constables' Accounts of the Manor of Manchester, Vol. 3, 1743–1776* (Manchester:
Cornish, 1892), p. 176.

21 *Manchester Directory, 1772* (Raffald), p. 55.

22 M. M. Edwards, *The Growth of the British Cotton Trade 1780–1815* (Man-
chester: Manchester University Press, 1967), ch. 8; L. S. Marshall, *The
Development of Public Opinion in Manchester, 1780–1820* (Syracuse, New
York: Syracuse University Press, 1946); A. E. Musson and E. Robinson,
Science and Technology in the Industrial Revolution (Manchester: Manchester
University Press, 1969), ch. 12.

23 Wadsworth and Mann, *Cotton Trade and Industrial Lancashire*, p. 510; J.
Aikin, *A Description of the Country From Thirty to Forty Miles Round
Manchester* (1795; Newton Abbot: David & Charles, 1968), p. 192.

24 A. E. Musson, 'Industrial motive power in the United Kingdom, 1800–70',
Economic History Review, 2nd series, vol. XXIX (1976), p. 417.

25 Aikin, op. cit., p. 129.

26 Sleath & Co.'s career is recorded in a series of advertisements in the
Manchester Mercury, 30 August 1796, 14 February, 22 August 1797, 29
May 1798.

27 The main sources for this episode are the *Manchester Mercury* and *Manchester Journal*; also E. Vale, *The Mail-Coach Men of the Eighteenth Century*
(London: Cassell, 1960), p. 119.

28 *Lowndes London Directory*, 1789: Guide to Stage-Coaches, Waggons . . ., p.

99; P. Barfoot and J. Wilkes (eds), *The Universal British Directory of Trade and Commerce* (London: C. Stalker; Brideoake & Fell, 1790), Vol. I, pp. 479, 506; W. Holden, *Holden's New Easy, and Complete Referance to all . . . Stage-Coaches, Mails, Waggons . . . Barges* (London: 1799), pp. 63, 96.

29 Register of Boats and Barges, 1795, Cheshire Record Office, QD.

30 *Manchester Mercury*, 12 July 1803.

31 *The Gentleman's Magazine*, vol. LXIX (1799), p. 815.

32 Innholders' Company Freedom Admissions Register, 1673–1820, 3 March 1795, p. 188, Guildhall Library MSS 6651/1.

33 *Manchester Directory, 1794* (Scholes), p. 194; V. I. Tomlinson, 'Early warehouses on Manchester waterways', *Lancashire and Cheshire Antiquarian Society*, vol. 71 (1961), pp. 145–6.

34 Copy letter, William Wright to Joseph Baxendale, 25 May 1852, referring back to the 1790s, Pickford papers KS/2/5(b); *Manchester Directory, 1781* (Raffald), p. 92; *Annals of Agriculture*, vol. 42 (1804), pp. 96 ff., 379 ff.

35 Information from private papers belonging to Mr E. Halfpenny of Ilford. My thanks are due to him for permission to read and quote from them.

36 List of subscribers, pp. xvi ff.

3

Back from the Brink,
1800–47

Pickford's history during the first half of the nineteenth century reads almost like the script of a classic business drama. The old heads which had guided the firm to fame and fortune had passed on, leaving young men of little experience to take up their inheritance. The succession went off smoothly, the business was conducted sensibly and for a dozen or so years everything was to all external appearances proceeding satisfactorily. The storm which broke in 1815, when the record first reveals the firm to be sliding into bankruptcy, was thus quite dramatic and threatened to sweep Pickfords away. Two of the four young partners lost their nerve and quit. The other two battled on but could not stem the flood-tide of debts. To save the firm they brought in new partners, in pursuit of fresh capital. The manoeuvre was successful, but at the cost of losing control and watching from the sidelines as one of the newcomers put the business back on its feet. Even then, a neat touch of theatre, there was a further twist to the story. No sooner had one threat been overcome than another arose, in the shape of the steam locomotive which promised to destroy road and canal transport entirely. There was a final battle to be fought, but this time one which could not be won.

DECLINE AND FALL, 1800–17

Conditions favoured inland transport during the early years of the nineteenth century as generally high levels of economic activity ensured a steady demand for transport services. Only a handful of years between 1800 and 1815 were marked by depression; the severe recession of 1811 might be set off against the booms of 1802 and 1810, while the moderate boom of 1815 followed four years of continuous recovery.[1] Such conditions were promising enough, but when set in the context of long years of war with France and the consequent weakening of coastal shipping they added up to a powerful stimulus to inland transport. But dangers lurked ahead. More capital was drawn in than could be profitably employed in peacetime. After 1815, therefore, inland transport was likely to be severely disturbed, even without the sharp instability of the economy which accompanied the return of peace.

In the meantime the sun shone and inland transport flourished. The canal system was substantially extended. The promotions of the 1790s matured, new routes were opened to Worcester, Leicester and across the Pennines. The opening of the Blisworth tunnel on the Grand Junction canal in 1805 completed the through canal route from the midlands direct to London. Canal traffic could pass more quickly, more cheaply and over longer distances. On the roads the long debate on wheel design was shelved and Parliament, following the advice of Telford and MacAdam, put its weight behind raising the quality of road surfaces. The efficiency of road and canal transport was greatly increased and in turn contributed positively to the further development of the economy. The provision of transport services increased markedly, as did the number of firms engaged in their supply. Underpinning both of these was a substantial growth in the volume of traffic conveyed. But by how much the level of traffic grew can be indicated only in very general terms. The toll revenue of canal companies and turnpike trusts, a reasonable measure in that, allowing for discounts, both appear to have charged at close to their statutory maxima, suggests a large growth of traffic around the turn of the century, fairly high levels thereafter, and a new peak about the time of Waterloo. Canals were the major beneficiary, but it appears that road traffic was also increasing.[2]

Both roads and canals featured in Pickfords' development during these years. The wagon service was maintained and in fact reinforced by the introduction in 1814 of a new service of high-speed vans which, completing the journey between Manchester and London in thirty-six hours, introduced a new quality of rapid transit. But the mainspring of the business was increasingly the canal trade. New depots strengthened the firm's canal route between Lancashire and London, and included sideways extensions to Leicester and Worcester. The size of the barge fleet was rising – from ten in 1795 to twenty-eight in 1803, to fifty or more by 1810. An isolated set of toll payments to the Coventry Canal Company, which controlled part of the through route between London and the north midlands, provides the only clue to the growth of Pickfords' canal traffic. For the six months March to August 1803, the firm paid tolls of £808; four years later the total was £2,171, a margin not explained by different levels of prices or of economic activity. The growth of the canal trade attracted many new entrants, but the signs are that Pickfords was building up a prominent position. If toll payments are a valid measure of customer use, Pickfords' trade was twice that of the next largest customer on the Coventry canal and by implication accounted for a fair share of the trade to London. Another measure of customer use is the purchase of licences from the Coventry Company for permission to pass its locks by night. Pickfords' fifty licences well exceed the next largest number taken up, fifteen by Bache & Co.[3] The firm's operations at this stage drew the attention of a contemporary commentator:

> *Mr Pickford* has a great number of boats, which proceed regularly day and night upon this canal [Grand Junction] and the other canals north of it, as the mail coaches do on the roads, although with less expedition . . . [the boats] arrive in London with as much punctuality from the Midlands and some of the more distant parts of the Kingdom, as the waggons do.[4]

Whether the compliment was merited or not, it was no longer quite correct to identify the firm with 'Mr Pickford'. The question would be, which Mr Pickford? Thomas Pickford retired soon after his brother's death, allowing the third generation of the family to take over. The business was divided into twenty-four shares, the bulk of which were distributed equally between the direct heirs. Figure 2 explains the distribution.

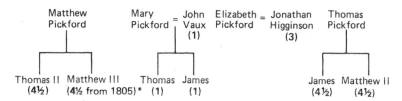

Fig. 2   *Distribution of shares, Thomas and James Pickford & Co., 1800*
    Note: Until 1805, the date of his majority, his shares were attached to Thomas II
    (*Source: Partnership agreement, 1 October 1800, Pickford papers*)

The sons of Matthew Pickford, Thomas II and Matthew III, replaced their father in Manchester, while James and Matthew II, the sons of Thomas Pickford, took control in London. They were all fairly young; James was the oldest at 27 years of age and the youngest, Matthew III, was still a minor. It thus made sense to draw on the advice and experience of their uncle Jonathan Higginson who joined the partnership but without giving up the right to continue his own, competing, carrying business. The remaining three shares were taken by other relatives by marriage, who had in fact been taken into partnership by Matthew Pickford shortly before his death. One of them, James Vaux, a nephew of Matthew Pickford, had held the position of principal clerk and cash keeper in Manchester, still the headquarters of the business. His right to continue in the post was written into the new deed of partnership, together with the provision that he could not be dismissed without the written consent of the majority of the partners. Deliberately or not, the two sets of brothers were balanced off against each other. The Manchester Pickfords, should they wish it, could not get rid of James Vaux without the assistance of other partners, and neither pair could alone exercise a decisive influence in the business. Are these hints of a family wrangle over the succession? Even if no more than a fair distribution of the inheritance, the neat counter-balance of share-holdings was not necessarily in the best interests of the firm. When decisions were required, they might be difficult to obtain.

The partners were expected to be, as the deed of partnership put it, 'honest and faithful to the others in all their business accounts and to take their fair share and concern for the business'. Quite what each of them contributed to the business is unknown, since no records have survived which might illuminate the internal history of the firm during these years. Day-to-day management seems to have been left in the hands of depot managers or agents, even in London. The employment of agents, paid by salary plus commission on the business they trans-acted, was common enough, a sensible solution to the problems in-herent in an extended chain of operations. But where the inducement of commission, effectively a share in the business, did not work and/or overall supervision was lax, the results could be disastrous. Randle Brereton, the agent at Preston Brook, had to surrender his own carrying business to Pickfords to make good debts he owed the firm as agent,[5] and another agent reduced the firm's Birmingham office to a state of financial chaos. What was at best a flexible system, combining initiative with local autonomy and releasing the partners from the major burden of management, does not seem to have worked too well for Pickfords.

Overall strategy must have rested with the partners, but again little detail is available. Their known actions in developing the business, however, appear to have been sound. One important step was the purchase of the road haulage business of Robert Clarke of Leicester, completed in 1803.[6] Clarke was a substantial carrier whose operations between Sheffield and London employed 16 wagons and 130 horses. His entire stock in trade and business premises were bought. As well as a depot in Sheffield, these comprised a number of buildings, stables, warehouses and a counting house, in the innyard of The White Bear, Basinghall Street. For a time, all of Pickfords' road vehicles were transferred to The White Bear.

Clarke also owned a large establishment in Leicester, which included a blacksmith's shop and a wheelwright's shop. This was put to special use, and became an important focal point of the firm's road haulage operations. All of Pickfords' road services, to Manchester or to Sheffield, followed a common route out of London, passed through Leicester and diverged at Loughborough. The Sheffield service bought from Clarke fitted easily into the firm's existing scheme of operations, entering territory new to Pickfords only beyond Loughborough. Leicester was roughly the halfway point for both services and formed a suitable spot from which they could be controlled. Vehicles and wagon space could be saved by trunking along the common route from London as far as Leicester, and partial loads in the other direction could be consolidated there. For these reasons Leicester became, with Manchester and London, one of the three places from which the firm was later managed, a step which emphasises the importance to the firm of its road haulage business.

It is possible to outline the main stages of Pickfords' growth in the early years of the nineteenth century. The deed of partnership in 1800 listed premises at Blisworth, Brentford, Macclesfield, Manchester and Stoke (presumably Stoke Bruerne), in addition to The Castle in London. More information is available three years later. In July 1803 the Duke of York, commander-in-chief of the armed forces, received a letter offering him the emergency assistance of Pickfords should Napoleon's threatened invasion materialise. The accompanying detail, summarised in Table 3.1, is a useful guide to the firm's trading activities.

Table 3.1 *Pickfords' Organisation, July 1803*

| Road Operations | | | Canal Operations | |
Place	Horse Strength	Manager	Place	Manager
Castle, Wood Street	40	James Pickford	Paddington	Mr Wright
Market Street	60	Thomas Pickford Snr	Stoke Bruerne	Mr Horsefull
Stony Stratford	60	W. Godfrey	Braunston	Mr Lea
Northampton	10	Thos. Hartup	Coventry	Mr Shaw
Kings Norton	9	Wm. Dane	Derby	Insp. Oakes
Harborough	9	Insp. Ashton	Preston Brook	Mr Brereton
Leicester	30	T. Thornicroft	Liverpool	Insp. Barber
Kegworth	8	Insp. Barrow	Manchester	Insp. Poulson
Derby	8	Insp. Baker		
Ashbourne	8	M. Bass		
Poynton	20	Thos. Pickford II		
	262			

Source: T. and J. Pickford & Co. to Duke of York, 1 July 1803, Pickfords Removals Ltd.

The north–south line of Pickfords' road and canal operations is clearly spelled out, and with a number of interesting features. One of these is the distribution of horse strength, which it will be noted related only to wagons. Of a total of 400 horses, 138 were always on the move. The location of the other 262 indicates the pressure points of the system. Poynton was still a functional part of the business, Leicester also stands out, but most other places evidently mark off stages at which teams were changed and rested. The heavy concentration in and close to London is perhaps partly explained by local cartage, but probably more by the higher wear and tear inflicted on horses by the poorer road conditions close to the capital. The focal points of the firm's canal operations are also indicated, but not their relative importance. On the management side, Thomas Pickford still kept an eye on the wagon horses at Market Street, and deposited their dung on his fields, but of the younger family only James and Thomas II are represented.

During the next dozen or so years, the number of Pickfords' outlets grew rapidly, prompted chiefly by the canal trade. William Wright, the agent at Paddington, remembered these years:

> 1801. Canal open to Paddington: first boat loaded . . . with *cotton* . . . Warehouse soon finished and house built . . . Within six months stable built. One horse and cart placed for West End: business increases – a second cart placed – deliver all west of Fleet Market . . . 1804. A second warehouse built: horses increased at Paddington. 1807–8. The next wharf taken . . . trade increases . . .[7]

To accommodate this expansion premises had to be taken in a large number of other places, in addition to Paddington. And details of their insurance, recorded in 1817,[8] make plain how much more extended the firm had become during the intervening years.

The total stock of premises was insured for £46,000. Paddington alone, the centre of the firm's canal trade, was valued at £16,000. That, together with The Castle and a new warehouse in Fore Street, comprised more than half of the capital sum insured, clear evidence that London had already become the prime focus of the business. Manchester was second in importance. The range of warehouses, stables, offices, dock, boatyard and saw pits, for the construction and repair of barges, was insured for £9,700. London and Manchester still remained the dominant poles of the business, but they were now supplemented by a number of sub-depots. The most important of these, insured for between £4,000 and £1,000, were at Birmingham, Braunston, Coventry, Derby, Macclesfield, Leicester and Stoke Bruerne, with lesser ones at Blisworth and Warwick. In addition were a chain of forty-two small depots, the great majority strung along the line of the London-to-Lancashire canal route. In 1803 Pickfords had traded from a dozen or so places; in 1817 the number had reached about fifty-six. Whatever else might be said about the young partners, they had not stood still.

Perhaps, indeed, they had expanded too well, too quickly, for in 1817 Pickfords was in desperate trouble. The contrast between appearances and reality was stark. The crisis which finally engulfed the firm seems to have blown up suddenly and progressed very rapidly. A number of debts were owed, but that due to the Grand Junction canal, £15,000, dwarfed the others. Indeed it was so large that the canal company insisted on a special mortgage to guarantee it.[9] The preceding stages are the puzzle. A debt of that size could not have occurred overnight, nor indeed gone unnoticed by the partners. Something had evidently gone very wrong. But what? Trading conditions had been favourable, so the explanation must lie within the firm.

It would be easy to construct an elaborate, socio-psychological theory of management failure – untried young men, over-speedy expansion, lack of commitment and attention to the business. The less the hard evidence, the greater the opportunity to speculate! But reading between the lines as the story unfolds, a more mundane and all too common explanation presents itself, namely, that the business suffered because of a lack of financial expertise. Pickfords had reached the stage at which financial management, the planned allocation of revenue between current and long-term needs, had become perhaps as important as the traditional skills of the carrier. The firm's recent growth had presumably absorbed considerable capital in boats and premises. And when cash-flow problems appeared there was evidently no one who could run a tight budget on the revenue earned in the business or, as a last recourse, get hold of stop-gap loans. This is essentially to rationalise the course of events, but the contrast between the Pickfords' seemingly uncomprehending slide into bankruptcy and the means by which the firm was ultimately saved could not have been sharper.

Pickfords was already in such a bad way in 1815, a favourable trading year, that it was virtually too late to put things right. The depression of 1816 was perhaps the death-knell. The canal trade slumped, forcing other carriers into trouble, although none so large or so desperate as Pickfords. Competition was acute as the pressure of surplus capacity, now that the war was over, in both road and canal transport pushed carriage rates ever lower.

Pickfords' plight, therefore, got steadily worse. Little headway was made in discharging the debt to the Grand Junction Company. Instead the canal company became increasingly insistent, demanding additional guarantees and threatening the ultimate sanction of refusing further credit. Other trading debts were due to the Birmingham and Grand

Union Canal Companies, and an account of £30,000 was owing to the
bankers, Daintry & Ryle of Macclesfield and Wilson, Crewdson & Co.
of Kendal. The last thing the business could tolerate was an internal
drain of capital, but that is precisely what happened. At least one
partner, James Vaux, had already left although more than half of his
£18,000 capital remained to be paid off. The fatal blow came when
James and Matthew II, the London branch of the family, decided to
run for it and withdrew their joint capital of £26,000. Thomas II and
Matthew III attempted to struggle on, but the burden of trying to
carry the firm's accumulated debts and pay off their cousins proved too
much. They recognised defeat and looked to the only possible solution,
the injection of fresh capital from new partners. They thereby saved
the business, but could not escape bankruptcy themselves.[10]

REORGANISATION

The first day of April 1817 marks a distinct break, a fresh start in
Pickfords' history. It acquired, in retrospect, the status of a red letter
day, formally enshrined as the commencement of the firm's financial
year, when three new partners joined the business, Zachary Langton,
Charles Inman and Joseph Baxendale who was to be the agent of
renewal. The firm's recovery and ascent to primacy in the carrying
trade by the 1830s was as emphatic as its previous collapse. How is
the transformation to be explained and why did the new men succeed
where the Pickfords had failed?

The incomers brought various assets to the business, but none so
valuable as the capital available to them. Not that they themselves
actually owned a great deal of money; indeed Baxendale, and probably
Inman, too, borrowed their entry capital. No, what mattered was that
through their kinship ties they possessed what the Pickfords had so
acutely lacked, access to considerable financial resources, especially in
Lancashire. The ties of kinship which bound the three together were
real and effective, however remote they might appear to modern eyes.
Kinship, by blood or marriage, provided entry and acceptability to
social groups of wealth and influence, the opportunity of seeking
financial backing and the guarantee that it would not be abused.
Unlike the Pickfords, the new partners could drum up capital, sufficient
to stem the tide of debts, and were willing to employ it in the business.
It was, indeed, crucial for the business that they were able to dig considerably deeper into their relatives' pockets than their half share,
subscribed in equal proportions, of the £48,000 capital on which the
new firm of Pickford & Co. was floated.

The core of the kinship ties which bound the three newcomers together was provided (see Figure 3) by the Langton, Birley and Hornby
families of Kirkham, in the Fylde of Lancashire.[11] They shared business

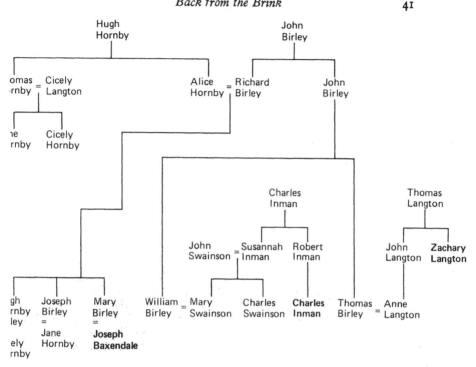

Fig. 3 · *Family relationship between Baxendale, Langton and Inman*

ventures in flax-spinning, sail-cloth manufacture and trade with Russia, the Baltic and the West Indies, and flourished especially in the later eighteenth century when the economy of Lancaster and its hinterland enjoyed its brief flush of prosperity. Business ventures were cemented by interlocking partnerships, and further reinforced by marriage alliances.

This was Zachary Langton's background, although his family's bonds with the other two were stronger in the counting house than in the marriage bed. Zachary was in his twenties when he moved to London, in 1785, and began business as a warehouseman dealing in Manchester goods. One of his suppliers was the cotton firm of Birley, Cardwell & Co. of Blackburn. Richard Birley of Kirkham was one of the co-founders of this firm, and was joined by his brother-in-law, Thomas Hornby, who in 1784 invested £10,000 as a sleeping partner. The value of such contacts was shown in 1793 when the firm, together with other members of the Birley and Hornby families and several Blackburn merchants, collectively stood surety for Zachary Langton for a loan of £15,000 put up by a group of London merchants.[12] Langton

could bring to Pickfords a credit standing which was good both in
London and in the Lancashire business community of his birth.

The Birley family also featured in the life of Joseph Baxendale.
His early business career was in the cotton trade, first in London with
Samuel Croughton, warehouseman of St Paul's Churchyard, another
customer of Birley, Cardwell & Co., and then in partnership with
Charles Swainson in a calico-printing business at Bannister Hall, near
Preston. In 1816 he married Mary Birley, the daughter of Richard
Birley of Blackburn, and subsequently borrowed from the trustees of
his wife's dowry the £8,000 he needed to buy a stake in Pickfords.
The personal relationship between Baxendale and Langton might be
tenuous; in precise terms, the wife of Mary Birley's first cousin was
the niece of Zachary Langton. But what really mattered was that they
both belonged to the same family group.

Charles Inman, the third of the partners, was attached to the others
by more distant ties. His link with the group came through his first
cousins, Charles and Mary Swainson. Charles Swainson was the
senior partner to Baxendale at Bannister Hall; his brother-in-law was
William Birley, married to his sister Mary. Charles Inman can be
placed, therefore, in the same network of family alliances, but little
else is known of him except that he came from Lancaster, like Baxendale,
and that his family just possibly had some dealings in the West India
trade, like the Birleys. However, he did not need to have the same
prominent links as the others. Business enterprises had long been built
on interlocking partnerships and family alliances. The business community was small and locally concentrated, to be largely identified by
enumerating a small group of families. To gain membership of it was
itself a promise of further opportunity.

The Birley family quietly made the transition from merchant in the
mid-eighteenth century to industrial manufacturer in the early nineteenth. It stood at the centre of a complex web of family and business
connections. The Birleys, together with the Langtons and the Hornbys,
were variously active in promoting the industrial life of south Lancashire, contributing money and energy to railway schemes, joint-stock
banks, chambers of commerce, and also took part in local and national
politics. They provide the main unifying link between the three
partners, and possibly also explain how the connection with Thomas
and Matthew Pickford arose. In March 1817, James Pickford mentioned in a letter to his brother, Matthew II, that negotiations were
being conducted on behalf of the new partners by a 'Mr Birley'. This
was probably Hugh Hornby Birley, Joseph Baxendale's brother-in-law,
who two years later acted as trustee in respect of the Pickfords' bankruptcy. He was, therefore, presumably already known and acceptable
to them. But how well they knew each other is uncertain. The only
evidence of a direct connection between the Pickfords and the Birleys

is a run of entries, from 1797 to the 1820s, in the name of 'M. Pickford' in the ledger accounts of Birley, Cardwell & Co.

When the new partnership commenced, on 1 April 1817, Manchester was still Pickfords' headquarters.[13] Responsibility for that end of the business was allocated to Thomas Pickford and Joseph Baxendale. Matthew Pickford and Zachary Langton had control in London and Charles Inman took up station at Leicester. The firm traded under the name of T. and M. Pickford & Co. in Manchester, and Messrs Matthew Pickford & Co. in London. No particular arrangements were made in the deed of partnership for the management of the business beyond the partners' presence at the three places named. The partners each received an annual salary of £500, about the going rate for the period, plus 5 per cent on their capital. Profits could not be withdrawn without the consent of all the partners and misuse of funds was penalised by a £1,000 fine and expulsion from the partnership.

The debt burden which had brought Pickfords down was the first priority to be tackled. The new partners were indemnified against past debts, but there were special problems. Premises employed in the business in Manchester, London and elsewhere had been mortgaged, at £10,000, to Wilson, Crewdson & Co. of Kendal as part security for a larger debt. The new firm would have been seriously embarrassed if the bank had occasion to foreclose, so Langton, Baxendale and Inman agreed to join the two Pickfords in a bond guaranteeing that amount. In return for this further assistance half the firm's goodwill, estimated at £10,000, was made over to them. There were also other debts which could not be escaped. The canal companies which were owed money by the old firm presented the bill to the new one, and threatened to refuse credit if it was not settled. In order to trade on the canals the new men had no option but to pay up.

Langton and his colleagues became steadily embroiled in the rest of the Pickfords' debts. Thomas II and Matthew III remained responsible for the debts of the old firm, but were unable to pay. Their new associates seem to have been quite ignorant of the depth of their insolvency and their inability to settle. Langton was patently shaken to discover, as he did in November 1818, that the Pickfords were on the verge of bankruptcy, for, as he wrote to Baxendale, 'what so much concerns them I cannot look at as a matter of indifference to us'.[14] If they abandoned the Pickfords to their fate the business would be brought down in the ensuing crash, their own capital with it. Baxendale and Inman shared his fears, and agreed to bail them out. It proved an expensive rescue attempt. Repeated requests for help were met, each presented apparently as positively the last, until by April 1821 they totalled £17,000. Bankruptcy followed.

The terms on which Thomas and Matthew Pickford settled with their creditors reveal their now total dependence on their three col-

leagues.[15] The latter's price for yet further assistance was full control
of the business. The Pickfords had indeed already been reduced to a
minority position. The distribution of shares in the business had been
adjusted in 1819, in recognition of the fact that the additional resources
put in by Langton, Baxendale and Inman, by way of propping up the
Pickfords, entitled them to a greater say. The five partners were placed
on an equal footing, thereby according a majority holding to the newcomers. Two years later, when bankruptcy could no longer be de-
ferred, their hold had strengthened even further. In return for yet more
advances, they now held a general lien over the entire property, stock
and profits of the business. But that still was not the finish. The Pickfords' creditors, at least all except their former partner James Vaux
who insisted that the £10,000 capital due to him be paid in full,
agreed to a composition of 10 shillings in the pound on the debt of
£67,500, but even that could not be paid without the continued help
of their partners. Again they agreed, provided that Hugh Hornby
Birley was appointed as trustee to effect compulsorily what the Pickfords
had conspicuously failed to do voluntarily. The Pickfords were allowed
to participate in profits, but the income was disbursed by Birley – in
order of priority, 5 per cent interest on the £17,000 owed to their
partners, then £500 for their personal needs and the balance to their
creditors. It was 1835 before all the creditors were paid off.

Not surprisingly finance was a continuous problem, at times stretched
so tightly as to approach breaking point. In November 1818 Langton
reported to Baxendale, 'besides the £1,000 which you direct me to
advance . . . there has come today from Liverpool £500, and as much
from Manchester. This keeps the wolf from the door today and to-
morrow . . . [and] enables me to pay £500 borrowed yesterday.'[16]
Limited funds had to be strictly rationed. Hence Baxendale's remark,
some time later: 'Cash matters have due attention but do not pay the
Grand Junction canal account on the first lest you may want the money
for the following days' payments.'[17] The business must have been
daily operating on a fine balance between credit and crisis. Progress
was slow and the firm seemed to be trailing behind its competitors.
Bache & Co. was believed to be coping better with the depressed
conditions of 1819. Its boats and operations were anxiously examined,
but no obvious explanation could be found for its superior performance.[18]

Slowly, at first very slowly, conditions improved. The violent
fluctuations of the postwar economy gave way, from about 1820, to
rather more stability. The demand for transport services followed the
peaks and troughs of the trade cycle, but the general trend was for slow
expansion. Other changes were internal to the firm. The settlement
with the Pickfords' creditors removed a major area of uncertainty. More
decisively, Langton and his colleagues chose to convert their ownership of the business into control. Joseph Baxendale began to assume

wider managerial responsibility on behalf of the new partners. He initially remained in Manchester, away from the real centre of the business, but when Matthew Pickford III retired in 1823 Baxendale promptly took his place in London and assumed responsibility for the total concern. At the same time Pickfords' canal depot at City Basin replaced The Castle in Wood Street as the firm's headquarters. The canal trade was duly recognised as the heart of Pickfords' business, and London as its main nerve centre.

Baxendale quickly learned that his future was to be arduous. In February 1820, soon after commencing his wider duties, he visited the firm's Birmingham agency and what he found there so appalled him that the memory of it never faded.[19] The stock was badly run down, the books were in chaos. There were unsettled accounts dating from 1812, paid-up accounts had not been entered, unpaid accounts entered as paid. Baxendale prosecuted the agent for fraud, sacked most of the staff, and himself settled down to sort out the mess 'until I either kill or cure'. He succeeded, but only after two months of assiduous toil, working up to nineteen hours a day, and employing four part-time clerks. In contrast, when visiting Worcester as a temporary break from Birmingham, Baxendale was delighted to find everything in order. But there were other reminders; at Liverpool soon after, a newly appointed clerk was caught with his hand in the till. The business clearly needed a good dose of discipline, and Baxendale was the man to administer it.

REVIVAL

Pickfords' fortunes were eventually restored, but it took considerable toil and effort. In 1828 the business was said to be 'very prosperous'[20] but if so its prosperity was of recent date. It is impossible to make firm statements about Pickfords' financial condition at this time since few appropriate records survive. Some figures have been derived from Baxendale's private papers, drawn up as a personal memorandum of his income, outgoings and net worth. From these figures, which are tabled and analysed in Appendix 1.1, a series of notional distributed profits has been estimated. These are graphed in Figure 4. To proceed far with these figures it would be necessary to know the accounting practices by which they were arrived at, including any prior charges before the net revenue was determined. However, there seems no reason to reject Baxendale's record of his own share of profits from the business, one of the sources employed. And what was 'paid out', notionally, since the partners were obliged to reinvest their profits, ought to have borne some broad relationship to what was coming in – assuming that the new partners' financial control was sufficient protection against overdrawing. With this caution in mind, it seems reasonable

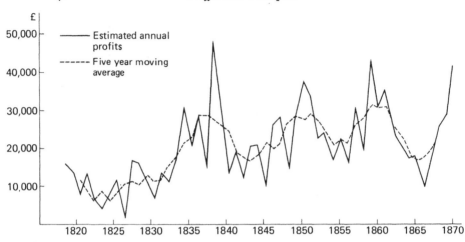

Fig. 4 *Pickfords' estimated profits, 1818–70*

to regard the figures as a crude guide at least to the general directions in which the earnings of the business were moving.

The degree of fluctuation makes the annual figures confusing. A five-year moving average, minimising but not removing the swings, shows the trend more clearly. The early 1820s are revealed as lean years, and the recession of 1826 as particularly sharp. The years 1827 and 1828 were a lot better but on trend appear as no more than recovery from the previous low level. Forward movement remained slow and hesitant until about 1832, from which date there was marked and largely sustained upward progress. The trend reaches no plateau but rather describes several phases of rise and fall, which continued beyond the years immediately under consideration.

It was, then, probably the early 1830s before Pickfords' fortunes were firmly re-established. The firm's recovery no doubt owed something to improved economic conditions, but most likely far more to the effort and resources invested in it by Langton, Baxendale and Inman, and the staff of head-office clerks and local agents, many of whom put in long years of continuous service. The number of carrying firms proliferated. In 1825 Pickfords was one of seventy-five firms trading from Manchester. Only three others operated both by land and water, and only a handful paralleled its structure of services, but even so on the majority of routes the firm faced competition from several other carriers. There was room for all to stretch, although Pickfords seems to have grown rather more than the rest. The barge fleet was expanded from some 80 boats in 1820 to 116 in 1838, all but 4 of which were employed on the canals. The firm then owned about 800

PICKFORD & Co.

Have Establishments at all Places on the above Sketch, or convey
Goods without any intermediate Carrier.

Map 3   '*A sketch of Pickford & Company's line of land and water conveyance*' *redrawn from Robson's* Commercial Directory of London, 1835

horses, half of which hauled the canal boats, and about a sixth were stationed in London. The overall picture is perhaps best indicated by the number of local branches. Approximately eighty agencies in 1830 had swollen to forty-four major depots and about a hundred smaller ones eight years later.[21]

A map of Pickfords' services, published in 1835 by way of advertisement, illustrates the maximum extent of the firm's activities at the peak of the pre-railway transport system. Two features stand out, the heavy concentration of agencies and services within the traditional territory between London and Lancashire, but with outriders to Bristol, Worcester and the West Riding, and the continued employment of road transport as feeder to, and parallel with, canals. The core of services was provided by canal conveyance. Pickfords became increasingly associated with canals, emerging as the recognised premier firm of canal carriers. Simultaneously it was becoming identified with just one of the partners, Joseph Baxendale. By the mid-1830s Pickfords had become 'his' firm, to the extent that John Moss, chairman of the Grand Junction Railway Company, could affirm, 'Mr Baxendale was the greatest carrier on the canals'.[22]

As Moss's comment implies, Pickfords' revival owed a great deal to the one man. In time Joseph Baxendale so stamped his personality on Pickfords that the two became synonymous. The single-handed nature of his achievement became legendary in the firm. His success rested on the support of others but there is no doubt that it was his driving force and energy which powered Pickfords' new-found momentum. Who was this man, and what were the reasons for his success?

JOSEPH BAXENDALE

Joseph Baxendale was born in 1785, the son of a Lancaster surgeon.[23] The Baxendales were originally a Liverpool family, cabinet-makers, and freemen of the borough of Lancaster, the county town. His father, Josiah Baxendale, moved to Lancaster in the early 1780s. In December 1784, Josiah married Mabella Salisbury, the daughter of a lesser gentry family, and Joseph was born the following September. Little is known of Baxendale's childhood and youth. He is reported to have received 'a good education', although he himself later described these years as 'very wretched'. Josiah Baxendale seems to have been a forthright man, with an independent turn of mind, and in this son clearly took after father.

In September 1804, at the age of 20, Baxendale left Lancaster for Preston, 'to fight my way through life', as he wrote in old age. From there he went to London where, in March 1806, he was established with Samuel Croughton, wholesale linen draper of 33 St Paul's Churchyard. Baxendale was apparently representing the interests of a

Mr Swainson there. Croughton's warehouse was the London outlet for Bannister Hall calico-printing works, near Preston, founded in the late eighteenth century by Richard Jackson and John Stephenson.[24] In 1804 the partnership was extended to take in a John Swainson, presumably the Mr Swainson whom Baxendale was representing. Correspondence exchanged between Baxendale and his father in 1808 implies that this Swainson was a partner at Bannister Hall. Jackson, one of the other partners, also features prominently.

One letter which Joseph Baxendale received soon after arriving in London is of particular interest. It was from his father and contained Josiah's advice to his son on how to prepare himself for his life's work. Such letters were a convention of the period, although Josiah's is marked by its practical tone, business oriented, rather than the more common instruction in the social graces. After cautioning against joining military associations or wasting time in clubs and meeting houses, Josiah warmed to his main theme:

> I would wish you to endeavour to make yourself a perfect master of Book-keeping, which you may accomplish very easily, by paying a little attention and court to your Book-keeper. The advantage you will ultimately receive from it, there is no appreciating. I would advise you to read, occasionally the best French authors, for at some period your knowledge of that language may be of essential service to you. If you have leisure and inclination to improve yourself in the Italian language, I would recommend you to make yourself a master of it; but above all things, I would wish you to make yourself acquainted, which you may do of an evening, with all the best English authors, as it will be a source of improvement and continual amusement . . . and if you get the character of having a little more learning and knowledge than your neighbours, it will not be any disadvantage to you.

A daunting training programme, but not beyond the disciplined will-power of Joseph Baxendale.

Baxendale did not stay long in London. Early in 1809 he left Croughton and returned to Lancashire, where he borrowed £4,000 and bought a one-fifth share in the Bannister Hall concern, in partnership with Charles Swainson. He acquired a cottage at Walton-le-Dale, near the factory and bleaching grounds, and from there travelled in search of orders. Few events of this phase of his life are known. One, which remained a vivid memory, was being shot at during the bitter calico-printing strike of 1815.[25] An altogether happier event in the same year was his engagement to Mary Birley. When Baxendale retired from the Bannister Hall partnership in December 1816, he had netted about £6,000 in profits and interest, enough to pay his way, and discharge part of his borrowings.

Baxendale's correspondence with his father conveys the impression of a competent, self-assured young man. Independence and self-reliance were features which Josiah Baxendale stressed. When Baxendale found himself in difficulties his father was willing to help but on terms which left the ultimate responsibility to his son. Accordingly the £2,000 which Josiah Baxendale made available in 1809, half the capital Joseph needed to go in with Swainson, was as a loan charged at the customary rate of 5 per cent interest. Joseph was reminded that life was a harsh school, but what it had to teach could be learnt in only one way. 'An early lesson [in life] sometimes makes a lasting impression, which makes people cautious in their money transactions.'

When he joined Pickfords, Joseph Baxendale had briefly shared the experience of running a business, and perhaps picked up the ground rules of effective management, although there could have been few similarities between a calico-printing factory and a transport firm. However, in so far as entrepreneurial success depended as much on character and personality as specific skills,[26] some transfer of experience should have been possible. Baxendale had also ventured borrowed capital in Bannister Hall, and did so again when he entered Pickfords. But a certain self-confidence and willingness to take moderate risks are not sufficient explanation of Baxendale's success in regenerating Pickfords. For this it is necessary to probe deeper and discover, by combining what is known about the young and the mature Baxendale, what particular qualities he possessed which were relevant to the task at hand. Those which stand out are a sound business judgement, a forceful yet attractive personality, a large capacity for hard work, a thorough, methodical mind and a competent knowledge of accounts.

The last-mentioned qualities, method, orderliness and accounting ability, were highly relevant to the mess Pickfords was in. Baxendale found the firm's accounts in 'the most wretched state of confusion', so that the new partnership itself only avoided bankruptcy by keeping its own accounts strictly separate from those of the 'old' firm. It might be an exaggeration to say that Baxendale was obsessed with figures, but his surviving papers abound with collections of figures and their analysis. At the level of contemporary accounting knowledge, Baxendale appears to have been more than competent. Conventional mercantile accounts, although inadequate for the more sophisticated needs of capital accounting, could be adapted sufficiently to provide a guide to overall profitability, provided they were executed with care and method. Baxendale possessed these crucial qualities. The chaos at Birmingham was sorted out not by complex technique but by perseverance, long hours of careful checking, reconstituting the books. The primary requirements were personal discipline and strong motivation.

No doubt the threat of bankruptcy helped to concentrate Baxendale's mind and will.[27]

How far could Baxendale use his skills as a 'tool of management'? At the least he expected an examination of the books to guide the firm in its progress. His dictum was that problems should be 'sifted to the marrow', and an analysis of the figures was an essential component of the sifting. His surviving personal memoranda books contain the most detailed unit cost/revenue analysis. Labour charges of all categories and rates, the itemised construction costs of a new boat, daily working costs, including wear and tear, of two boats working between Manchester and Liverpool, all were carefully noted. He could calculate the average quarterly earnings of selected fly boats over roughly comparable periods in 1827, 1830, 1832 and 1837, down to earnings per day and per mile. Either he was simply fascinated with figures or he found the exercise useful.

In his own notes, Baxendale depreciated the fixed capital tied up in Pickfords' boats. The horses were also written down at the annual stock-taking.[28] But what principles were applied and how capital was charged to the accounts is unfortunately again unknown. An interesting development in this respect, however, was the creation of a reserve fund, when the partnership was revised in 1838, to which one-fourth of the profits were allocated. This was probably by way of a sinking fund, to cover bad debts among other things, rather than the proper provision of reserves to meet depreciation, and the amount allowed suggests a round rather than a calculated sum. When the partnership was further adjusted in 1843, the share devoted to reserves was reduced to one-eighth.

Baxendale was, in addition, a skilled administrator, with the ability to simplify and thereby strengthen Pickfords' organisation. David Stevenson, a long-serving railway official who knew Baxendale well, paid tribute to these qualities. He wrote that 'the success of Pickford & Co., and the general efficiency of that establishment, proved his administrative powers . . . His clear system of forms and arrangements, by which a hold of the goods conveyed is maintained from the time they leave the consignor until they reach their destination, continues to be the basis of the carrying business all over the kingdom.'[29] The Eastern Counties railways took Pickfords as a model for dealing with its correspondence. To each outgoing communication a letter of the alphabet was attached as a reference code denoting the office or clerk responsible for it. As a result all queries or business arising could be channelled promptly in the appropriate direction.[30] The earliest example of this system which has been found is a letter from Pickfords to the Oxford Canal Company in 1824. This may be explained by the chance survival of records, but, significantly, that was the year in which Baxendale took over responsibility for the total concern. His dictum 'method is the hinge of business' was no empty preaching.

Baxendale was an energetic man, an essential quality in view of Pickfords' wide geographical spread of agencies. He spent much of his time travelling, checking the operational efficiency of the business. He undertook successive rigorous tours of inspection. For example, between mid-December 1834 and the same time the following year he spent 127 days on the move, travelling by boat, coach and post-horse, a total distance of 4,622 miles. A special boat, the *Joseph*, was allocated for this use, to be replaced in 1827 by the *Lark*, a purpose-built, specially-fitted craft, which cost £350 as opposed to £190–200 for a normal trading boat. The canal companies were accommodating; the Warwick & Napton committee agreed to let Pickfords' representatives pass free of toll when using their boat for business or pleasure purposes.[31] Baxendale wasted no time on these trips. His father accompanied him on one trip and kept a diary of their journey.[32] The presence of guests was not allowed to slow the pace. The continuous record of late nights and early risings, at between 5.00 and 6.00 a.m., suggests that the requirement for prolonged travel was a pretty robust constitution.

In the later 1830s Baxendale was able to relax his efforts on Pickfords' behalf, but he retained sufficient energy to take on additional business interests. In 1836 he joined the board of the Regent's Canal Company, and remained for three years. He also became a prominent figure in railway affairs. In 1839 he acted as adviser on goods traffic to the London & Birmingham railway and was for a few months also superintendent of the outdoor department but that, in conjunction with his other activities, overtaxed him and had to be given up. He had already, in 1837, joined the board of the South Eastern Railway Company, and as chairman in the early forties was instrumental in pushing the line through to Folkestone and establishing a through route between London and Paris by way of Boulogne.

Baxendale's railway interests were not confined to Britain. In the late 1830s he acted as consultant for the construction of the Belgian state railway system.[33] His promotion of the cross-channel route from Folkestone would explain his directorship of the Amiens & Boulogne railway. He also had a substantial investment, and was possibly a director, in the Compagnie du Chemin de Fer du Nord. Another directorship in the 1840s was of the East India Railway Company.

Along with energy went enterprise. On many occasions Baxendale's foresight, to which David Stevenson paid tribute, proved invaluable. He quickly appreciated the opportunities offered by railways, and approached the Liverpool & Manchester and Grand Junction Railway Companies for facilities well before their lines were complete. In 1838 he correctly anticipated a failure of the water supply at Tring Summit on the Grand Junction canal, and when the time came he had the details of an arrangement with the London & Birmingham railway all tied up, so that he could smoothly transfer his essential traffic to the railway, leaving all his rivals floundering. Again, convinced that the accommodation for goods traffic planned by the London & Birmingham railway would be inadequate, he bought a site at Camden Town next to the company's terminus and built a warehouse on it for his own use. Events quickly confirmed his judgement.

Baxendale was supported by a forceful personality. His portrait, presented to Mrs Baxendale in 1847 by Pickfords' agents as a tribute to his achievement in the previous thirty years, has the pose of a confident, self-assured man. His was a dominant personality, without being domineering. Stevenson considered him 'cheerful and witty in conversation, ever had a word of encouragement for the youngsters, and was universally beloved by those whom he employed'.[34] He was fond of aphorisms such as 'Nothing without labour', and 'He who spends all he gets is on the way to beggary', a selection of which he had posted in Pickfords' offices and warehouses. He was, in short, Victorian thrift writ large, exhibiting all the virtues so highly esteemed by Samuel Smiles, and enjoying the appropriate awards.

In 1836 Baxendale was voted a gift of £500 by his partners in recognition of his exertions on behalf of the firm. Pickfords had been reinvigorated and its profitability restored. He might then have reasonably expected a few years of rest during which to enjoy the fruits of his labours. Instead he had to plunge straight into another battle, to meet the challenge of railways. The new mode of transport which had at first seemed to be a powerful addition to the carrier's range of services was turning out to be the instrument of his destruction.

The early years of railways were fraught with uncertainty for carrying firms,[35] but Baxendale soon signalled his intention to move with the times and dispatch traffic by rail where that seemed preferable to road or canal. As the network of rails progressed, services employing them were extended. It was as a carrier by rail that Pickfords became a truly national transport firm. Agencies remained predominantly in the traditional areas, but new ones were opened wherever the railway led, in south Wales and south-west England, through the north of England to Edinburgh and Glasgow, across the counties south of London, and even across the Channel to Calais. The new warehouse and office block at Camden Town, intended to replace City Basin as the firm's headquarters, was the focus of Baxendale's railway ambitions.

But hopes so strongly kindled were to be bitterly frustrated. The canal companies did not take kindly to being downgraded to a residual role. More to the point, the railway companies did not prove accommodating. They decided to shut the carriers out. Baxendale fought a protracted legal battle with the Grand Junction Railway Company in an attempt to force access to its rails. He won every open encounter in the courtroom but lost the guerilla war in the station yard. Eventually he withdrew in disgust and left his sons to strike a bargain with the railway companies.

Railways wrought one kind of decisive change on Pickfords' history, retirement and death another. In 1838 the long-running partnership between Langton, Baxendale, Inman and the two Pickford brothers reached full term. Matthew Pickford III had already left the business and now Langton and Inman also retired. Joseph Baxendale and Thomas Pickford continued in partnership; Baxendale became senior partner, holding a half-share to Thomas's quarter.[36] It was also time for the new generation to join the firm. No more Pickfords entered the business, but Baxendale had several sons to follow him. His eldest son, Joseph Hornby Baxendale, joined Pickfords in 1836 at the age of 19, and was later followed by Lloyd, Richard and Salisbury. In 1843 Joseph Hornby and Lloyd were admitted to the partnership. So things remained until the death of Thomas Pickford in 1846. His interest was bought out and the business passed entirely out of the hands of the Pickford family.[37] Just as Joseph Baxendale's railway ambitions crumbled, he finally gained control of Pickfords. The ultimate irony could not have been lost on him.

REFERENCES: CHAPTER 3

1 A. D. Gayer, W. W. Rostow and A. J. Schwartz, *The Growth and Fluctuation of the British Economy, 1790–1850* (Oxford: Clarendon Press, 1953), Vol. 1, pp. 346 ff. In order to review the development of the business during these years it is again necessary in this chapter to anticipate briefly some events which are discussed fully later.
2 J. R. Ward, *The Finance of Canal Building in Eighteenth-Century England* (London: Oxford University Press, 1974), p. 165; R. G. Wilson, 'Transport dues as indices of economic growth, 1775–1820', *Economic History Review*, 2nd series, vol. XIX (1966), pp. 110–23.
3 Coventry Canal Company memorandum book, 1802–1808, Public Record Office (PRO)/British Transport Historical Records (BTHR) Rail 818/196; licence payments, minutes of general meetings, 9 January 1810, PRO/BTHR Rail 818/27.
4 A. Rees, *The Cyclopaedia: Or Universal Dictionary of Arts, Sciences and Literature* (London: 1819–20), Vol. VI, article on canals, written in 1805.
5 Indenture, 7 October 1812, Pickford papers CHP/16.
6 *Leicester Journal*, 6 September 1793, 26 February 1802; for the Pickfords' deal with Clarke, trading bond, 25 June 1803, Pickford papers CHP/8, and counterpart of lease of premises 25 May 1803, Pickford papers CHP/12.
7 Wm. Wright Jnr to Joseph Baxendale, 25 May 1852, Pickford papers KS/3/5(b).
8 Payments journal, Manchester office, PRO/BTHR Rail 1133/126.
9 Draft and final version of mortgage agreement, Pickford papers CHP/19, 20; also Regent's Canal Company, minutes of general committee, 20 September 1815, PRO/BTHR Rail 860/8.

10 Grand Junction Canal Company, minutes of general committee, 29 February 1816, PRO/BTHR Rail 830/43, board minutes 11 June, 5, 27 September, 10, 17 October 1816, PRO/BTHR Rail 830/1; Birmingham Canal Company, letter of 12 June 1817, PRO/BTHR Rail 810/587; Grand Union Canal Company, committee minutes, 7 January 1818, PRO/BTHR Rail 831/2; letter of licence between T. and M. Pickford and their creditors, April 1821, PRO/BTHR Rail 1133/26; see also E. Halfpenny, ' "Pickfords": expansion and crisis in the early nineteenth century', *Business History*, Vol. 1 (1959) pp. 115–25.

11 For the background to this section R. Shaw, *Kirkham in Amounderness. The Story of a Lancashire Community* (Preston: Seed, 1949), *passim*, esp. pp. 692 ff.; H. Fishwick, *The History of the Parish of Kirkham in the County of Lancashire* (Chetham Society, vol. CXII, 1874); J. Porter, *History of the Fylde of Lancashire* (Fleetwood and Blackpool, 1876), pp. 363–401; M. M. Schofield, *Outlines of an Economic History of Lancaster, 1680–1860*, (Lancaster Branch of the Historical Association, 1946, 1951), pt 1, chs III–VI.

12 Records of Birley, Cardwell & Co., English MSS 1199/1, John Rylands Library, Manchester.

13 Draft partnership agreement, 1 April 1817, Pickford papers CHP/25; also draft agreement, 1 April 1817, assigning Pickfords' assets to the new partnership, Halfpenny papers; *London Gazette*, 8 April 1817, p. 872.

14 Langton to Baxendale, 27 November 1818, Baxendale papers.

15 Letter of licence between Thomas and Matthew Pickford and their creditors, April 1821, PRO/BTHR Rail 1133/26.

16 Langton to Baxendale, 28 November 1818, PRO/BTHR Rail 1133/149.

17 T. and M. Pickford & Co., Manchester (Baxendale), to Messrs Matthew Pickford & Co., London, 25 January 1820, Baxendale papers.

18 Thomas Pickford to Joseph Baxendale, 7 January 1819/20, Pickford papers KS/2/5(a); T. and M. Pickford & Co., Manchester (?to London), 12 August 1819, Baxendale papers.

19 The following is based on a group of eight letters written by Baxendale in Birmingham, February–March 1820. All are in the Baxendale papers, except one at PRO/BTHR Rail 1133/129.

20 Halfpenny, ' "Pickfords": expansion and crisis', p. 124.

21 E. Baines, *History, Directory and Gazetteer of the County Palatine of Lancaster* (Liverpool: 1824–5; reprinted Newton Abbot: David & Charles, 1968), Vol. II, pp. 405–9; deed of arrangement, 3 May 1838, Pickford papers KS/2/2; number of horses returned for assessed taxes, PRO/BTHR Rail 1133/147.

22 Fifth Report and Evidence, *SC on Railway Communications*, PP, 1840, vol. XIII, Q. 3468.

23 Most of this account of Baxendale is based on his surviving personal papers. Specific references are not given. There is a brief and not very reliable memoir of Baxendale in S. Smiles, *Thrift* (London: John Murray, 1883), ch. IX.

24 A series of articles based on Bannister Hall records appeared in *The Connoisseur*, 1957–8.

25 G. Turnbull, *A History of the Calico-Printing Industry of Great Britain* (Altrincham: Sherratt, 1951), p. 191.

26 See Coleman's assessment of Samuel Courtauld III: D. C. Coleman, *Courtaulds. An Economic and Social History* (Oxford: Clarendon Press, 1969), Vol. 1, pp. 120 ff.

27 S. Pollard, *The Genesis of Modern Management* (London: Edward Arnold, 1965; Harmondsworth: Penguin Books, 1968), ch. 6.

28 Stock of horses, 31 March 1831, PRO/BTHR Rail 1133/147.

29 D. Stevenson, *Fifty Years on the London and North Western Railway* (London: McCorquodale, 1891), p. 14.
30 G. P. Neele, *Railway Reminiscences* (London: McCorquodale, 1904), p. 8.
31 Warwick & Napton Canal Company, board minutes 1 August 1820, 7 September 1821, PRO/BTHR Rail 882/9.
32 G. L. Turnbull, 'A tour by canal' (mimeograph).
33 Second Report and Evidence, *SC on Railways*, PP, 1839, vol. X, QQ. 5702–52.
34 Stevenson, op. cit.
35 G. L. Turnbull, 'The railway revolution and carriers' response: Messrs Pickford and Company, 1830–1850', *Transport History*, vol. II (1969), pp. 48–71.
36 Deed of arrangement, 3 May 1838, Pickford papers KS/2/2.
37 The *London Gazette* 27 August 1850, announced the expiry of the partnership, and the continuation by the Baxendales; also, deed of arrangement and release, Mrs Elizabeth Pickford to Messrs Pickford & Co., 20 July 1865, Pickford papers CHP/27.

4

Pickfords and Road Transport, 1750–1850

Pickfords started as a road carrying concern, conveying passengers and goods between Manchester and London. There are two significant words in that sentence, 'road' and 'goods', elements of the transport industry which, certainly in combination, have been largely neglected by historians. A fair amount is known about roads themselves; central and local authorities were responsible for their upkeep and demands for finance for their repair gave rise to inquiry as to their condition and extent. Town Books, Quarter Sessions, records of Parliament, all have something to say. Of the traffic which passed over them, however, little is known beyond the common complaint that it was excessive and destructive of road surfaces. Eventually, from 1747,[1] Parliament imposed taxes on travel by coach, chaise or post-horse and from the fiscal records an outline of the subsequent development of passenger traffic can be obtained. Except for brief periods road haulage was not taxed and never in a way which yields an insight into the volume or the composition of road goods traffic. There are no sources for road transport comparable to the Port Books, which have proved so valuable in the study of the coasting trade. Although a few chance surveys provide some clues, to set a firmer context it is necessary to try to formulate the sort of demand which road transport met. The subject merits sustained analysis, but only the main headings can be outlined here.

THE SPHERE OF ROAD TRANSPORT

The demand for transport services spans a broad spectrum. Goods traffic consists of a wide range of commodities, the needs and characteristics of which vary enormously. There is the volume and value of the item, its liability to damage, convenience of handling or need for special facilities, the location of the consignor or consignee, the urgency

or otherwise of dispatch. The possible permutations of these factors
are immense, such that no one mode of transport could possibly
accommodate them all. Instead there have to be several transport
modes, to a large extent complementary, each undertaking those
functions for which it is best fitted, but also to a greater or less extent
competitive, the choice between modes resting on changing circumstances and the precise formulation of demand. In the eighteenth
century the basic choice was between road and water transport, super-
ficially a choice between expensive and cheap transport.

It is easy to see road transport fulfilling a role complementary to
water transport. Imports had to be distributed inland, goods conveyed
to coastal or riverine ports for onward transmission, final deliveries to
be made locally. Again in many circumstances road transport was
manifestly not competitive: cheap, high volume, heavy goods (merchandise and raw materials) were either transported at low cost or not
at all. How could road transport secure a preference, its own protected
segment of demand, and even mount effective competition for traffic
which could choose between rival modes?

Part of the answer lies in the qualitative service provided by road
transport. It was direct, almost door to door, and goods could be
transported undisturbed for long distances. It was flexible, the complex
carrier system capable of reaching every town and village in the country.
It was reliable and less disrupted by bad weather than river or coastal
shipping; while vessels were storm-bound or held up by unfavourable
winds, a wagon could battle through. In some cases the land route was
a good deal shorter and in others delays protracted what ought to have
been a quick sea passage. In the early eighteenth century London was
nominally twelve hours' sailing from Colchester but the round trip
was rarely completed in less than a week. The London carrier took three
days for the same round trip.[2] At its best, road transport offered certain
advantages which water transport could not match.

The traffic to be conveyed provides another part of the answer.
For some goods the burden of carriage was quite small, less than $2\frac{1}{2}$
per cent of the final price in the case of the homespun stockings dispatched by Abraham Dent from Kirkby Stephen to army contractors
in London.[3] Light textiles generally and other light consumer goods
fell into this category, especially those easily spoilt by water damage.
This risk could be minimised by careful packing, adding to the expense,
and eliminated if water was avoided entirely. Especially was this the
case for fine cloths which, as John Smith of Stourport told the committee on the Worcester & Birmingham Canal Bill, 'manufacturers do
not choose to risk . . . by water'.[4]

A third part of the answer concerns the relative prices of road and
water transport. Measured by ton/mile rates, the latter was always by
far the cheaper, by a considerable margin where the weight/value ratio

of commodities was extreme. But ton/mile rates do not necessarily tell the whole story. There were other dues to be paid as well and when these were added up the gap between water and road costs could be considerably narrowed. In 1770 Henry Hindley, woollen cloth manufacturer of Mere in Wiltshire, complained that increased wharf charges at London and Newbury had so inflated the cost of river carriage as to bring it 'within a small matter of the price I have been offered to have [goods] brought wholly by land carriage'.[5] His product occupied the mobile middle band of traffic which perhaps relatively small adjustments could attract either way. Bulk flour would not be expected to fall into the same category yet William Thurnal, miller and maltster of Duxford and Cambridge in the 1830s, maintained that carriage by barge from Ware to London was less than the cost of warehousing, wharfage and cartage in London. 'I can deliver flour to the consumer as cheaply by land carriage as I can by water and land because there are additional charges in London at the wharfs.'[6] This is not to deny the primacy of water transport as regards the volume of traffic conveyed, only to argue that judgements based on comparative ton/mile figures need to be looked at cautiously.

In normal peacetime conditions, traffic divided predominantly in favour of water transport but when war broke out, as it did rather frequently in the eighteenth century, dramatic changes took place. Traffic was immediately diverted inland in much greater quantities, to escape the attention of privateers or because coastal shipping had practically ceased to operate. Declaration of war was the signal for the press-gang to get busy and equally for sailors of the merchant marine to disappear quietly from their home ports. For several months there might be no sailings at all. William Stout found that when his expeditions to London to buy stock for his Lancaster shop coincided with the outbreak of war, it was land carriage to get them home or nothing.[7] Convoys, protected by naval frigates, were eventually set up, but only after some delay, and they were in any case not sufficiently secure to remove the need and cost of insurance. At 2 to 3 per cent of the value of the cargo the cost was significant, sufficient to persuade John Wilson, a Leeds linen merchant, to abandon coastal shipping during the Seven Years' War and rely on land carriage to fetch home to Leeds his supplies of raw linen from the counties of Angus, Perth and Fife. Moreover, he continued in that way for some years after the war had ended.[8]

Both road and water transport progressed. Ports were improved, the size and efficiency of the coastal fleet raised, the mileage of navigable river was extended and canal construction begun. Development in road transport took two main forms, the turnpiking of roads and the substitution of wagons for packhorses, both of which enabled the road carriers to meet the rising pressure of demand from the economy without an undue escalation of costs. The influence of turnpikes is

difficult to determine exactly, but at least some well-informed contemporaries were satisfied they had positive, beneficial effects on the
cost of carriage. Defoe commented at length on the 'great progress'
and 'wonderful Improvements' arising from turnpikes which were
already apparent in the 1720s and forty years later Henry Homer was
sure that during the intervening years an 'astonishing revolution' in
road conditions had taken place. Defoe believed that by reducing the
wear and tear on horses turnpikes reduced carriers' costs by about a
third, an estimate which Malachy Postlethwayt later confirmed.[9]

Whether after mid-century turnpikes continued to be accompanied
by the same savings is less clear, especially as the pressure of provender
costs, the most crucial and highly volatile element in horse-based
transport, became more consistently upwards. If so it was probably
because turnpikes fostered the substitution of wagons for packhorses.
Although packhorses survived into the second half of the eighteenth
century, wagons were progressively introduced from the early years of
the century where traffic was densest, that is, on the London and major
provincial routes, which, too, were the first to be turnpiked. The Broad
Wheels Act of 1753 also greatly encouraged the adoption of wagons.
The road from Kendal to London, one of the longest hauls, was among
the last, in 1757, to see wagons introduced. The comparative advantage
of the wagon and horse team was further enhanced by the upward drift
in the weight taken by the carrier's wagon, as indicated by the increase
in the permitted payload from less than 3 tons at the beginning of the
eighteenth century to over 6 tons at its end. The packhorse had a
limited potential, each animal confined to a pack of 240 pounds. By
combining capital (wagons) with labour (wagon horses, in this respect
the equivalent of manpower in manufacturing), the productivity of
road transport was greatly advanced.[10]

The supply of transport services, therefore, ranged across a spectrum
equivalent to the demand for them. Of that spectrum, road goods
transport was an integral part. It served a certain band of the spectrum,
but not uniquely particular types of commodities. Part of the band it
shared with water transport, which is why carrier traffic contains so
many common elements with that recorded by the coastal Port Books.
It was a normal, regular component of the industry, with a full part
to play in meeting the transport needs of the economy.

ROAD TRANSPORT: MANCHESTER AND ELSEWHERE

Road transport was very important to Manchester. Removed from
coast or major river, it lacked the advantages of cheap water transport
which favoured economic growth. Only to the west did it enjoy a
water outlet, the Mersey & Irwell navigation created in 1721, which,
however, remained a difficult sail because of its bends and shoals.

The Bridgewater canal, which reached Manchester in 1764, marked a substantial improvement but it was the later 1770s before the canal linked Manchester to Liverpool, and both with London. There was no river to north or to south, whilst to the east lay the Pennines, a natural barrier to water transport not breached until the trans-Pennine canals of the 1790s. Traffic seeking the London market, the most important outlet beyond the local market, faced a difficult choice. It could go by coaster from Liverpool or Hull, the latter route being promoted by the Airmin Company, set up in 1752, by way of wagons to Wakefield and thence down the Aire & Calder,[11] or it could go by road. Allowing for the costs of multiple handlings and trans-shipments by either of the water routes, road transport was a competitive alternative.

Manchester was one place where, by reason of its topography, the margin between road and water transport was likely to have been more than usually balanced in favour of the former. There is evidence of a considerable flow of traffic by road from Manchester to London, composed especially of the woollen and fustian cloth on which south Lancashire's industrialisation was based. Cloth produced in the Bolton area was generally traded in Manchester and taken to London by road. Already by the late sixteenth century much of the cloth output of the region was exported through the port of London, having arrived in the capital by road. In the seventeenth century trading links between the two places were underpinned by road transport. And commodities conveyed were not confined to cloth. An early eighteenth-century petition to Parliament from merchants, shopkeepers and wagoners in Manchester and adjacent parts of Lancashire and Cheshire claimed that 'the greatest part of the manufactures and trades [of the area] is conveyed by Land Carriage . . . to London in waggons'. This included heavy merchandise, loads of up to 10 hundredweight, which could not 'be divided to be carried on packhorses without very great damage'. The wagons returned with a wide range of goods, including the orders of the four grocers, two mercers, the chapman, dyer and haberdasher who supported the appeal for relief of William Garnett, a Manchester carrier, to the Buckinghamshire magistrates in 1704 when the goods he was carrying were destroyed by fire.[12]

Garnett was just one of a long line of carriers who plied the London route from Manchester. In the late sixteenth century the Shuttleworth family, near Bolton, employed several London carriers and in the early decades of the next century the Chetham brothers of Manchester dispatched their raw cotton and made-up fustians from and to London by carrier.[13] Taylor recorded three groups of carriers from Manchester, as well as others 'that doe passe through divers other parts of *Lancashire*'. From then on the various carrier guides provide a continuous record of carrier services between the two places. In the 1680s there were two services from Manchester and three others which served a number of places including Manchester. In 1715 four firms provided four services per week, a level which was more or less maintained to mid-century. By the late 1750s the number of firms had risen to six and the number of services to ten per week.[14]

Supplementing these London services was a whole network of carriers trading to other places. By 1772, when the overall picture can be seen for the first time, they formed a substantial transport system. Of the 101 services per week from Manchester, about two-thirds were local, the rest, other than those to London, directed to important provincial centres, most of them fairly nearby, Derby, Nottingham, Leeds, Sheffield, but others a considerable distance away, Birmingham, Bristol, Cambridge, Newcastle-upon-Tyne.[15] A large part of the country was, therefore, directly accessible by road transport and, of course, Manchester carriers linked up with colleagues from other parts. For how long this precise system had existed is difficult to establish. The Manchester newspapers of the 1750s identify local carriers from Rochdale, Chorley and Bolton, together with Joseph Bucknall, a Coventry carrier, John Bostock, a wagoner of Wakefield, and a bankrupt carrier, Thomas Berisford of Gorton, whose stock was offered for sale at The Ram Inn, Northampton.[16] This suggests at least part of the later system already existed by mid-century and some of it must have originated much earlier.

The 1730s was perhaps the crucial decade. Those years marked the onset of a major phase of development of Manchester's trade. Aikin explained how in the forty years from 1730 the so-called 'Manchester men' made the transition from travelling chapman to master manufacturer. Like their counterparts in Leeds, they stayed at home to organise production and maintained contact with the market through specialist agents, commercial travellers and carriers. In both places the extension of trade coincided with substantial improvements in road transport. In the 1740s, Leeds merchants undertook a large programme of turnpike construction in the West Riding, in part because of their dissatisfaction with the Aire & Calder navigation. The first turnpike from Manchester was that to Buxton, in 1724, promoted, significantly, as the shortest route to London and was followed in 1732, 1735 and 1741 by three trans-Pennine promotions, indicative of a drive to gain better access to the port of Hull through which an increasingly important trade with northern Europe was conducted.[17] Aikin associated this phase with the substitution of wagons for packhorses but there is every reason to believe that it also marked in Manchester a stage of increased reliance on road transport in general and on the services of common carriers in particular.

It would follow that by about mid-century opportunities in this Manchester-to-London trade ought to have improved. Carrier services did increase, from four to ten per week, but otherwise change came only slowly. For two or three decades more the trade retained much of its traditional form. The half-dozen or so firms carrying to London all operated from inns or warehouses in innyards, even if, like Pickfords, their real base was elsewhere; they worked their wagons at the same speeds and journey times, and acted jointly when increasing their rates of carriage. That a strong competitive element nevertheless remained, though not overtly conducted by way of price or speed, is suggested by the rapid turnover of firms engaged in the trade. Of thirteen signatory firms to joint advertisements, giving notice of rates' increases, published by the London carriers in the *Manchester Mercury* in 1765 and 1767,[18] only four remained to be listed in the first Manchester directory published in 1772. Indeed if all firms trading in the mid-1760s signed both notices, six had disappeared during the intervening two years and three new ones come forward to replace them. Even in this early period, therefore, when the overtly competitive element was perhaps more muted than it later became, firms passed freely in and out of the trade and only the occasional one survived for very long.

The 1772 directory provides a brief perspective of the Manchester-to-London carrying trade.[19] Six firms were listed, Pickfords, Bass & Co., Cooper & Co., Hulse & Co., Washington & Co. and Wood & Co. Of these, Cooper and Wood were new firms since the 1760s. The joint services of the six totalled ten per week, the same as in the 1750s. Bass and Wood provided one service per week each, the others two. As journey times were also still, so far as is known, the same as in the 1750s, their scale of operations remained largely unchanged. Bass and Wood needed four wagons for their weekly service, the rest six, giving a total of thirty-two wagons employed in the trade. At three weeks' duration and 8 tons carried per round trip, they could perform 544 trips and convey about 4350 tons a year.

The traditional pattern of the trade began to change in the 1770s. In road transport generally and in places other than Manchester, the frequency of services was increased, speeds were accelerated and journey times cut.[20] 'Flying' wagons were already travelling some roads, but the emphasis on speed became much more marked, as did the more directly competitive running of one wagon service against another. Not enough is known about the eighteenth-century road haulage industry to be able to explain this phase of its development satisfactorily. Why did it occur in Manchester later than in some other places? What did it owe to competitive forces within the trade, what to possible technical improvements in vehicle design or road conditions, what to anticipated competition from the nearly completed Trent & Mersey canal?

The break came in Manchester in May 1776 when a new firm of carriers, Swaine & Co. and Frith & Co., cut the journey time to London from nine to eight days and followed this up in the autumn with a further reduction to six days.[21] The rest of the trade seems to have ignored the first cut, but responded vigorously to the second. Pickfords and Cooper & Co. countered with an even more dramatic reduction, to four and a half days, halving, within a matter of weeks, what had for decades been the standard journey time between Manchester and London. However, although the advertised four and a half days was sustained in practice, it proved to be an awkward timing for scheduling purposes, being inefficient in the use of wagons, and was replaced by a timing of five days. Speeds were then stabilised at this rate to the end of the century.

Quicker transit times led naturally to more frequent services. At these higher speeds two services per week could be performed by four wagons instead of the six or more which the firms operating at that level owned. There was, therefore, the choice of either getting rid of two wagons or moving to three services per week. Cooper & Co. and Hulse & Co. took the latter course and soon announced an extra service and Pickfords, although there is no direct evidence, most likely followed suit. And again this first increase was quickly followed by others. In 1780 Pickfords was operating four services per week, by 1788 six per week, effectively a daily service since Sunday travel was still technically prohibited and commercial transport observed the ban. In both speeds and levels of service, therefore, once the traditional stability had been broken changes occurred rapidly but after a brief transitional phase a new stability emerged.

The 1781 directory of Manchester bears witness to the expansionary years of the late 1770s. Both the output of carrier services and the number of firms supplying them had grown by about 50 per cent, although in the London trade the growth of services was less and the number of firms had fallen by one. The next directory, in 1788, indicates that during the intervening years a recession had occurred, of minor proportions generally but, if the information is accurate, quite sharply in the London trade. Only two firms were recorded, Pickfords and Bass & Morris, which together provided only eight services per week instead of the previous thirteen, a fall perhaps explained by the first impact of canal competition. These losses were, however, more than made good in the next decade when, with the outbreak of the French wars and despite canals, road transport was once more at a premium. Three new firms entered the London trade in the 1790s, two only fleetingly, and services recovered to reach twenty per week by 1797. In that year, of the four firms engaged in the London trade, only Pickfords had been established for more than a handful of years.

Although the absolute number of long-distance carrier services slowly increased through the 1780s and 1790s, the overall balance between these and local services remained largely unaltered. Certain quite important changes were, however, taking place. The two groups were moving slowly towards their later segregation, for classification purposes, into 'country' carriers, those who continued to use the inns, and the 'principal' carriers, those who worked from independent warehouses or took premises of their own. In 1772 both groups were to be found in close physical proximity with each other, and with the coaching trade, clustered together in the inns of Deansgate, Market Street and Shudehill, the heart of the old township of Manchester. While the coaching trade remained in Deansgate and the county carriers in Shudehill, several of the major carriers, including Pickfords, had moved out by the 1790s, westwards to Bridge Street, off Deansgate, when that area was redeveloped with the building of the new bridge, and eastwards to Fountain Street, York Street and Dale Street. To the east especially the commercial and manufacturing interests spread rapidly and, whether for the sake of lower rents or closer proximity to potential traffic, leading carriers moved with them.

Twenty-five years later this divergence was even more marked, by which time the road-based carriers had been joined by a large number of firms carrying by canal. In 1824, of seventy-four principal carrying firms in Manchester, forty-five carried by water, twenty-five by land and four combined the two.[22] All of these had premises in the town and in addition there was about twice that number, chiefly of country carriers, operating from the nearby towns and villages of Lancashire and Cheshire, and even some from Yorkshire, to the inns at Shudehill. The principal road carriers were still grouped around Bridge Street and Fountain Street/York Street, the water carriers being necessarily located elsewhere, in the main grouped either at Castle Field, the head of the Bridgewater navigation, or the terminal wharfs of the Ashton and Rochdale canals. The impact of canal transport on Manchester's carrying trade had by then been quite striking, although the large number of concerns which were recorded as being exclusively road carriers, including such important firms as Deacon, Harrison & Co. and John Hargreaves, is a clear indication of the scope remaining to road transport.

Indeed it is worth dwelling briefly, as a preliminary to looking at the development of Pickfords' own road services in the period, on the growth of road transport during the first half of the nineteenth century. In Manchester itself the expansion of trade was sufficient to feed a swelling volume of traffic to both road and canal carriers. The author of the *Manchester Guide*, published in 1804, remarked that despite the proliferation of boats on the Bridgewater and Mersey & Irwell navigations, 'the land carriage between [Liverpool and Manchester] has been so far from decreasing that there are twenty times the goods carried by land now' than when the water routes had been first opened. Some 120 carriers were said to connect Manchester by road with all parts of the country.[23] And if water transport took the lion's share, perhaps later replacing some of these connections, road transport continued to be needed. Short-haul market services were considerably expanded; produce, coal and other heavy goods from nearby carted rather than boated into the town; traffic carted to and from the head wharfs of the Bridgewater, Ashton and Rochdale canals. By carriage and cartage, the volume of traffic passing over Manchester's roads on the eve of the railway was rising.[24]

The expansion of road transport in the nineteenth century owed a great deal to the outbreak of war with France. Not only was the demand for carrier services immediately boosted, but a programme of road building was put in hand which, under the guidance of men like Telford and McAdam and after the final turnpike boom of the 1810s and 1820s, raised the standard of the nation's roads to a peak. The effect on road haulage was to encourage further expansion and to increase its flexibility. Customers were presented with a widening range of speeds to choose from (appropriately priced since speed, as always, was expensive), slow and fast wagons and, especially in urban areas, regular services of even faster carts and vans. Around London there was a marked growth of carts and vans serving places within a distance of 10 to 15 miles while elsewhere the comparable development, especially in the 1820s and 1830s, took the form of short-haul market services linking provincial centres more strongly with their immediate hinterland.[25] Of the overall expansion of the industry there can be no doubt, even though appropriate and reliable statistics are, as yet, lacking. But if the number of firms in the trade is adopted as a rough and ready yardstick – and it can be no more because, since firms provided different levels of service they cannot, without serious risk of misrepresentation, be equally weighted as units of transport – then the count for London rises from 350 firms in 1790 to 500–550 in 1815, about 730 in 1823 and about 950 in 1840.[26] The size of the increase is significant, but more so the fact that it continued to rise steadily throughout the period. There was, especially in the 1820s and 1830s, a flowering of road goods transport, comparable to that in coaching, which has not yet received the attention it warrants.

Pickfords made a distinctive contribution to these developments. In July 1814 it inaugurated a new quality of road goods service, its famous caravans or fly-vans 'on springs and guarded',[27] which might fairly be regarded as a significant innovation in the technology of road transport. Vans of a kind were already in general use, but they were confined to relatively short distances and were unsprung vehicles, in effect light-weight wagons. The sprung van was a distinct advance in vehicle design. It enabled higher speeds to be maintained for greater distances, at less wear and tear to the horses and at less disturbance to the merchandise conveyed.

In design and operation Pickfords' vans were modelled on coaches. They were, indeed, described as 'a large oblong vehicle, like an immense box, on springs, drawn by four horses, with a coachman in front and a guard behind'.[28] They carried a pay-load of 3 tons, at an average speed of 6 miles per hour, roughly halfway between the faster speed of coaches and the slower speed of wagons. Fast journey times were achieved by continuous running. Like coaches, the vans kept moving day and night, employing successive relays of horses, comparable in calibre to the best coach-horse. Indeed some of Pickfords' drivers could not resist the temptation of racing against coaches. The emphasis, other than speed, was on punctuality. The journey was divided into a number of stages, each carefully timed and, again like the mail coaches, contractors who horsed the vans were fined if they failed to keep time. If customers were to pay a higher price, they had to be offered a quality product.

The innovation was highly successful. A daily service was introduced between Manchester and London, the journey being completed in thirty-six hours instead of the four or five days by ordinary wagon. The Manchester-to-London line remained the core of Pickfords' van services, but in time others were added. A branch van from Sheffield was started in 1819, taking in Chesterfield, Mansfield and Nottingham and linking with the Manchester vans at Leicester. Leicester was the control point. Loads were redistributed or duplicates put on from there as the traffic required. The same year saw a further extension, to Liverpool. Initially it was served by an extension van from Manchester, but a more direct service was soon provided by way of a branch van from Macclesfield. Again careful timing was a feature of the operation. The down London van arrived in Macclesfield at 2.35 a.m. and at 4.00 a.m. a van left for Liverpool. It returned the same day, in time to connect with the up van which arrived in Macclesfield from Manchester at 10.00 p.m.[29] Other short van routes worked at this time were between Macclesfield and Congleton, and Sheffield and Leeds. The network of vans, therefore, mirrored the line of the firm's established road services, resting on the same focal points of Manchester, Sheffield, Leicester and London. Pickfords' vans became 'as familiar as the railway trains of today',[30] and, of course, it was not long before competitors followed the firm's lead.

Van speeds fell about halfway between coach and wagon, and so did van prices. Daniel Deacon's statement, that of an experienced carrier, of the relative costs of carriage between London and Yorkshire in the late 1830s, 18 shillings per hundredweight by coach, 12 shillings by van and 6 shillings by wagon, nicely exemplified the balance of speed and price. These prices reflected several years of keen competition.[31] Pickfords' charges were rather higher, opening at 20 shillings per hundredweight, or 2 pence per pound, between Manchester and

London and being raised to 23s 4d per hundredweight in July 1822. Competition later forced them down, but the lowest known charge was 16 shillings per hundredweight. A special rate was charged for parcels under 14 pounds, 2 shillings for 6 pounds or less and then at 3 pence per pound. This was the traffic the van service was particularly aimed at, those small parcels plus urgent and/or expensive items which could be enticed away from the coaches.

Some of the vans' customers can be identified. 'Two, at least, of the old Manchester banks were accustomed to send their heavy London packets by Pickfords' van.' The main demand for speed came from London dealers in fancy goods and silk who visited Manchester each week to make their purchases from the warehouses. Only by van could they get their wares to London in time to inspect them before they travelled north again. The first van to leave Manchester after the week's buying was on a Sunday night and so great was the pressure for space that financial inducements were offered by some dealers, or so it was alleged, for preferential treatment.[32]

How profitable this line of business was is uncertain. One statement, by Samuel Salt, usually a reliable source, put Pickfords' van profits for the years 1818 to 1825 at the very healthy figure of £24,000 per annum.[33] Salt apparently intended to imply that the profit was very large, but there is reason for scepticism of the figure he quoted. A fully loaded van, 3 tons at 20 shillings per hundredweight, would have earned £60 per trip between Manchester and London. Averaging the claimed profit over the maximum number of trips per annum over that one route, ignoring the others for the moment and the fact that many vans were not full, implies a clear profit of £40 per trip. Such a profit margin is at least unlikely and moreover conflicts sharply with the express view of Pickford officials who flatly denied in the mid-1830s that the vans were so profitable. In fact they claimed that the vans covered their expenses by only a small amount but were nevertheless of great value to the firm since by sending its correspondence, some 40,000 letters a year at the time, by the vans it escaped an otherwise enormous postage bill.[34]

There was more road traffic, however, than that carried by the vans. The conventional wagon services remained, operated by broad- and narrow-wheeled vehicles. Pickfords' fly-wagons continued to run between Manchester and London, three times a week in 1836, and carrying about the same load as the vans. In an emergency, frost in winter, drought or the annual stoppage of the canals in summer, road transport came back into its own. Otherwise the main scope for road haulage, and where it continued to expand, was in areas where it provided the more efficient means of transport. For Pickfords this was concentrated in the hill country of the Pennines where roads could provide a much shorter route than river or canal. Leeds and Sheffield were 36 miles apart by road, Chesterfield and Sheffield only 20 miles, but both were separated by 100 miles of water. The water route between Leeds and Derby was 150 miles compared with 72 by road; a journey which a wagon could perform in two days took two weeks by water and involved two or three trans-shipments. Delay and multiple handling both narrowed the margin between road and water transport.[35]

The area between Manchester, Leeds and Sheffield was where Pickfords' wagon services were particularly extended in the 1820s and 1830s. One of the first routes was between Manchester and Sheffield, commenced as a daily service in the early 1820s and stepped up to twice daily in 1835. Another, started in September 1820, was from Sheffield to Nottingham, six days a week. Others were concentrated in the West Riding. One was from Manchester, linking with the Calder & Hebble navigation at Halifax, and there were daily services from Huddersfield to Leeds, Bradford and Halifax. Huddersfield and Halifax were being used as canalheads to and from which traffic was being dispatched by road. Pickfords evidently employed the Huddersfield canal to enter Manchester but other carriers sent traffic the whole way by road. Witnesses supporting the Manchester and Leeds Railway Bill in 1836, insisted on the preference for road transport. 'There are very few goods sent from Leeds to Manchester except by waggons, the canal route is very circuitous indeed.'[36]

ROAD TRAFFIC

The traffic carried by road from Leeds, Bradford and Halifax to Manchester was, of course, the woollen and worsted cloth produced in those towns. The conveyance of cloth and other textiles is a recurring theme in the history of road transport. Its place in the origins and early days of the road carrying trade has already been observed and it occurs again prominently in the 1830s. What other traffic was conveyed by the road carrier? For reasons already explained it is misplaced to conceive of particular categories of goods as being pre-eminently carrier traffic or, taking the contrary view, excluded from his wagon. Having said that, certain types of goods were more commonly carried than others and it is worth probing a little deeper to discover what these were. Here the lack of surviving records of carrier businesses is a great weakness but enough can be gleaned for a reasonable picture to be pieced together.

One carrier's traffic is known in some detail, that of William Bass of Burton-on-Trent. In the 1760s the contents of his Manchester-to-London wagons included butter, cheese, game, hops, honey, malt, wool, rushes, leather, furniture and a myriad of sundries which defy categorisation or enumeration. These were the sort of products which any carrier might convey in any area. But, especially on the London routes, there was another segment of traffic characteristic of the local economy which the carrier served. In Bass's case this comprised the felt hats taken to London for James Oliphant, among others, from a number of local hatters; spades, engine-plates and other metalware for Thomas Thornewill and screws for Job Wyatt, both local iron merchants; to say nothing of his own product, ale, in large quantities.[37]

Only a few customers actually served by Pickfords can be identified. One was Samuel Oldknow whose fine muslins were conveyed by wagon in the 1780s from Mellor to his warehousemen, S. and W. Salte, in London. Returns loads to Mellor included bags of superior quality Barbados cottonwool, a piano 'packed up very carefully', and frequently boxes of £200 cash, presumably to help Oldknow pay his wages. Oldknow can not have been the only cotton firm in the Manchester area to employ Pickfords. Light textiles were also carried for John Swanwick, high-class mercer and draper of Macclesfield. Swanwick obtained his cloth, gloves and buttons from all over the country, but especially London. One of his London suppliers, Nichols & Co., wholesale haberdashers and whalebone cutters of Cateaton Street, sent regular consignments to Macclesfield from the 1780s to the early 1800s by means of Pickfords' wagon. There were metal goods as well, files for Peter Stubs of Warrington delivered by Pickfords, and other carriers, to 'customers in all parts of the kingdom', and, the contents of a wagon sunk beneath floodwater by a foolhardy driver, 'besides hosiery and other goods, a ton of cutlery from Sheffield'.[38]

The best evidence on the composition of road traffic, and the continuing vigour of road transport, is contained in the testimony of the numerous witnesses appearing before parliamentary committees in support of railway promotions in the 1830s. It provides only an impressionistic guide to the volume of traffic then being conveyed by road but as to its content it is highly informative. Swift road transport was the only way by which fresh produce, like meat and butter, could get to London markets in prime condition. Gloucestershire woollen cloth merchants were emphatic that for the conveyance of fine Saxony wools from London and the dispatch of their high-value woollen cloth to the capital only road transport would do. 'We send all the goods we can by carrier, preferring the quicker and certain though more expensive mode of conveyance to the uncertainty at a small expence.'[39] John Early, of the famous firm of blanket makers at Witney, was equally emphatic. He employed water transport only for oil, 'it being a raw article we are not so particular, the time is not so much an object, but when the manufactured article is sent we like to have it sent as early as possible'.[40] From the Reading draper, Oxford wine and spirit dealers, the Horsham grocer, Nottingham hosiers and lace dealers, Norwich worsted and silk manufacturers, the Leeds woollen merchant, representative evidence was presented of their dependence on road transport. And wagoners from Birmingham, Leeds, York, Manchester and Southampton explained the other circumstances in which road was preferred to water transport.[41] Without elaborating further it is plain that there was plenty of business for road transport in the 1820s and 1830s, as there had to have been to explain the size and growth of the industry in those years.

ROAD AND RAIL

That railways soon bit deeply into road traffic is not surprising since they were built for that very purpose. Witnesses who spoke so firmly about their preference for road transport were equally sure of what they hoped to gain from railways. They looked for the quality of service provided by road transport, its reliability, regularity and directness, but at a higher speed and lower cost. What railway promoters had their eye on, and never failed to include in the supporting 'traffic cases' they presented to Parliament, was, in addition to passenger business, precisely those categories of traffic, produce, light merchandise and urgent goods, which had figured in the witnesses' evidence. What these goods might lack in volume, compared with heavy goods conveyed by canal, they more than made up for in value and formed a potentially very lucrative source of revenue. As one question and answer so clearly put it: 'The greatest portion of the income for the carriage of goods is expected from those denominated light goods?' 'Yes; that is the carriage by waggon.'[42] It is too simple, and misses a crucial step in promoters' calculations, to draw a line between passenger traffic drawn from roads to railways, and goods traffic drawn from canals.

For a time promoters themselves were not too sure which category of business to go for. The case for the Liverpool & Manchester railway had hinged largely on the needs of the goods traffic between the two places, and the inadequacy of the water routes to accommodate it. The next cluster of promotions, influenced by the then astonishing success of the Liverpool & Manchester's passenger business, gave much greater prominence to road traffic. No road carrier gave evidence on the Liverpool & Manchester Railway Bill but thereafter few Railway Bills came to Parliament without expert witnesses both as to the potential passenger traffic, buttressed by coaching statistics certified by the Stamp Office, and to goods traffic currently handled by road carriers. The fact that it was thus marked out as a prime target is perhaps the best evidence of the importance attached to road traffic.

The transfer from road to rail was, when it came, decisive, although not quite so abrupt as is often implied. It occurred more slowly for goods than for passenger traffic, for short-haul than for long-distance routes. Indeed for a time, to the 1850s, local market services continued to expand. There were still many miles of railway yet to be built in 1850, including a large number of local branch lines, and until they were ready, roads and road carriers had to be relied on for access to the nearest railhead or market town. Of the three tiers of the traditional carrying trade only a handful of the bottom rank, the local or village carriers, survived, some of whom, or rather their descendants, lived long enough to see the first stirrings of revival at the turn of the century.[43]

The opening of the Liverpool & Manchester railway, in 1830, provided Pickfords with a foretaste of what was to come, although of itself was no great immediate threat. As a relatively short, detached line of rails, and unsupported by any others for several years, it touched only the fringes of Pickfords' operations. It soon became the preferred means of conveyance between Manchester and Liverpool, at least for the type of goods which had previously gone by van, and traffic was transferred with little disturbance to the rest of the business. Sheffield goods, including the steel and metalware carried for Stubs, which had previously been sent on from Manchester 'by caravan, waggon and canal' were instead 'forwarded to Liverpool by the railway'.[44] A substantial volume of business was built up, sufficient for the railway company to provide Pickfords with a warehouse, rent free, in Liverpool for its van and Sheffield goods.[45]

During the 1830s more Railway Bills were passed and longer lines of railway laid down. By the middle of 1837 a continuous rail link between London and Lancashire was rapidly approaching completion. The northern section, between Liverpool and Birmingham, was opened in July 1837 and the southern section, to London, early the following year. In the early summer of 1837, therefore, road interests likely to be affected began to prepare for change. The trustees of the Ashbourne to Leek turnpike, part of the route employed by Pickfords, met in the June to consider their future 'in consequence of the railroads intended shortly to be opened'.[46] They realised that the good times were over, toll receipts in fact peaked that year, but hoped that the offer of rebates to stage-coach operators inclined to give up would moderate what even so would inevitably be a substantial fall in their revenue.

The same month Pickfords decided to abandon its van service. The van horses were put up for sale, in London, 'twenty remarkably fine, powerful, young, fresh, good-actioned, short-legged horses, in beautiful condition . . . just taken off their well-known London, Manchester and Liverpool van, in consequence of the intended opening of the railroad from Liverpool to Birmingham'.[47] Pickfords' action was part of a wider strategy to adopt railway conveyance, and it is not surprising that van goods were the first to be switched, but the move proved to be slightly premature. Conditions on the Grand Junction railway, the Liverpool-to-Birmingham line, were a little confused at first and some of Pickfords' clients, bullion merchants in particular, preferred to continue with the service they knew. For a short time, therefore, a limited van service, three days a week, was restored but continued only until the southern section, the London and Birmingham railway, was opened. The vans were taken off this route for good in May 1838.[48] An offer to the firm of reduced tolls by the trustees of the Ashbourne-to-Leek turnpike was not pursued.

This was not quite the end for Pickfords' road services. Railways were built piecemeal and for several years, until an outline network was complete, there were gaps in the system which road vehicles were able to plug. The main scope was in the provision of temporary road links to towns just off the main line, until a branch was built to them, or to towns on the planned route which the rails had not yet reached. As gaps were filled, the vans and wagons were moved on to new locations. For several years in the late 1830s and early 1840s there was a fair amount of scope. In May 1841, for example, a van was put on from Stoke to the railhead at Birmingham, and others ran from Derby to Manchester and from Derby through Leek and Ashbourne to Macclesfield. Bradford, Bristol, Canterbury, Hastings, Halifax, Warwick, Wakefield and many other places were all linked at this time to the rail network by wagon and van. From the mid-1840s the main outlet was in the north of England, a shifting frontier as the line of rails crept on from York to Darlington, to Durham, to Newcastle. The frontier was closed in July 1847 when the Berwick-to-Newcastle line completed the east coast route to Scotland.[49]

One of the drivers employed by Pickfords in the borders was a certain James Paterson. He provides a link between the traditional role of road transport, reaching back to the origins of the carrying trade itself, and its new form in the second half of the nineteenth century as short-haul, urban cartage, ancillary to the railway industry. James Paterson was still a young man when his job came to an end and like many before him and since he decided to try his luck in London. There with the moral and financial support of Walter Carter, a Manchester carrier, he founded the firm of Carter, Paterson & Co. From tiny origins it grew into a major transport firm, with which in the future Pickfords itself became inextricably bound up.

REFERENCES: CHAPTER 4

1 20 Geo. II, c.10.
2 Burley, 'Economic development of Essex', p. 231.
3 Willan, *An Eighteenth Century Shop-keeper*, p. 109.
4 House of Lords Record Office (HLRO), minutes of evidence, HL, 1791, Worcester and Birmingham Canal Bill, fol. 7.
5 Mann, *Wiltshire Textile Trades*, p. 373.

6 HLRO, minutes of evidence, HC, vol. 18, 1836, London and Cambridge railway.

7 J. D. Marshall (ed.), *The Autobiography of William Stout of Lancaster, 1665–1752* (Manchester: Manchester University Press, 1967).

8 G. L. Turnbull, 'Trends in the development of the road haulage industry in the eighteenth century', paper presented to the Economic History Society Conference, Swansea, 1978, pp. 7–11.

9 D. Defoe, *A Tour Through the Whole Island of Great Britain* (London: Everyman Library, 1928), appendix to the second volume; H. Homer, *An Enquiry into the Means of Preserving and Improving the Public Roads of This Kingdom* (Oxford: 1767), p. 8; M. Postlethwayt, *The Universal Dictionary of Trade and Commerce*, 2nd edn (London: Knapton, 1758), Vol. I, p. 616.

10 For an illuminating example of the comparative advantage between wagons and packhorses, *House of Commons Journal*, vol. XXVIII, pp. 133–44.

11 *Manchester Mercury*, 24 July 1753.

12 N. Lowe, *The Lancashire Textile Industry in the Sixteenth Century* (Chetham Society, 3rd series, vol. XX, 1972), ch. V; HLRO, Main Papers, HL, 2 February 1719; W. Le Hardy and G. L. Reckitt (eds), *Buckingham Sessions Records*, Vol. II 1694–1705 (Aylesbury: Buckingham County Council, 1936), pp. 405–6.

13 Harland, *The Shuttleworth Accounts*; Wadsworth and Mann, *Cotton Trade and Industrial Lancashire*, pp. 31, 33, 36–48.

14 J. Taylor, *The Carriers Cosmographie* (London: A.G., 1637), p. 15; T. De Laune, *The Present State of London* (London: Larkin, 1681); *The Merchants and Traders Necessary Companion* (London: Hinde, 1715); G. J. Ghent, *Great Britain's Vade Mecum* (London: 1720); *The Intelligencer: or Merchants Assistant* (London: 1738); J. Osborn, *A Compleat Guide to . . . London* (London: Osborn, 1740 and successively to 1783).

15 *The Manchester Directory for 1772*, pp. 55–7.

16 These are mentioned in the *Manchester Mercury* between 1753 and 1756.

17 Aikin, *Description of . . . Manchester*, p. 183; R. Guest, *A Compendious History of the Cotton Manufacture* (Manchester: 1823), pp. 10–11; Defoe, *Tour Through the Whole Island*, Vol. III, pp. 102, 154; R. G. Wilson, *Gentlemen Merchants, the Merchant Community in Leeds 1700–1830* (Manchester: Manchester University Press, 1971), pp. 137–49; Wilson, 'Transport dues'; for Manchester turnpikes, *House of Commons Journal*, vol. XX, p. 363; vol. XXI, p. 805; vol. XXII, p. 372; vol. XXIII, p. 649.

18 *Manchester Mercury*, 24 September 1765, 1 December 1767.

19 Five directories were published before the end of the century, in 1772 (Raffald), 1781 (Raffald), 1788 (Lewis), 1794 (Scholes), 1797 (Scholes). Further references to these are not given.

20 P. T. Marcy, 'Britain's roads and communications on the eve of the Industrial Revolution, 1740–1780', *Transactions of the Bristol and Gloucestershire Archaeological Society, 1967*, vol. LXXXVI (1968), pp. 158–9; *York Courant*, 14 July 1772, acceleration of Leeds–London wagons.

21 The following is based on the Manchester newspapers and directories of the period.

22 Baines, *History, Directory and Gazeteer of Lancashire*, pp. 405–6.

23 J. Aston, *The Manchester Guide* (Manchester: Aston, 1804), pp. 282–4.

24 Musson, 'Industrial motive power', p. 431: a third of the coal brought into Manchester in 1836 was transported by road, and much of the rest would have been carted from the canalheads; for cartage in Manchester generally, HLRO, minutes of evidence, HC, vol. 24, 1836, Manchester and Salford Canal Bill; B. W. Beacroft, 'The streets and street traffic of Manchester, 1890–1914' (unnpublished MA thesis, Leicester, 1963), ch. 1.

25 Developments around London are observable from the contemporary directories; M. J. Freeman, 'The carrier system of south Hampshire, 1775–1851', *Journal of Transport History*, new series, vol. IV (1977), pp. 64–9.

26 *Universal British Directory*, 1790, Vol. I; Critchett and Woods *Post Office Directory*, 1815; Pigot & Co., *London and Provincial Commercial Directory for 1823–4*, quoted by P. S. Bagwell, *The Transport Revolution from 1770* (London: Batsford, 1974), p. 57; *Robson's London Commercial Directory*, 1840.

27 *Manchester Mercury*, 5 July 1814; most of the other details of the van operations are from a journal, 1817–22, and a memorandum book written up in the 1830s, PRO/BTHR Rail 1133/126, 129.

28 J. T. Slugg, *Reminiscences of Manchester Fifty Years Ago* (Manchester: Cornish, 1881), p. 226.

29 I. Finney, *Macklesfelde in ye Olden Times* (Macclesfield: 1873), p. 80.

30 Slugg, op. cit.

31 *SC on postage*, PP, 1837–8, vol. XX, Q. 7267.

32 L. H. Grindon, *Manchester Banks and Bankers*, 2nd edn (London: 1881), p. 173; *SC on London Grand Junction Railway Bill*, HL, Sessional Papers (SP), 1836, vol. XXXI, evidence of Joseph Derham.

33 S. Salt, *Railway and Commercial Information* (London and Manchester: Smith, 1850), p. 11.

34 Derham's evidence to *SC on London Grand Junction Railway Bill*.

35 *SC on North Midland Railway Bill*, HL, SP, 1836, vol. XXXII, evidence of J. Hubbard, T. Coxe, F. Saunders; details of these wagons are from the same sources as in note 27.

36 HLRO, minutes of evidence, HL, vol. 2, 1836, Manchester and Leeds Railway Bill, H. Dawson's evidence.

37 Transcripts of William Bass's book, 1760–70, kindly provided by Mr Ben Ward.

38 Unwin, *Samuel Oldknow and the Arkwrights*, chs 4, 5; Swanwick papers, kindly made available to me by their owner, Mrs M. Moss of Prestbury; T. S. Ashton, *An Eighteenth Century Industrialist. Peter Stubs of Warrington, 1756–1806* (Manchester: Manchester University Press, 1939), p. 91; *The Gentleman's Magazine*, vol. LXXXIX (1809), p. 81.

39 *SC on Cheltenham and Great Western Union Railway Bill*, HL, SP, 1836, vol. XXXI, evidence of C. Stephens.

40 *SC on Oxford and Great Western Union Railway Bill*, HL, SP, 1837, vol. XIX, evidence of J. Early.

41 Published or MSS evidence on the following Railway Bills, excluding those already mentioned in other notes: Great Western, London and Brighton, Midland Counties, London and Norwich (Eastern Counties), London and Birmingham, Birmingham and Derby, York and North Midland, Hull and Selby, London and Southampton.

42 *SC on Oxford and Great Western Union*, evidence of W. Hemming.

43 A. Everitt (ed.), *Perspectives in English Urban History* (London and Basingstoke: Macmillan, 1973), ch. 8; and 'Country carriers in the nineteenth century', *Journal of Transport History*, new series, vol. III (1976), pp. 179–202.

44 *Sheffield Directory* (Sheffield: Gell, 1825), p. 178; *Sheffield Directory* (Sheffield: White, 1833), p. 143; Stubs papers, steel book 1834–40, Archives Department, Manchester Central Reference Library

45 *SC on Railway Communication*, 1840, QQ. 3729–33.

46 A. E. and E. M. Dodd, 'The old north road from Ashbourne to Leek', *Transactions of the North Staffordshire Field Club*, vol. LXXXVIII (1948–9), p. 56.

47 *The Times*, 14, 20 June 1837.
48 *SC on Railroad Communication*, PP, 1837–8, vol. XVI, Baxendale's evidence.
49 G. Neville to W. Lewis, 15 May 1841, Pickfords Removals Ltd; *Derby Directory* (Derby: Glover, 1842/3), p. 158; publicity maps of Pickfords' rail services, 1839, 1841, 1844, copies in the possession of the author.

5

Pickfords Canal Carrier, 1785–1850

That canals made a vital contribution to Britain's industrial growth can not be doubted. Industrial growth went hand in hand with large-scale production, and scale and concentration of production in turn required the support of bulk transport services, cheaply provided. Before the railway, only water transport could fill this need; and before the canal, water transport was inevitably confined to the coast or navigable river. Sites favoured by cheap transport facilities rather than abundant local resources tended to prosper as centres of growth. Canals removed that constraint. As a conduit of cheap transport capable of being introduced in most places where economic need demanded it, the canal necessarily exerted a profound influence on the shape of future development. Not only was the pattern of inland transport transformed, the sharp fall in transport costs, especially in the basic traffics of minerals, agricultural produce and heavy goods, could not fail to have powerful, multiplier effects across the whole structure of the economy.

Change, however, came slowly. Britain's system of inland waterways took a lot longer to be completed than is often realised.[1] The canal age began in the 1750s in Lancashire, with the Sankey Brook and the Duke of Bridgewater's schemes, but it was a full fifty years before traffic could flow easily and continuously through anything like a national network of inland waterways. There could be many years' delay between the ceremonial digging of the first turf of a new canal and its opening for traffic. Some of the early schemes in the midlands were completed promptly, but others, notably the important Oxford canal, took two or three decades to finish. Although by the mid-1770s parts of the midlands and south Lancashire were well served by canals, their effectiveness was limited to local traffic. Long-distance traffic by canal developed a lot more slowly. By the end of the 1770s the canals which connected the Mersey, Trent and Severn provided a limited number of long-distance routes, but the principal need was a through route to London.

London was the pivot of the nation's flow of traffic and until easy access was open to the capital from all parts an effective national system of canal carriage could not be expected to emerge. It was, however, one of the last routes to be developed. It required direct entry to London by canal, which the Grand Junction provided, partially from 1800 and fully, after the opening of the Blisworth tunnel, from 1805. From the turn of the century the trade to London, and the canal trade generally, expanded very rapidly, reaching its peak from the 1820s to the mid-1840s.

THE GROWTH OF THE CANAL CARRYING TRADE

The way in which the canal carrying trade developed generally can be illustrated by a brief outline of its growth in Manchester. The Mersey & Irwell navigation, completed in the early 1730s, formed one line of communication by water between Manchester and Liverpool. The Bridgewater canal provided a second. It reached Manchester from Worsley in 1764, and the extension along the north Cheshire boundary through to Liverpool was opened in March 1776. To the south lay a group of canals, as yet unconnected to the Bridgewater. The Trent & Mersey and the Staffordshire & Worcestershire canals stretched down through the industrial midlands to the canals around Birmingham, and on to Stourport on the Severn and Shardlow on the Trent. Both were progressively opened to local traffic from about 1770 but the need to construct tunnels at Harecastle and at Preston Brook, which gave entry to the Bridgewater, obstructed longer-distance flows. The two tunnels were opened in 1775, and the remaining stretch of the Trent & Mersey line between them was completed two years later. Uninterrupted canal conveyance then became possible between Manchester, Liverpool, the Potteries, Birmingham and the west midlands, and the towns, ports and catchment areas of the Trent and Severn river systems. This was the nucleus of a new transport system, uniting many of the most important centres of Britain's industrialising economy.

The growth of canal carriage from Manchester followed the progression of canal construction. Initially there was only local traffic, the duke's coal from Worsley, and his trading boats to and from Warrington.[2] Then in May 1774 the firm of Hugh Henshall & Co., already engaged in local trade on the Trent & Mersey canal, introduced a service from Birmingham and Stourport to Manchester and Liverpool. It catered for two main flows of traffic, one to Birmingham, Bristol and the west of England by way of the River Severn, the other to Derby, Nottingham, east coast towns and London by way of the Trent. Henshall's advertised carriage rate between Manchester and Birmingham was £2 12s 6d per ton, a substantial reduction on the previous land rate of £4 per ton. But this was only the first stage of an even bigger cut. Until the connection was made between the Bridgewater and the Trent & Mersey, goods had to be taken by road from Stockton Quay, Warrington, to Burslem wharf, at the south end of the Harecastle tunnel. When through conveyance became possible three years later, the canal rate was reduced further to £1 10s 0d per ton.[3]

Hugh Henshall & Co., named after the Trent & Mersey Company's chief engineer who was responsible for the completion of the canal after the death of James Brindley, his brother-in-law, was in effect the trading arm of the Trent & Mersey Canal Company, being set up by a group of directors to promote trade on the canal. Henshall & Co. was successful and built up a commanding position on the Trent & Mersey. In the early 1790s it controlled most of the traffic passing off the canal on to the River Trent and employed as many as seventy-five barges, then one of the largest barge fleets on the canals.[4] However, there was competition. In 1782 a new firm of carriers, Worthington & Gilbert, began a rival service to the midlands. This firm, too, enjoyed privileged connections in the person of John Gilbert, who was the son of the Duke of Bridgewater's agent. As a result his firm received, probably intentionally, favoured treatment at Castle Quay and hence a preference in respect of traffic originating in Manchester. The firm's success in taking business from Henshall & Co. precipitated a sharp clash between the duke and the Trent & Mersey Company.[5]

Pickfords was the first fully private firm to enter the canal trade in Manchester. Its move followed the revival of construction by the Coventry and Oxford Canal Companies in 1785, promising the completion of a canal route from Lancashire to London by way of the Thames at Oxford. The final sections, to Oxford in the south and Fazeley in the north, were finished in 1790. By then some traffic was already passing part of the way between London and Manchester by canal. A London directory for 1783 included among the carrying services to Manchester 'carriage to the canals and thence in barges' from The Saracen's Head, Snowhill. The name of the carrier was not recorded. Perhaps it was Henshall & Co., since it is known that the firm was operating just such a service three years later. It was conveying goods from Manchester down the Bridgewater and Trent & Mersey canals to Shardlow and taking them on from there to London by road. Pickfords entered the canal carrying trade by acquiring this portion of Henshall's business.[6]

From the end of 1786, when the takeover was announced, it is possible to piece together an outline of the development of Pickfords' canal services. At that time barges were dispatched from Manchester four times a week, and in order to speed up the delivery of goods in London the transfer to wagons was moved from Shardlow to Rugeley, farther north on the Trent & Mersey canal but in a more direct line for London. A couple of years later, this service had probably been stepped up to a frequency of six departures per week, the equivalent of a daily service.[7]

During the next fifteen years Pickfords progressively adopted canal conveyance for its traffic between Manchester and London, exploiting new canals and additional sections of existing canals as they became available. Negotiations were undertaken with the various companies whose line of water formed part of the canal route between London and Lancashire, contact usually being established some time before a particular stretch of water was ready for use. In May 1788, for example, eighteen months or so before the through route was finished, Matthew Pickford negotiated terms with the Coventry and Oxford Canal Companies for wharf and warehouse accommodation on their respective canals at Polesworth and Braunston. He also secured a temporary concession of reduced tolls from the Coventry canal for as long as he had to transfer to road wagons to get past its unmade section at Fazeley.[8] However, although the Oxford line south of Banbury was also still unfinished, there is no sign of a similar arrangement with that company.

The first inland water route to London from Lancashire was, therefore, by way of the Trent & Mersey, Coventry and Oxford canals to Oxford, and then by the Thames navigation. Its value was limited, however. It was indirect, the southern arm of the Oxford canal below Braunston following a particularly winding course, and navigation of the Thames below Oxford could be difficult. Consequently it did not take long for an alternative route to be promoted, the Grand Junction canal from Braunston to the Thames at Brentford, which would provide, especially by the Paddington extension, direct access to London. Construction of the Grand Junction began in 1793, on a scale appropriate to what was expected to become the arterial route to the capital.[9] In July 1796, Matthew Pickford was in touch with the canal company, discussing terms for his use of the upper section of the canal, north of the Blisworth tunnel. In August the following year, Pickfords' traffic on the canal was reported to have become 'a most valuable trade . . . between London and the northern parts of the kingdom'.[10]

For several years Pickfords' canal traffic to London relied on road haulage connections. London goods were trans-shipped between canal and road at Braunston, the reason it would seem for Matthew Pickford being asked by the Oxford Company in November 1789 to give up the premises he leased there.[11] Another canal carrier, Gothard & Co., followed Pickfords' practice in dispatching barges from Shelton wharf, Newcastle-under-Lyme, 'down the canal to Braunston, from thence by land to London'.[12] Matthew Pickford's response to the Oxford Company's decision was to move north to Coventry. A contemporary remarked on the large volume of goods from the north flowing into Coventry by canal, 'from whence they are taken to London by Mr. Pickford's waggons who has large warehouses on the wharf to store goods'. In 1794 Pickford's canal boats sailed every afternoon from Castle Quay to Coventry, from where 'goods for London and beyond' were to be forwarded 'upon fly-waggons'.[13]

In 1797 the fly-wagons were moved south to Blisworth. This followed the opening of the upper section of the Grand Junction canal, north of the Blisworth tunnel, which allowed continuous canal conveyance most of the way to London. Special arrangements in Pickfords' favour meant that Blisworth became a particularly suitable place at which to transfer to road wagons. In August 1797 the Grand Junction Company agreed to build 'a good carriage road' from Pickfords' wharf to the turnpike at Blisworth and then continue it over Blisworth Hill to the turnpike road leading from Northampton to Old Stratford, and on to London. In 1801 the canal company was even more accommodating, and built an extension of its tramway over Blisworth Hill to Pickfords' wharf.[14] Despite the fact that the lower section of the Grand Junction canal, south of the Blisworth tunnel, was opened in 1800 and was used by Pickfords, the firm having taken premises at White Friars on the Thames and at Paddington, northern traffic was not conveyed by that route. Until 1805, when the Blisworth tunnel was opened, Pickfords' northern traffic entered London by road. The additional costs of a second or third trans-shipment were evidently not offset by lower canal freights.

The long-distance canal trade to London was little developed before 1800. By that date Pickfords had been joined in the trade from Manchester by only one other firm, Bache & Co. of Coventry. The next decade, however, witnessed rapid expansion. The completion of the Grand Junction canal was a powerful stimulus. The company's basin at Paddington rapidly filled up as firms hustled to secure the lease of wharfs and warehouses there. From slow, almost languid beginnings, the canal trade entered a forty-year phase of bustle and haste as enterprise flooded in and firms vied for leadership and dominance. Pickfords strove to match the best of them. It acquired a commanding position in the Manchester trade early on and by the end was widely regarded as the country's leading canal carrier.

London and Manchester continued throughout to be the primary centres of Pickfords' canal trade. The high level of competition in the trade called for swift movement of goods, as much through the termini as between them. Termini were best located close to shippers and merchant customers and although central sites were expensive, and associated with pressure on space, they were none the less desirable. Pickfords moved from its original warehouse at Castle Field, on the south-western edge of Manchester, to a more central position in Great

Bridgewater Street, on the link between the Bridgewater and Rochdale canals, near to its main offices and stables in Oxford Road. The same progression occurred in London, from White Friars at Brentford, the original terminus of the Grand Junction, to Paddington Basin and finally, in 1820, to central London, to the City Road Basin of the Regent's canal. Pickfords' depot at City Basin became the headquarters of its entire canal operations. A private cut was dug from the main canal, special lifting gear erected, loading bays and warehouses were put up, together with a range of administrative offices. When, in 1824, the site was severely damaged by fire, it was said to have contained, no doubt with some exaggeration, 'the greater portion of the product of the northern part of England'.[15] The buildings were well insured and soon rebuilt.

To a predominantly north–south flow of traffic between London and Manchester were added a number of routes from east and west, and one or two cross-country routes for good measure. Surprisingly, perhaps, it was not until 1800 that Pickfords began carrying by canal between Manchester and Liverpool. Moreover, few resources seem to have been committed to the route and the firm's presence in Liverpool was at a fairly modest level. In the early 1820s it flirted with the alternative canal route between the two towns, that by way of the Leigh branch of the Bridgewater to its junction with the Leeds & Liverpool canal, but the results were disappointing and the experiment was soon abandoned. Services from Liverpool to London seem to have been a relatively late development. Other extensions were from Derby to London, soon after 1800, and from Birmingham in 1805. This move into Birmingham preceded a fairly substantial build-up in the midlands, reaching out to Worcester and Bristol in the west and Leicester in the east.

Leicester was not joined to the Grand Junction canal, and hence the direct route to London, until the opening of the Grand Union canal in 1814. Prior to that date access to the canal system had been possible but only by a long detour, sweeping north to the Trent by way of the Leicester and Loughborough navigations, through to the Trent & Mersey at Shardlow, and then completing the arc by turning south at Fradley Junction. Such a cumbersome route was good reason for Pickfords to introduce a more direct service to Leicester which combined road and canal conveyance. The original intention had been to dispatch goods from London to Brownsover wharf on the Oxford canal, near Rugby, and to continue from there by wagon. The Ashby-de-la-Zouch canal, however, approached even closer to Leicester, at Hinckley. In 1802, two years before its completion, the Ashby Company decided to ask 'Mr Pickford to consider whether he might not advantageously to himself and the public in his proposed carriage of goods to and from Leicester' choose Hinckley rather than Brownsover for the place of trans-shipment. Pickfords agreed and the Oxford and Coventry Canal Companies consented to help the trade along by co-operating in a toll reduction on all groceries conveyed between London and Leicester.[16]

On the day of the Grand Union's official opening, 9 August 1814, two of Pickfords' boats were among the flotilla which passed along the canal to inaugurate the line. While others stopped at Market Harborough to celebrate, Pickfords' boats continued to Leicester and immediately returned with a London-bound cargo. This was evidently the inception of a new service, a cross-country 'run-about' from Birmingham. A pair of boats left Birmingham every Thursday afternoon and travelled to Leicester by way of Warwick, Banbury and Oxford, arriving at their destination the next Monday. They departed the same evening, completed the return journey to Birmingham on the Thursday morning, and were ready to set off again the same afternoon. A service was also instituted from Leicester to Nottingham.[17]

Although it was to serve the west midlands and Bristol trade that Henshall & Co. had initiated its canal services from Manchester, Pickfords had shown little interest in that part of the country. Evidence suggests that the firm made no use of the Staffordshire & Worcestershire canal before 1825 and only limited use thereafter.[18] The first entry to Worcester was in fact from Birmingham, on the heels of the Worcester & Birmingham canal, opened in 1815. Once established, however, Worcester became an important outpost of Pickfords' provincial business in the west of England. A number of trading boats employed on the Severn carried the firm's influence down-river from Worcester to Bristol.

As well as taking up wholly new lines of canal and straying into some fresh areas of territory in the process, across the Pennines to Huddersfield, for example, Pickfords was also prompt to adopt improved routes which served existing traffic more efficiently. The Macclesfield canal, completed in 1831, provided a shorter route into Manchester and the Gloucester & Berkely canal eliminated some of the worst hazards of the Severn. As soon as both were open, Pickfords' traffic was diverted through them. However, for all the modifications and extensions the emphasis of Pickfords' canal trade remained firmly concentrated in the central corridor from London through to Lancashire.

THE CANAL TRADE IN OPERATION

Transport services on the canals were supplied by all kinds of agent.[19] Firms and individuals who dealt in large, regular traffics, such as coal, iron-ore, or grain, owned their own fleet of boats. Certain canal companies were also carriers, either openly, or, as in the example of

Henshall & Co., in disguise. Especially prior to 1800, before the canal trade really got into its stride, some companies owned and operated boats in order to develop the trade over their stretch of water. Carrying beyond their own line of canal was much less common, at least until the Canal Carriers Act of 1845 cleared up any uncertainties concerning the legality of such activities. In general, therefore, and especially during the heyday of canals, companies confined their operations to the management of their waterways and did not seek to control the traffic passing over them. The trade was left clear to private enterprise. Its rapid growth was accompanied by specialisation, between private and public carriers, between small, one-man businesses and large-fleet operators, between local and long-distance traders, between swift and slow services – indeed, all the features already well familiar in the road transport industry.

The slow or 'stage' boats, as they were called, displayed the characteristics of a 'tramp' service. Cargoes, of the low-value kind, were sought wherever they could be found. Boats were hauled by a single horse, and tied up overnight. It was the typical trade of the owner-operated small business. The fast or 'fly' trade, by contrast, tended to be the property of an élite group of carrying firms, large-fleet owners like Crowley, Bache, Sutton, Kenworthy, Robins, and of course Pickfords, which maintained a national scale of operations. Speed was of the essence in the fly trade, up to 4 miles per hour between locks but less than that for journeys overall. Relays of horses were used, double crews employed and special licences bought from the canal companies which accorded registered fly-boats priority at locks, that is, entitlement to jump the queue, a fruitful source of altercation between boatmen, and also conferred the right to continue travelling by night, passing through locks which would otherwise be chained up until morning. Fly-boats were run by schedule rather than departing when full, and rates for traffic so conveyed naturally attracted a premium. Although the boats carried all kinds of goods, the fly trade was typically composed of high-value freight, especially merchandise and groceries.

Pickfords dabbled briefly in the slow trade. Stage-boats were run between Derby and London in 1801–2,[20] but there is no evidence of similar services elsewhere. For the rest, the firm specialised in the fly trade, focused heavily on operations to and from London, although it is a point of interest that the craft operating the midlands 'run-about' service mentioned above were described as 'fly stage boats'. Pickfords' services from Manchester were by fly-boat from the start. By the early 1800s regular schedules had been established, boats being advertised to depart 'with or without loading'.[21] The licensing of fly-boats seems to have come in during the 1790s and was certainly common from the first decade of the nineteenth century. Pickfords' practice, and that of other carriers too, was to pay an annual composition for a certain number of boats rather than paying for each boat journey. Payments of this kind to the Coventry Canal Company, among others, are recorded from 1808 and continued until the licence system was abolished in the 1840s.

The financial requirements of the canal carrying trade were substantial, in terms of both capital and current needs. Considerable resources were needed to finance the credit and discounts allowed to traders, the most common form of competition between carriers, while premises and working stock absorbed yet further sums. It is possible to outline the chief categories of Pickfords' investment in the canal trade and to indicate very roughly the capital cost involved. The main provisions were for boats, horses, wharfs, warehouses, stabling and offices.

Pickfords' fleet of canal boats was built up from ten in 1795 to about eighty in 1820. For a time a number of boats were hired, never more than a dozen or so, but this practice ceased in 1822. From about that date also, the firm's barge fleet was extensively overhauled. Of eighty-three boats in use in 1821–2, seventy-six were classed as 'old' and only seven as 'new'. During the next five years eighty boats were disposed of and sixty-nine new ones built, the bulk of them, fifty, between 1822 and 1824. The average cost of these boats was about £192, or a total of some £13,500 for the entire number. The purpose of this rebuilding seems to have been straight replacement of stock, as numbers were held stable at about eighty-five to ninety boats for the rest of the decade. A second, lesser phase of building in 1830 and 1834 suggests a deliberate policy of expansion as net additions to stock raised the total to 116 trading boats in 1838.[22]

The principle of hiring instead of purchasing stock was also adopted for the supply of horses to haul the canal boats, and continued for a longer period of time. Prior to 1825 Pickfords owned no boat-horses at all; haulage of the canal boats was put out entirely to contractors. In 1817 contracts were placed for a total of 1,640 miles at 10 pence per double mile per horse. One man, Samuel Lea, who also acted as Pickfords' agent at Braunston, worked a total of 863 miles. A first purchase of 110 horses in 1825 was increased to 150 the following year. That remained the total until 1835 when, in a second spurt, following the expansion of the barge fleet, it jumped to 320 and on to a peak of 398 in 1838.[23] Pickfords' records contain no information concerning the price paid for these horses. Mr W. B. Grime, the agent to, and a proprietor of, the recently established New Quay Company trading on the Bridgewater canal, claimed in 1825 that the price of horses for the company's boats had risen from £20 to 'nearer £30'. If a compromise price of £25 is applied to Pickfords' purchase of boat-horses, the stud of 400 would have cost £10,000, spread over several years. Whether such prices were invariably paid, however, may be doubted. Canal-horses were not renowned as the finest specimens of the breed. Prime boat-horses were valued by Pickfords, in a rare stock list of 1831, at 30 to 40 per cent below prime van and wagon horses. Moreover, the average value, after depreciation, of fifty boat-horses was only £7, compared with £17 10s od for van horses and £15 0s od for wagon horses. Once past their best for road work, many van and wagon horses ended their working life plodding along the canal towpath.[24]

Substantial investment in premises was also undertaken, the cost of which, however, was met only in part by Pickfords. Since canal companies stood to benefit from the traffic which a firm like Pickfords could bring to their line, they were generally willing to erect wharfs and warehouses for the carriers' use. The companies retained ownership of the premises and let them out on a lease. In 1818, for example, Pickfords approached the Warwick & Birmingham Canal Company for the use of a complex of buildings at Warwick, including a warehouse, an agent's house, a boatshed and a shed in which to house road wagons. In asking for this accommodation, the firm argued that the increased toll revenue which it would bring together with the capital improvement to the company's property would more than offset the costs incurred. The canal company agreed, built the premises and leased them to Pickfords for twenty-one years, charging a rent calculated at $7\frac{1}{2}$ per cent of the construction costs.[25] The equipping of such premises, however, fell to the carrier. Unfortunately few figures of what this cost have been found. The £20,000 spent on Pickfords' canal headquarters at City Road Basin was exceptional, but the total cost of the firm's string of premises alongside the canals navigated by it must have added up to a sizeable sum. According to Baxendale, Pickfords had, in 1824, already spent £45,000 on premises and equipment since he had joined the firm. The one agency at Wolverhampton was later said to have cost £5,000, and a former agent claimed to have been told that three of Pickfords' provincial depots had cost £30,000, presumably in aggregate.[26] There is no sense in trying to total such shaky figures into an overall estimate of the capital employed, but it is clear that one is talking in terms of thousands rather than hundreds of pounds. In 1820–1 Pickfords' premises, the bulk of them employed in the canal trade, were valued for fire insurance purposes at £67,250. In the same year the firm also took out insurance for goods in transit to the value of £44,000.[27]

The organisation of canal traffic was highly complex. Full throughloads which could be trunked direct to their destination were the most desirable traffic but represented a relatively small proportion of the total tonnage between London and the north. The bulk of Pickfords' traffic was of an intermediate kind which came on to the main north-south route from east and west. This was directed to various staging points, sorted, and then sent forward to its appropriate destination. Cross-country traffic of this kind was tricky to organise, and required very clear methods of procedure. A cargo of 15 tons could, according to Baxendale, involve up to 150 consignees and therefore an equal number of invoices. To avoid chaos and ensure that cross-flows were dealt with promptly and accurately, constant care and attention were necessary.

Traffic from the east midlands was assembled at Shardlow. The employment of a few large Trent boats and, at a later date, establishments at Newark, Gainsborough and Hull, were the means by which Pickfords was able to draw on the river system of these eastern counties. Traffic to and from the west midlands and the west of England was channelled through Braunston, which stood at the junction of the Oxford and the Grand Junction canals. At Napton, nearby, the Oxford canal connected with the Warwick canals, giving entry to Birmingham and the west. Situated on the north–south line and with easy access to the west, Braunston was in many ways the focal point of the canal network of the south midlands. The central position of Braunston as an entrepôt was certainly important for Pickfords. The cost of a regular, timed schedule of fly-boats was the conveyance on occasion of only partial loads. To fill empty spaces goods might be picked up along the way, but in particular sufficient cargo to complete a load could usually be guaranteed at Braunston. This was especially important for the operation of boats returning from London since the balance of traffic was weighted heavily in the opposite direction. Boats which left London light could be filled up at Braunston or, if more appropriate, the boat might be taken off completely and its contents distributed between others.[28]

Canal carriers gained a reputation for great regularity in the conduct of their business. In 1840 supporters of the canal interest claimed that from the time their goods reached the carrier in Manchester they could calculate to within a few hours their time of arrival in London.[29] But it was not all plain sailing. The high cost and high loading factor of the typical canal boat rendered it an unwieldy unit of transport outside of categories of goods which easily lent themselves to bulk consignments. Capacity could, however, be maximised by reducing delays, shortening turn-round times and maintaining a keen regard to working efficiency. Swifter journey times allowed the more intensive use of stock – hence the system of licences in the fly-boat trade. Over and above these constraints was the central problem of peak loading, intrinsic to every branch of the transport industry. No carrier could afford to hold a margin of spare capacity sufficient to meet all temporary shifts in demand. Given notice boats could be called in from elsewhere, but even the most efficient carrier was unable to cope immediately with a sudden press of traffic.

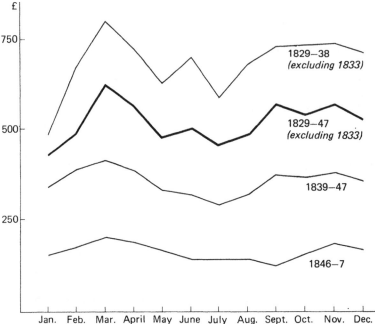

£

Fig. 5   *Seasonality in the canal trade: Pickfords' average monthly toll*
payments to the Oxford Canal Company, 1829–47

Even in normal times the canal trade was strongly seasonal in
character, as Figure 5 demonstrates.[30] The graph of Pickfords' average
monthly tonnage payments to the Oxford Canal Company for all but
one of the nineteen years from 1829 to 1847 displays distinct fluctuations. The most striking features are a marked peak in the early spring,
which sometimes occurred in April rather than March as shown in the
graph, together with a secondary peak in the late summer. The same
seasonality remained in the late 1840s, despite a sharp fall in traffic
by then. This traffic pattern was not particularly new, nor was it
confined to the canal trade, although it might have caused special
problems there because of the large-scale units employed. One explanation is to be found in the timing of export shipments overseas. In
1794 road carriers drew Parliament's attention to the exceptional
pressures on their services in March and April. More goods, they said,
were conveyed to London for export at this time than during any
other two months of the year. The seasonal export of manufactures,
following and preceding the hazards of winter voyages, can be found
in the East Anglian cloth trade of the early seventeenth century[31] and
there is plenty of evidence, in parliamentary proceedings on Railway

Bills in the 1830s, of merchants rushing their goods to the ports before the weather closed in for the autumn. Such fluctuations of demand inevitably raised difficult questions as to the optimal size of fleet. No carrier could afford capacity which, measured by the peaks, would be idle for up to half the year.

The lesson of experience was cautious creation of additional capacity. It is noticeable that in a period when the volume of canal traffic was still expanding, Pickfords' stock of canal boats remained stable through the 1820s and increased only slowly after 1830. Just when to expand is one of the decisions for which hindsight helps enormously! Presumably it did not take too long to build a canal boat so that once the decision had been made the shortcomings on the supply side could be quickly made good. The difficulty would have been to discriminate between the usual short-run peak and a permanent shift in demand. The carrier's reply to criticisms of delay was that his level of stock was adequate for normal conditions and could moreover cope with a far larger volume of traffic *provided it were regular*. Rail and bus commuters experience the same frustrations of peak-loading problems every day, and are equally unsympathetic to the complex economics to which they give rise.

The inadequacy of the water routes between Liverpool and Manchester was a key argument in the case for the rival railway project. The dilatoriness of those notorious bales of cotton which could be transported across the Atlantic in a shorter time than it took to remove them from Liverpool to Manchester is one of the favourite chestnuts of transport history. Mather, Richards and Hadfield have together reduced the wilder claims of Sandars and other railway propagandists.[32] The Bridgewater canal, the prime target of hostility, which was in turn personalised in the figure of R. H. Bradshaw, displayed many features of the special case, not the least of which was the dead hand of the duke's will which pre-empted the very considerable profits earned by the canal for uses other than reinvestment in it.

In presenting their arguments against the proposed railway, the Bridgewater trustees had a coherent case to make.[33] They rejected the principle of the railway promoters' claims, that there was a chronic deficiency in the supply of transport services between Liverpool and Manchester, and instead insisted that the problem lay in the irregularity of canal traffic. The trustees' fleet of boats had steadily increased with the years and could have absorbed twice the volume of traffic had it flowed regularly. In 1825 they could only cite the exceptional growth of traffic since 1823, occasioned by the onset of boom conditions in the economy; during the first quarter of 1825 traffic from Liverpool to Manchester was already 50 per cent higher than in the corresponding quarter of the previous year, which itself must have been the highest for several years. But commerce was fickle and instinct advised that such levels were unlikely to last. When the Bill was re-examined the following year, the boom had broken and the trustees had the evidence to complete their case. Traffic in the first two months of 1826 had been 75 per cent below the peak level of August 1825. Even after subsequent recovery in the March, boats were still not fully employed. The economic rationale of the canal carriers' attitude to capital expansion was thus roundly endorsed. To write thus is not to reject all criticism of the canal carriers but to argue its proper perspective. Variability of demand is an inescapable fact of the transport industry. Historically it affected road as much as canal transport, and, as one witness predicted, 'that will be the same if there are waggons upon the Railway'.

It is worth pausing to look briefly at the composition of the canal carrier's traffic. For reasons already explained, it is misplaced to think too rigidly in terms of specific categories of canal traffic. If the companies' rates were low enough to compete with other modes of transport, traffic, of whatever kind, would go by canal. It is possible, however, to provide some descriptive detail. Pickfords' correspondence with the Oxford Canal Company, for example, mentions Cheshire cheese, Shropshire cheese, steel, ale, earthenware, Derbyshire goods between Birmingham and London, cast-iron boxes, wrought iron, timber, nails in bags, steel in bundles, grinding stones, castings, iron chains, ingot brass, coal, steam-engine parts, provender, zinc, salt, earthenware in crates from the Potteries to London, pottery flints, guano, rags and old rope from Lancashire to papermills in London. The list could be extended almost indefinitely, but to no real object. Piece for piece, many of these items could equally well have appeared on the carrier's wagon. But not, of course, in the same quantities or at the same cost. The great value of the canals, and of the canal carriers' services, was surely that together they extended enormously the range of goods which could be conveyed through inland means of transport cheaply and over long distances. What the traffic totalled and what the proportions of the various categories of traffic were is as yet unknown. Probably no more than partial answers will ever be possible. In Pickfords' case, one isolated statistic is that the firm handled an estimated 902,000 tons of canal traffic in London in 1845, together with a further 345,119 tons at Birmingham, but the evidence does not exist to confirm, deny or extend these figures.[34]

The canal carriers were accused of various forms of collusion and restrictive practice, in particular of keeping their rates a close secret, charging differentially according to category of customer rather than type of traffic and rigging the market by agreeing not to underquote a competitor. Some of these can be confirmed, others qualified. Myles Pennington, sometime agent to John Hargreaves, candidly admitted that 'rates of freight were based on *caste*'. He explained that 'esquires, reverends, military officers, the nobility, etc., had to pay for their titles', as, indeed, they had earlier to the road carriers. As a young agent he had found the principles of charging, and in particular why one trader paid more than another, distinctly puzzling. Hargreaves had not provided a schedule of charges but set minimum rates and left his agents to get the best they could. On seeking further advice on the rates in force, he was referred to Joe, one of the outside staff.

I have to remark that Joe Hornby was the carter who collected and delivered goods in the town of Preston. I call him 'Joe'. He is a clean-shaved, rather pleasant looking fellow; he comes into the office, strokes his hair in front and looks wondrous wise. The way-bill is from Manchester to Preston (30 miles); we charge by the 112 lbs., the ton is not used. We start with bales, boxes and trusses of cotton, cloths, linens, etc. (dry goods). I say, 'Tommy Careful, one bale.' 'Fourteen pence,' says Joe. 'Billy Sharp, one bale.' 'He'll only stand one shilling,' says Joe. 'Peter Careless, one truss.' 'He'll stand eighteen pence,' says Joe. And thus he went on, parties paying different rates for the same description of goods from the same place. Rates were fixed at what a man *would stand*.[35]

Pennington hastened to explain that this was not, as it might appear to be, a system of deliberate discrimination. What had happened was that a special rate genuinely conceded to one merchant reached the ears of a second who demanded equal treatment but not of a third who went on paying the original charge, and so on until the whole structure of rates actually in force had departed from any recognisably rational basis. It is not surprising that he found the whole set-up difficult to follow and having compiled a private ratebook kept it 'securely locked up in my drawer'. Pickfords likewise kept its rates-book out of the public view, insisting to several parliamentary committees that they were private property and would not be disclosed. The secrecy surrounding canal charges and the unpredictable nature of them exposed the carrier to unfavourable comparison when railway companies trumpeted the open publication of their own rates.

The charge of collusion, in the form of non-competitive quotation of rates, also draws some support from the available evidence. For example, a set of rates for various traffics drawn up by the Peak Forest Canal Company in 1839, partly to illustrate the effect which railways had had on canal charges, displayed a striking degree of parallelism. Rates were given for three carriers, Pickfords, Kenworthy & Co. and Robins & Co., but the sample of quotations for all three firms is limited to only six categories of goods. Of these, identical charges were made by all three for two categories of goods and Pickfords and Kenworthy were identical for two more. Of the remaining two categories, Pickfords and Robins agreed on one, and Kenworthy and Robins on the other. A more revealing series is for Kenworthy and Robins alone. Comparative charges were recorded for twenty-six categories of goods; before the railways, twenty-two of these had been identical, but the number had by then (1839) been reduced to twelve. A bland gloss on these figures would be that they demonstrate how the free working of perfect competition had reduced rates to their lowest remunerative level. A hint that the market did not work quite so freely is suggested by a note in a manuscript book of Pickfords' canal rates, of the period 1828–36: 'In the event of any goods offering for conveyance that are not provided for by a specific rate, no agent of the parties to have power to state terms, except in concert with agents of the other carriers, nor under any circumstances should such authority be exercised if there is time to correspond with the Principals.'[36]

Such a practice should cause no surprise. A free trader like James Lock, agent to the Sutherland family, opposed price cutting among the independent traders on the Bridgewater as ruinous, preferring 'a competition of services within a framework of agreed rates'.[37] Except when pressed sharply by competing modes of conveyance, competition within sectors of the transport industry has generally been prosecuted by way of service rather than by price. The canal carriers were no exception, at least before railway competition began to bite. Custom was attracted by a variety of means, such as offering different lengths of time for which accounts could be left unsettled, allowing discount for the prompt settlement of accounts, carrying empties and samples free of charge, allowing free warehousing for as long as a month. The firm with the best name for efficiency and prompt attention to business, together with the resources to finance the most tempting inducements, attracted the most custom. Merchants sending goods off regularly, therefore, tended to employ one carrier and used their trading account to negotiate favourable terms. Kenworthy & Co., for example, allowed a rates reduction of 25 per cent to regular customers.[38] Measures of this kind are likely to have been of more value to the merchant than occasional price wars.

By discharging his transport requirements through a single carrier a merchant could simplify enormously his book-keeping problems: not so the carrier, who faced a highly complex and onerous burden on this score. Canal charges were sufficiently complex in themselves, but the task was made far worse in the case of through routes by the need to engage in protracted negotiations with each canal company concerned for any alteration in rates. Individual companies were reluctant to commit themselves unilaterally and would only agree to any proposed change provided all the other companies concerned also gave their consent. The absence of any type of clearing house, either for processing routine traffic or regulating through traffic agreements of this kind, was a serious handicap. Instead of being able to discharge their tonnage payments through a central agency, they were obliged to keep a separate account for each canal used, in Pickfords' case probably twenty or more different sets of accounts.

The administration of these accounts further compounded the complications. Over and above the basic schedule of charges there was an intricate system of drawbacks, special rates or reductions in favour of particular routes or particular categories of goods, some purely temporary, others on traffic in one direction only. Not only were there disputes about overcharging by the canal companies or false declarations by the carrier, but the figures, on the basis of which accounts were rendered, were often neither complete nor compatible. The confusion got worse as time went on so that, as Pickfords wrote to the Oxford Canal Company in 1832, 'the canal accounts are now becoming so complex that it is difficult to know where we stand – some things being charged different rates, according as they are coming up or going down – and in some cases where a reduction is made, part of the goods are charged the reduced rate and part the full rate in the tonnage accounts leaving a portion to be obtained by way of overcharges, and again some allowances are made from statements furnished by us and some from accounts rendered by other canal cos.'. In this situation it is not surprising that Pickfords was finding the cost of keeping its tonnage accounts in order 'no light tax upon the drawbacks'.[39]

The truth of this complaint was later appreciated by the Grand Junction Canal Company when it commenced carrying on its own account. A sub-committee investigating the existing structure of rates reported that it was 'not based on any uniform principle or general rule, and it comprehends many differential and exceptional rates, the reasons for which are not always apparent and when apparent do not appear to justify the inconsistencies involved in such differences and exceptions'.[40]

No doubt the canal carriers shared in the canal companies' monopoly profit, but traders' complaints that because they were sheltered by monopoly conditions the carriers were indifferent to the merchants' needs should not be accepted without closer investigation. Traders complained of the delays in getting goods cleared, especially at busy times, but it seems that the carriers had a genuine grievance against those merchants who demanded the earliest possible delivery while delaying sending their goods to the wharf until the last possible moment. This pattern of behaviour, it was repeatedly alleged to the Lords' Committee on Sunday Trading in 1841,[41] was the cause of late working on Saturday nights and the need for boats to keep moving, instead of resting, the following day. Manchester factors were said to expect orders placed at the beginning of the week to be ready on the Saturday. Packers were kept at hand and the carriers required to collect any time up to midnight. Having waited so long for his freight the carrier was then under pressure to get it to London, where the recipient merchant wanted it the earliest day possible and at the earliest time of day. Traffic leaving Manchester late on Saturday night was due in London the following Thursday morning. Any carrier able to deliver only a few hours ahead of his rivals would sweep the board. The Saturday night charge to the first set of locks out from Castle Quay must have resembled that to the first fence at Aintree!

For other reasons, too, the transmission to and delivery of goods in London was carefully controlled.[42] Pickfords possessed only limited storage space at City Road Basin, so goods had to be moved through the depot quickly and in an orderly manner. The secret was careful planning. Every evening as each boat left Manchester the consignment notes of its contents, the weight, charge, consignee/consignor of every item, were sent off to London by the firm's fly-van. In this way City Basin received three days' warning of the incoming traffic. A second signal was sent when the boat entered the Grand Junction canal, from which point it was possible to estimate within a couple of hours the time of its arrival in London. In the meantime details of the awaited cargoes were entered into the porters' books and allocated to the appropriate delivery round. Discharging the goods on arrival then became a simple procedure. As each item came off the boat, a clerk identified it, looked it up in the book, and called off the numbered delivery round. The goods were taken by porters to the waiting line of wagons, loaded up, and off they went to the customer.

The clatter of iron-shod hooves and wheels began early. The boats from Manchester generally arrived in London between 2.00 a.m. and 5.00 a.m. Early arrivals had to wait until unloading began at 4.00 a.m. A line of carts and wagons, twenty-nine in all, were drawn up in readiness. By 5.00 a.m. the first wagons were pulling out, heading for warehouses which opened at 6.00 a.m. to receive them. By 8.00 a.m. the day's first delivery round was complete. Goods were sent off on a rota system, designed to meet customers' wishes and to speed the priority traffic. Light goods went first, said to be 99 per cent of the total traffic and up to 25 per cent of it heading for the docks for export, Macclesfield silks, boxes of hats and the like. For this privilege they, together with traffic from Liverpool, Derby and the Potteries, paid a delivery charge of 6 pence per item below 1 hundredweight, 1 shilling for items between 1 and 4 hundredweight, and 4 pence per hundredweight for weights higher than that. Heavy goods from Birmingham and Wolverhampton enjoyed no priority, being retained until the afternoon round, but were not charged separately for delivery. The aim throughout was to beat rival firms to the first delivery. Supervisors were employed to travel the streets to make sure there was no slacking on the job and that carters completed their rounds promptly and then speeded back to City Basin for another load.

At every stage, to the terminals, between the terminals and from the terminals, there was constant pressure for haste. The strain was borne particularly by the men who navigated the boats and worked the delivery rounds. Transport has been notorious for long hours, low pay and little job security. The pressure to be the first to deliver and the last to collect was the cause, in the late nineteenth century, of carters being required to work sixteen hours or more a day, and it is likely that conditions in these earlier years were much the same. Moreover, tramping a wet, sloppy towpath in the pouring rain teaches the lesson that the bargee's life was less than idyllic. The canal boatmen's ill repute, especially their penchant for poaching pheasants and raiding brandy barrels among their cargoes, was, of course, legendary. It is worth noting, however, that Baxendale was quite sure that the popular view of the boatmen was much exaggerated and that their pilfering was trivial when set against the value of the traffic conveyed.[43] The boatmen were skilled and subtle thieves and despite fines, payments to informers, the locking and sealing of holds and other devices, the owners failed to overcome their craft. There are many rich stories of boats found drifting helpless while their steerers enjoyed alcoholic bliss, of crews blowing themselves up by attacking barrels containing gunpowder instead of rum, but these were the exceptions, the exciting high spots for men whose lives were otherwise lacking in that respect. The regularity and success of the canal trade is proof enough that most shipments arrived intact and on time.

CANALS AND COMPETING MODES OF TRANSPORT

Canal conveyance did not operate in a vacuum. It interacted with other modes of transport, partly in competitive, partly in complementary fashion. Canals fed sea-borne shipping at Goole, Liverpool or City Road Basin, and road vehicles were employed for local cartage or forward conveyance from the wharf. Pickfords' canal rates from London to Manchester and to Birmingham and Warwick explicitly included cartage and delivery. The rate to Stafford incorporated delivery by road from Radford, the nearby wharf on the Trent & Mersey canal, a facility which was continued despite the construction of a branch canal to the town.[44] There were also a number of connecting services by road, from places like Chester, Shrewsbury and Bridgnorth, which, although served by water transport, were not linked to the main midlands canal system until towards the end of the canal age. Road transport was also provided to Aylesbury, although served by canal, and for a time Pickfords' wharf at Stoke was the focus of wagon services from Leek and Macclesfield. Over time, however, the canals were increasingly pressed by rival transport modes, roads, coastal shipping and, eventually, railways.

Comparisons between road and canal charges are subject to many of the reservations expressed earlier in respect of land and water transport. Canals were usually cheaper per ton/mile, but where their course was indirect or interrupted for other reasons the additional total journey cost left them open to the encroachment of more direct, swifter road transit. It was reported in the 1790s that agricultural produce was conveyed extensively by road to London from places in Hertfordshire located on the very banks of a canal, while in Oxfordshire barley was taken by road the 44 miles from Banbury to Birmingham and, moreover, coal brought back and sold as cheaply as that carried by canal. How typical these cases were has yet to be established but it is certain that even in the 1840s the Grand Junction canal's circuitous approach to London caused it to lose traffic to road transport.[45]

Road transport could, indeed, sometimes compete with canals even over long distances. A case in point was a regular service of road wagons between London and Leicester begun in 1828 by Messrs Deacon, Harrison & Co. For a charge no higher than that by canal, customers were offered at least comparable and possibly shorter journey times. Baxendale's reaction was to cut Pickfords' canal rate by 10 shillings per ton and he accordingly approached the various canal companies on the route for appropriate reductions in their tolls. The Grand Union Canal Company, more dependent on through traffic, readily agreed, but the Grand Junction Company was on this occasion slow to respond. However, a scheme was already in existence which allowed preferential tolls on goods declared for places north of the Trent, intending thereby to divert traffic from the coastal to the inland route, and it was eventually agreed to extend the preference to Leicester for an experimental period of three months. The experiment was subsequently continued for a further three months and the concessions extended to include traffic to Market Harborough, but there is no sign that the wagons were driven off. Indeed, the competitive position of the canals in that area seems to have deteriorated further, since in 1835 both the Leicester and Loughborough navigation companies were being outbidden by road transport for traffic to and from Birmingham.[46]

At much the same time Pickfords was losing trade between London and Oxford to competitors using the Thames navigation, supported by road haulage connections. Early in 1828 it suggested to the Regent's Canal Company that in order to combat this the company should cut its rates as the Oxford and Grand Junction Companies had done. However on learning that the reductions referred to had occurred some time previously and that neither of the other two companies intended any further measures to meet the immediate threat, the Regent's Canal Company declined to act on its own.[47] The loss of traffic continued and from 1830 Pickfords repeatedly pressed the

Oxford Canal Company in particular for improved facilities, but without success.

Another rival was coastal shipping. Before the advent of steam-powered ships, the canal fly trade held the advantage for merchandise, but otherwise goods were sent by whichever route offered the better price. Heavier goods between London and the north went by canal if it could beat the coastal rate by way of Liverpool, Gainsborough or Hull. The Grand Junction was active in proposals to attract traffic to the inland waterways. A scheme to draw cargoes intended for Birmingham away from Gainsborough was turned down by the Birmingham Canal Company, but the Grand Junction's own reductions on heavy groceries to Leicester and places farther north by way of the River Soar were taken up by Pickfords and Deacon, Harrison & Co.[48] In competing for such traffic the canal carriers were acutely conscious of their dependence on the canal companies for adequate reductions in toll. In 1830 John Robins, of Robins, Mills & Co., had been asked to quote for the conveyance of 3,000–4,000 tons of iron cisterns from London to Liverpool and as his down-tonnage had been particularly light recently he was anxious to secure the traffic. 'But we are aware that no reduction we can make in the freight will prevent the cisterns going by sea – unless we are met by a proportionate reduction of tonnage on the part of the canal proprietors.'[49] It is not known whether Robins got the traffic, but at least the Oxford Company was willing to make appropriate reductions, provided that the Grand Junction did likewise and that each boat containing the cisterns carried a certificate that the Grand Junction had in fact made the allowance.

The 1830s marked a new phase of competition from coasters, by the introduction of steam-powered vessels. Steamships were first employed between London and Goole early in 1834 and were soon competing successfully for traffic to Manchester. Their swifter services were not easily countered. Appeals from Pickfords, Bache and Kenworthy for improved co-operation from the canal companies received serious attention from the Grand Junction Company but elsewhere fell on deaf ears. A further initiative of the Grand Junction Company in October 1838 met a similar fate, despite the well-publicised decision of two leading canal carriers to turn to steamers. Steam also left its mark on the west coast trade. Carriers employing the canal route from Stourport to Liverpool and Manchester, a five-day passage, trailed far behind the two days' sailing it took steam vessels to reach Liverpool from Bristol.[50]

Canal companies were not quite so feeble in the face of railways as was once believed. Individual companies, admittedly the exceptions, attempted to turn the advent of railways to advantage. The Manchester, Bolton & Bury Canal Company, for example, intended to convert itself into an integrated railway and canal enterprise, the canal to take

heavy traffic, the railway passengers and merchandise.[51] Some companies had been taking measures to speed the flow of traffic, as much,
however, for the purpose of improving their competitive position
against other canal routes as from any intention of heading off railways.
Certain stretches of canal were widened or straightened, but most
attention was devoted to lockage since it was the number of locks to
be passed as much as the total mileage to be covered which determined
overall journey times. At some particularly troublesome bottlenecks
parallel flights of locks were built in order to double the number of
boats which could be accommodated at one time. This was done at
Runcorn by the Bridgewater trustees in the 1820s, and at Hillmorton
by the Oxford Canal Company in 1840.[52] A simple but apparently
effective alternative adopted by the Grand Junction Company in 1833
was to fit extra paddles to the upper gate of a lock. These caused water
to flow into a lock much more quickly. Using this device, boats could
be passed through a lock, on a 7-foot rise of water, in one and a half
minutes compared with about five minutes previously. A favourable
report from Pickfords on its effectiveness caused the Grand Junction
to decide to extend the device as soon as possible.[53] But such innovation
was too sporadic; more often it was a case of too little and too late.
Moreover it was in some ways self-defeating since some companies
sought to recover their capital expenditure by withdrawing discounts
previously allowed. What ought to have been a means of meeting
railway competition instead became an excuse to refuse repeated pleas
from Pickfords and other carriers for the canal companies to match
railway charges by lowering their rates.

Things might have been different had it proved possible to adapt
steam-power to canal use. Experiments with steamboats were made on
the Forth & Clyde canal as early as 1789 and on the Sankey Brook,
the Mersey & Irwell and the Bridgewater navigation in the 1790s.[54]
The main requirement was to propel canal boats directly by steam-
power, but this proved too difficult to achieve. What success there was
mainly took the form of steam-powered tugs pulling 'barge trains', or
shunting boats through the longer canal tunnels. Other ideas included
the use of locomotives to haul canal boats, working from a track laid
along the canal bank.

Apart from its potential as a competitive form of transport, the
canal carriers' interest in steam-power had a logic of its own. Successful
innovation of the new technology would powerfully threaten the existing
structure of the canal trade. The commercial viability of steam-power,
therefore, warranted careful attention. At least these were the terms
in which Zachary Langton seems to have construed the position. In
1819 a Mr Maibon approached Langton with an invention for which
he evidently made large claims and apparently offered Pickfords exclusive use of it. Although doubtful that this would be any more

successful than previous devices of a similar kind, Langton reckoned he could not afford to ignore it, 'for if it should so turn out that he really can perform what he proposes to undertake and that he disposes of his invention to others who may adapt it to canal navigation, a competitor, with such an exclusive right, would be more than we could contend with'.[55]

The sustained experimentation with steam-power from the mid-1830s was probably more directly motivated by the onset of railway competition. Pickfords and Robins, Mills & Co. were, among others, involved in a number of trials with steam boats. A paddle-boat belonging to Robins & Co. was tested on the Macclesfield canal in 1838 and although reported capable of travelling at 5 miles per hour it could not achieve that speed, nor could it haul much more than a conventional barge drawn by a horse. Pickfords' experience was much the same. A trial run of a steamboat pulling an ordinary barge between Manchester and London, in September 1836, failed to produce significant results. Further trials on the Grand Junction canal in 1842 were similarly inconclusive.[56]

Only by the closest co-operation could the canal companies have put up any serious opposition to railways. But the pursuit of self-interest, which in the past promoted vigorous inter-company competition to the benefit of customers, now became perverted into obstructive individualism. They proved incapable of effective, united action. Joint conferences between canal company representatives and the carriers achieved nothing, except, perhaps, to give a further stir to the deep waters of canal politics. There was a time, in 1824, when Baxendale felt so closely identified with the canal interest that he offered to head the opposition to a proposed railway between Liverpool and Birmingham provided that the various canal companies would get together and undertake capital improvements, the absence of which he regarded as the prime cause of railway promotions.[57] By the late 1830s any hopes of that kind must have long since evaporated.

The outcome of an initiative by the Grand Junction Company is particularly revealing. In an attempt to force some joint action, that company introduced a system of preferential tolls designed to deflect traffic away from those canal companies, notably the Coventry and the Oxford, which would not agree to an average toll on through traffic of 1 penny per ton/mile. An unintended result was to further worsen the trade of the Macclesfield, Peak Forest and Ashton canals which was already being hit by railway competition. A delegation from the three canals was therefore sent south to try and repair the damage. Bouverie, manager of the Grand Junction, explained the purpose of his policy and agreed to extend the concession if the delegates could persuade either or both the Coventry and Oxford Companies to co-operate. The Coventry Company proved willing, but they drew a blank in Oxford. A spokesman for the Oxford Company suggested that the carriers were up to their old tricks, but this time attempting to play the canal companies off against the railways instead of against each other. Informed that Pickfords had already begun carrying by rail and that others were about to follow suit, he remained unmoved. Committees hoping for a constructive response to their problem of failing trade must have been thoroughly depressed by the final remarks of their delegates' report.

> To show the feeling which exists between the several canal companies in the south we may incidentally mention one member of a committee in allusion to the late meeting at Birmingham asked us somewhat roughly 'why the devil we had not joined them in black-guarding Bouverie'.[58]

In addition to this internecine rivalry, railways further highlighted the fatal divergence of interest between the canal companies and the canal carriers. Firms like Pickfords which specialised in the conveyance of merchandise were immediately and acutely vulnerable to railway competition, especially over long distances. Most canal companies, however, derived the bulk of their revenue from relatively local and low-unit-value traffic. They could lose their through merchandise traffic and still return a comfortable dividend. The Grand Junction did most to foster through traffic, but that in any case was in its own interest. It was a long line of canal, closely shadowed by the London & Birmingham railway to which it lost traffic as soon as the latter was open. Elsewhere self-interest encouraged the opposite view. A brief glance at the early railway map indicates why the Oxford Canal Company, for example, which controlled a key section of the north–south route, felt in no way threatened before the mid-1840s nor inclined to sacrifice revenue in order to assist the carriers. Other companies faced awkward decisions. The Trent & Mersey Company was obliged to treat through and local traffic equally: toll reductions conceded to the one would have had to be extended to the other. That was not a step to be taken lightly.

The carriers had no such difficulties. Their whole business was at stake. They warned the canal companies that unless everything was done to foster the fly trade, reduce all charges to the minimum and speed the traffic, it would be quickly lost to the railways. Some companies were sympathetic, but not enough. And when the rest saw the danger it was already too late. The carriers had gone with the merchandise trade to the railways.

THE END OF THE CANAL TRADE

Pickfords' withdrawal from the canal trade came, as Figure 6 shows,[59] in two sharp breaks followed by a final ebbing away. The firm's stock

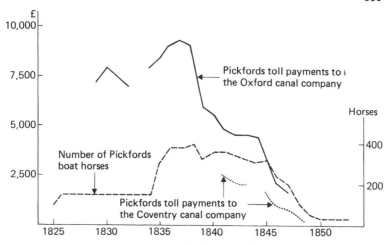

£

10,000

7,500

Pickfords toll payments to
the Oxford canal company

Horses

5,000

400

Number of Pickfords
boat horses

2,500

200

Pickfords toll payments to
the Coventry canal company

1825   1830   1835   1840   1845   1850

Fig. 6   *The stages of Pickfords' withdrawal from canals*

of boat-horses and its toll payments to the Oxford Canal Company peaked during the years 1836–8. Railway competition first bit sharply in 1839. Payments to the Oxford Company dipped by a third while the firm's traffic on the Peak Forest canal fell by a half during the first three months of the year.[60] Although the decline was never reversed, the position was stabilised a little in the early 1840s, the limbo years before the basic railway network was completed and during which the canal companies could not decide which way to jump. The final break came in 1844–6 when despite an expanding economy the canal trade again slipped sharply, soon to fall away to nothing. The decline of Pickfords' boat-horses tells the same story. After correcting for an initial over-reaction, the number fell year by year. By 1841 the barge fleet had been reduced by a quarter and in 1843, a significant move, Pickfords' head office was transferred from City Road Basin back to The Castle Inn, Wood Street.[61] In 1845 the final run down began, from 380 horses that year, to 230 the next and only 14 in 1852, the last year they were recorded.

Pickfords' canal trade, which had taken decades to perfect, was dismantled in a matter of years. Between 1845 and 1847 the Coventry, Oxford, and Worcester & Birmingham Canal Companies all received notice terminating the firm's lease of premises from them, while in October 1847 it was reported that Pickfords had decided 'to abandon at Christmas next the canal as a means of transit for goods'.[62] Why all the rush? There is an obvious and single-word answer – railways. Not only were railways breaking beyond mineral traffic into merchandise and general goods by the mid-1840s, they were also organising in such a way as to strike hard at the carriers' livelihood. Those who wished to survive, and Pickfords was naturally one, were obliged to behave as the railways demanded. And what the railways demanded was the abandonment of all competing canal services. Pickfords had no option but to comply.

REFERENCES: CHAPTER 5

1 Details of the chronology of canal construction are drawn freely from Charles Hadfield's regional histories of canals. His precise knowledge of the exact line of canals and their dates of openings saved me from a number of errors.
2 *Manchester Directory*, 1772, p. 59.
3 *Manchester Mercury*, 3 May, 18 October 1774; T. Baines, *History of the Commerce and Town of Liverpool* (London: Longman, 1852), p. 440.
4 C. Hadfield, *The Canals of the West Midlands*, 2nd edn (Newton Abbot: David & Charles, 1969), the early pages; A. C. Wood, 'The history of trade and transport on the river Trent', *Transactions of the Thoroton Society of Nottinghamshire*, vol. LIV (1950), p. 35; Register of Barges, Q/RUB/1, Staffordshire Record Office.
5 Hadfield, op. cit.
6 *Compleat Guide to . . . London* (Osborn), 1783, entry for Manchester; *Manchester Mercury*, 19 December 1786.
7 *Kent's London Directory*, 1788, incorporating the *Shopkeeper and Tradesman's Assistant*, 1788, p. 72.
8 Coventry Canal Company, general meetings and minutes of committee of proprietors, 7 May 1788, PRO/BTHR Rail 818/3.
9 C. Hadfield, 'The Thames navigation and the canals 1770–1830', *Economic History Review*, vol. XIV (1944–5), p. 172; 'The Grand Junction canal', *Journal of Transport History*, vol. IV (1959–60), p. 96; *The Canals of the East Midlands* (Newton Abbot: David & Charles, 1966).
10 Grand Junction Canal Company, minutes, meetings of general assembly of proprietors and general committee, 27 July 1796, 8 August 1797, PRO/BTHR Rail 830/39.
11 Oxford Canal Company, minutes of committee of proprietors, 10 November 1789, PRO/BTHR Rail 855/4.
12 T. Allbutt, *Views of the Staffordshire Potteries* (1800), quoted by A. L. Thomas, *Geographical Aspects of the Development of Transport and Communications Affecting the Pottery Industry of North Staffordshire during the Eighteenth Century* (Collections for a History of Staffordshire, 1934), 1935, pp. 141–2.
13 Coventry Canal Company, rough minutes of committee meetings, 5 January 1791, 5, 12 December 1792, PRO/BTHR Rail 818/23; *Universal British Directory*, Vol. 2, 1791, p. 618, description of Coventry; *Manchester and Salford Directory*, 1794, p. 186. In 1795 Pickfords' barges were registered as operating between Manchester and Coventry: Register of Barges, QD, Cheshire Record Office.
14 Grand Junction Canal Company, minutes, meetings of general assembly of proprietors and general committee, 8 August 1797 to 26 May 1801, *passim*, PRO/BTHR Rail 830/39, 40; V. A. Hatley, 'The Blisworth Hill railway, 1800–1805', *Northamptonshire Antiquarian Society* (1962–3), p. 14.
15 *The Courier*, 27 February 1824; for Pickfords' dealings concerning City Road Basin, see Regent's Canal Company, committee minutes, 18 February

1818–13 December 1820, PRO/BTHR Rail 860/14, 16, 18; Grand Junction Canal Company, board minutes, PRO/BTHR Rail 830/1; case and opinion of counsel, PRO/BTHR Rail 1133/45.

16 Ashby Canal Company, minutes of proprietors and committee, 22 January–19 April 1802, PRO/BTHR Rail 803/3; Coventry Canal Company, minutes of general meetings of committee of proprietors, 9 March, 11 May 1802, PRO/BTHR Rail 818/27; generally, P. A. Stevens, *The Leicester Line* (Newton Abbot: David & Charles, 1972).

17 Stevens, *Leicester Line*, pp. 77–8; *Aris' Birmingham Gazette*, 28 November 1814; Wrighton's *New Triennial Directory of Birmingham*, 1815, p. 193; *Leicester Directory*, 1815, p. 80.

18 Staffordshire & Worcestershire Canal Company, minutes of committee, 11 October 1825, PRO/BTHR Rail 871/5. In 1826 the firm licensed only three boats, compared with the fifty usual on other canals.

19 For the canal trade generally, Rees, *The Cyclopaedia*, Vol. 6; T. Boyle, *Hope for the Canals* (London: Simpkin, Marshall, 1848); J. Hassell, *Tour of the Grand Junction* (London: 1819); W. T. Jackman, *The Development of Transportation in Modern England*, 2nd edn (London: Cass, 1962), pp. 436 ff.; C. Hadfield, *The Canal Age* (Newton Abbot: David & Charles, 1968); H. Hanson, *The Canal Boatmen, 1760–1914* (Manchester: Manchester University Press, 1975).

20 *Derby Mercury*, 17 September, 8 October 1801.

21 *Aris' Birmingham Gazette*, 9 November 1807.

22 Baxendale's memorandum book, 'Details of boats, etc.', Baxendale papers.

23 Statement of horses returned for assessed taxes, 1822–66, PRO/BTHR Rail 1133/147, p. 73.

24 Stock of horses, 31 March 1831, PRO/BTHR Rail 1133/147; Grimes' evidence, *SC on Liverpool and Manchester Railroad Bill*, HC 1825, PRO/BTHR Rail 1066/1515.

25 Warwick & Birmingham Canal Company, committee minutes, 14 December 1818; similar terms were negotiated for premises at Digbeth, 14 October 1811, and subsequently, also 12 December 1825, PRO/BTHR Rail 881/9, 10; for premises at Lowesmere, Worcester & Birmingham Canal Company, committee minutes, 28 July 1815, 14 February 1817, PRO/BTHR Rail 886/6, 7; premises at Leicester, Stevens, *Leicester Line*, p. 83.

26 Birmingham Canal Company, memorandum book, 17 November 1824, PRO/BTHR Rail 810/588; *SC on Railway Communication*, Fifth Report, PP, 1840, vol. XIII, QQ. 2179–2207 and 3799.

27 Journal, PRO/BTHR Rail 1133/126.

28 Grand Junction Railway Company, board minutes, 21 September 1836, PRO/BTHR Rail 220/1. For the importance of Braunston as described, Diary of Josiah Baxendale, PRO/BTHR Rail 1133/147, and G. L. Turnbull 'A tour by canal', (mimeograph).

29 Lainson and other merchants, *SC on Railway Communication*, Fifth Report, 1840.

30 The data for Figures 4 and 5 have the same source. Figure 4 is based solely on Pickfords' toll payments to the Oxford Canal Company, Figure 5 incorporates in addition some payments to the Coventry Company. The Oxford data contain four years of twelve observations, eight of eleven, five of ten and one of nine observations. Gaps have been filled by taking either the average for all other figures for the particular month, or the monthly average for the year, whichever accorded the better fit with the normal seasonal pattern. There is inevitably some error in the estimates, but it is not of a magnitude sufficient seriously to distort the major trends indicated by the data.

31 *House of Commons Journal*, vol. XLIX, pp. 439, 456; J. E. Pilgrim, 'The cloth industry of Essex and Suffolk, 1558–1640' (unpublished MA thesis, London, 1939), p. 180.

32 F. C. Mather, *After the Canal Duke* (Oxford: Clarendon Press, 1970); E. Richards, *The Leviathan of Wealth: The Sutherland Fortune in the Industrial Revolution* (London: Routledge & Kegan Paul, 1973); C. Hadfield and G. Biddle, *The Canals of North West England* (Newton Abbot: David & Charles, 1970), Vol. I, chs 4, 5. It was argued at the time that much of the delay complained of was illusory, in that Manchester dealers bought cotton speculatively and then deliberately left it at Liverpool until they wanted it.

33 *SC on the Liverpool and Manchester Railroad Bill*, 1825; *SC on the Liverpool and Manchester Railway Bill*, HL, SP, (68), 1826, vol. CCIX.

34 Oxford Canal Company, letter books, PRO/BTHR Rail 855/73–4, 81–101; *RC on Canals and Waterways*, 1909 (Cd 4840), Vol. V (pt II), Q. 41,189.

35 M. Pennington, *Railways and Other Ways* (Toronto: Williamson, 1896), pp. 29–30. I must thank Harry Hanson for this reference.

36 Peak Forest Canal Company, committee minutes, 27 March 1839, PRO/BTHR Rail 856/6; Pickfords' book of canal rates, pp. 57–8, PRO/BTHR 1133/130.

37 Mather, *After the Canal Duke*, p. 106.

38 Kenworthy's evidence, *SC on the Liverpool and Manchester Railway Bill*, 1826, p. 272; Boyle, *Hope for the Canals*, pp. 24 ff.

39 Oxford Canal Company, letter books, 24 December 1830, 13 March 1832, PRO/BTHR Rail 855/83, 85.

40 Grand Junction Canal Company, board minutes, 10 July 1848, PRO/BTHR Rail 830/10.

41 SC on Carriage of Goods and Merchandise on Canals, Navigable Rivers, and Railways on Sundays, *House of Lords Journal*, vol. LXXIII, appendix 2, QQ. 149–50, 237–8, 1009–20.

42 The following is based on Derham's evidence, *SC on the London Grand Junction Railway Bill*.

43 Baxendale's evidence, SC on the Carriage of Goods on Sundays, 1841; generally, Hanson, *The Canal Boatmen*.

44 Book of canal rates, PRO/BTHR Rail 1133/130.

45 W. Marshall, *The Review and Abstract of the County Reports to the Board of Agriculture* (London: 1818; Newton Abbot: David & Charles, 1969), Vol. 4, p. 453; Vol. 5, p. 23; Bouverie's evidence, SC on the Carriage of Goods on Sundays, 1841.

46 Grand Junction Canal Company, board minutes, 3, 30 December 1828, 19 March 1829, PRO/BTHR Rail 830/4; Grand Union Canal Company, committee minutes, 19 December 1828, PRO/BTHR Rail 831/2; Hadfield, *Canals of the East Midlands*, p. 82.

47 Regent's Canal Company, committee minutes, 27 February, 6 March 1828, PRO/BTHR Rail 860/30; Grand Junction Canal Company, board minutes, 26 July 1832, PRO/BTHR Rail 830/5.

48 Birmingham Canal Company, letter book, 19 April 1804, PRO/BTHR Rail 810/585; Grand Junction Canal Company, board minutes, 17 November 1823, PRO/BTHR Rail 830/3.

49 Oxford Canal Company, letter book, 7 May 1830, PRO/BTHR Rail 855/83.

50 Oxford Canal Company, letter book, 2 September 1834, PRO/BTHR Rail 855/86; Grand Junction Canal Company, board minutes, 7 October, 29 November 1834, 16 January 1835, 30 October 1838, PRO/BTHR Rail 830/5, 6; Heath's evidence, SC on the Carriage of Goods on Sundays, 1841.

51 Hadfield and Biddle, *Canals of North West England*, pp. 256 ff.

52 ibid., p. 98; Hadfield, *Canals of the East Midlands*, p. 161.

53 Grand Junction Canal Company, board minutes, 24 June 1833, PRO/ BTHR Rail 830/5.

54 J. Lindsay, *The Canals of Scotland* (Newton Abbot: David & Charles, 1968), pp. 26 ff.; T. C. Barker and J. R. Harris, *A Merseyside Town in the Industrial Revolution, St. Helen's 1750–1900* (London: Cass, 1959), p. 193; Hadfield and Biddle, op. cit., pp. 99–100.

55 Langton to Matthew Pickford, 31 August 1819, PRO/BTHR Rail 1133/149; Langton to Matthew Pickford, 4 September 1819, Baxendale papers.

56 *Macclesfield Courier and Herald*, 24 September 1836, 18 August 1838; Macclesfield Canal Company, committee minutes, 4 November 1835, 6 October 1836, PRO/BTHR Rail 850/2; Regent's Canal Company, committee minutes, 18 May 1842, PRO/BTHR Rail 860/38.

57 Birmingham Canal Company, memorandum book, 17 November 1824, PRO/BTHR Rail 810/588.

58 Peak Forest Canal Company, committee minutes, 30 January, 27 March 1839, PRO/BTHR Rail 856/4.

59 See note 30 for comments on the Oxford toll payments; the Coventry data is too spasmodic before 1841, but the trend shown thereafter usefully confirms that of the Oxford data. The figures for boat-horses are from: statement of horses returned for assessed taxes, 1822–66, PRO/BTHR Rail 1133/147, p. 73.

60 Peak Forest Canal Company, committee minutes, 30 January, 27 March 1839, PRO/BTHR Rail 856/4.

61 Baxendale's evidence, SC on the Carriage of Goods on Sundays, 1841; Diary of Joseph Hornby Baxendale, 1843, Pickfords Removals Ltd.

62 Coventry Canal Company, letter book, 19 December 1845, 12 June 1846, PRO/BTHR Rail 818/210; Oxford Canal Company, letter book, 20 June 1846, 27 September 1847, PRO/BTHR Rail 855/100–101; Worcester & Birmingham Canal Company, committee minutes, 8 October 1847, PRO/ BTHR Rail 886/11; Eerewash Canal Company, general meeting and committee minutes, 8 October 1847, PRO/BTHR Rail 828/2.

6

Railways, 1825–47: Hopes Raised and Dashed

In 1825, the directors of the Liverpool & Manchester Railway Company commissioned the engineer William Cubitt to visit Killingworth colliery, near Newcastle, in order to investigate and report on the working of George Stephenson's locomotive engines employed there. Cubitt was impressed. He advised that 'an iron railway with locomotive steam engines are [*sic*] a practical, eligible, and expeditious means for the transit of goods and merchandise and probably will become so for passengers in very many cases'. Canals, he believed, would, except in special circumstances, be superseded for all three categories of traffic.[1] A decade or so later much of Cubitt's prediction was close to fulfilment. The conveyance of passengers and light merchandise had been the spectacular success of the Liverpool & Manchester railway. The only uncertainty was whether canals would retain their heavy traffic.

Railway opinion remained divided as to whether heavy goods was desirable traffic or not, beyond the promotional phase. The early years of railways operations were, indeed, marked by conflicting practice. Some railway companies monopolised passengers and light merchandise and left the heavier freight to the carriers, whereas others took the view that a railway company ought to secure all the traffic it could possibly lay its hands on. Subsequent experience lent support to the latter view. Heavy merchandise turned out to be profitable business and was readily adopted once the railways were fully geared up to cope with it. Moreover pressed by competing lines and an unexpectedly high burden of capital charges, companies were obliged to pursue revenue wherever it could be found. Any lingering belief that a compromise between railway and canal would be possible was finally extinguished.

The canal carriers learned this lesson the hard way. All the major national firms, Bache, Kenworthy, Crowley, Robins as well as Pickfords, welcomed the arrival of the steam locomotive. They transferred capital from canal wharf to station yard, eagerly advertised new services by railway and stood poised to embark on new careers as railway carriers. But the dream soon faded; their ambitions crumbled. After a few bitter years nearly all retired, some to oblivion, others to a meagre existence as local cartage agents. How did Pickfords survive?

THE GROWTH OF RAILWAY CARRIAGE

Railways were built because they were needed.[2] The sharp boom of 1824–5 and each succeeding cyclical expansion served to emphasise the limitations of the existing system of inland transport by road and navigation, and the need for additional, probably alternative, means of conveyance.[3] The fact that railways were also speculative ventures, and therefore became at times the playthings of unscrupulous promoters, should not be allowed to destroy the essentially rational premise from which they began. The construction of the basic railway network was demonstrably rooted in current or foreseeable transport needs. Railways were built to convey passengers between large centres of population and freight through the major corridors of traffic. They were accordingly constructed in the areas and along the routes where both were to be found. These took the form, schematically, of an extended T, the horizontal arm of which reached from Liverpool through Manchester and Leeds to Hull and the vertical arm stretched down, as the canal route had done, through the industrial midlands to London. True there were other routes, especially passenger lines thrown off to the east, south and west from London and direct rails from the midlands to the west of England, but the earliest important commercial lines encompassed the traditional heartland of the nation's traffic. For that very reason they were also invading prime carrier country.

By 1839 a primitive system of rails extended between London and Lancashire, parts of the midlands and the West Riding. This in itself created a further demand for logical extensions and complementary lines. Thus, of over forty towns with a population of 25,000 or more in the census year of 1841, only seven lacked a railway connection by the end of 1844.[4] Of course the manic phase of promotions had its effect and even commercially sound companies later felt compelled to extend their mileage in order to shut rivals out of their claimed territories. But the fact remained that the successful railway companies were those which met a genuine demand, which had a solid traffic base on which to build.

Railways were built piecemeal. It took several years, to the mid-1840s, for the pieces to mesh together and form a reasonably articulated national network. In the meantime there was uncertainty, and inevitably disturbance to the carrier's traffic. Carrier and railway company had to judge the future by instinct rather than by guiding principles. Railways were a new form of enterprise; the operating companies had to feel their way, learning by experience,[5] and judgements as to best practice might vary between companies and over time. The carrier equally had a decision to make, since at least part of his traffic stood to be engrossed by the railways. His decision was not easy. The carrier anxious to employ railways had to risk offending the canal companies while simultaneously continuing to rely on them in areas where rails had not yet been laid. Variant policies adopted by railway companies in respect of goods traffic were one source of uncertainty for the carrier; having to gamble on the likely outcome of events was another. With the benefit of hindsight the overwhelming advantage of railways is perfectly obvious, but in the late 1830s and early 1840s, when the actual decisions had to be made, the carriers enjoyed no such luxury.

Carriers expected to have the same access to railways as they had to canals. The general belief was that, provided he paid the toll asked, the carrier was entitled to dispatch his traffic by railway. Accordingly, when Pickfords got in touch with the directors of the Liverpool & Manchester railway in October 1829, a few months before the line opened, the firm did not apply for permission but simply wrote 'stating their intention to conduct part of their business on the railway, and proposing they should provide waggons to be under their own lock and key, and that they should be charged one rate of tonnage for all goods'.[6] Terms were negotiable but the right of access was taken for granted. The directors were already discussing how best to deal with the goods traffic and as they had not yet come to a decision they delayed their reply.

The Liverpool & Manchester Railway Company was specifically charged by Parliament to convey all goods brought to its stations. Compelled thus to undertake common carrier obligations, it had to decide how to discharge them. Passenger and coal traffic would be carried by the company, but there was some doubt whether it should also carry merchandise. One possibility was for this to be contracted out to some of the carrying firms and the company confine itself to charging toll. The crux of the matter, which was immediately posed, was whether it would be better to forgo the carrier's income than to incur additional expenditure on wagons, warehouses, and so on. A working committee was appointed to investigate further. It sounded out carrying firms for terms, and eventually proposed that 'the railway company should be carriers of *general merchandise*, as well as of coals and passengers, without the intervention of separate carriers, (as Pickford, Kenworthy and others)', but without excluding the carriers, provided 'satisfactory terms' could be arranged.[7] Experienced personnel to manage the goods department could easily be acquired, especially at the sort of salaries railway companies could afford. Andrew Comber,

Pickfords' agent in Liverpool, was more than happy to receive twice his previous salary and a rent-free house as goods manager to the railway company in Liverpool. He was the first of many to be tempted (or in Baxendale's view overtly bribed) from Pickfords' employ into railway management.[8]

The Liverpool & Manchester railway board was, however, less welcoming of the carriers' traffic; 'satisfactory terms' proved elusive. The company did eventually agree to one arrangement which is of some interest. This concerned Pickfords' van traffic, for which it agreed to supply a special wagon 'to have a moveable body to be transferred to cart wheels at each end of the line'.[9] This has sometimes been seen as the origin of container-based, integrated road–rail transport but it is doubtful if the event has more than symbolic significance. Evidence given to the Gauge Commissioners in 1846 by employees of the firm implied that attempts to employ containers were not successful and were soon abandoned.[10] The railway company refused special terms of access to its line, but was, of course, happy to receive Pickfords' custom as part of its normal traffic.

The next railway to interest Pickfords was the Grand Junction line, which ran from a junction with the Liverpool & Manchester railway at Newton-le-Willows to Birmingham. It thus provided direct access by rail between Liverpool, Manchester and the industrial north midlands. It also bit deeply into prime canal territory, immediately threatening the northern arm of the through canal route to London. Pickfords could not afford to ignore it. Later on there were alternative railway routes out of Manchester from which to choose, but when the crucial decision had to be taken whether or not to transfer London traffic to the railway, it was the Grand Junction or nothing.

Again contact was made as the line approached completion, but this time Baxendale met the directors himself in order to put his case. He sought to impress the company by emphasising the scale and complexity of Pickfords' operations and its strong hold of the traffic between Lancashire and London. If the railway company wanted a share of the traffic a deal with Pickfords would be to its advantage. He expected to provide his own wagons but not his own locomotives.[11] If from his experience with the Liverpool & Manchester Baxendale had learnt a lesson, so too, perhaps, had the Grand Junction directors, many of whom also sat on the Liverpool & Manchester board. From the start the Grand Junction board was determined to control all parts of its operations and in particular not to allow the carriers to manipulate its traffic. Accordingly the directors who met Baxendale left him in no doubt as to the company's intentions. It was going to keep passengers and parcels, locomotive power and wagons under its own control and would also engage directly in carrying if that was deemed necessary to protect the company's interests. It was quite satisfied that the railway's superior speed would enable it to compete effectively with Pickfords. The Grand Junction board, therefore, did not hurry to give Baxendale an answer. He met the directors in September 1836 and the line was opened in July 1837, yet not until the following March did the company agree to set aside wagons for Pickfords' exclusive use.[12] In the meantime the firm had to rely on there being sufficient space on the scheduled services.

The Grand Junction Railway Company distrusted the carriers from the start and subsequently found little reason to change its mind. It would have preferred to do without them entirely and indeed began by monopolising the merchandise traffic. It was, however, forced to modify this policy. Much of the traffic which left Liverpool was consigned through to London and for that reason the lack of a continuous rail link to London was a serious weakness. For the first eighteen months rail carriage ceased at Birmingham, so that goods had to proceed the rest of the way by canal, thereby enabling the canal carriers to retain much of their business. They were probably no more than twenty-four hours slower to Birmingham, and the cost of trans-shipment there between rail and canal must have further reduced the attractiveness of a partial railway service.

Even when the London & Birmingham railway became fully operational for goods traffic, in April 1839, the position was not changed very much. Unlike the Grand Junction Company, the London & Birmingham did not act as carrier. There was thus no possibility of an 'end-on' agreement between the two companies and so the Grand Junction remained unable to provide for traffic south of Birmingham. To overcome this deficiency it looked for an agent to act for it both in London, for collection and delivery purposes, and on London & Birmingham rails. Time was lost on unsuccessful trials with Robins & Co. and John Jolly, both established carriers, and it was not until the spring of 1840 that an efficient agent, the new firm of Chaplin & Horne, was found. Before then the Grand Junction could offer a faster service from Liverpool but could not provide responsibility for goods in transit over the entire distance to London – a quality of service on which traders placed the highest emphasis. Consequently the carriers' service remained attractive, and if they made some use of the railway, the company's scarcely veiled hostility was every reason for restricting it to the lowest possible extent.

Until its agency arrangements were sorted out, the Grand Junction had to be more conciliatory towards the carriers if it wanted to break into their traffic. It therefore unbent a little. Fifteen months after its opening and following some pressure from Pickfords, it decided, in November/December 1838, to admit Pickfords, Bache, Kenworthy, and possibly others too, as independent carriers on its line. Formal contracts were exchanged and the details of them reveal how limited the concessions were.[13] The agreement was confined to through traffic from Liverpool to London. That between Liverpool and Birmingham remained the company's monopoly, and Pickfords' request to be allowed to operate from intermediate stations was also firmly rejected.[14] The terms on which the carriers were admitted were clearly spelt out. They had to provide a minimum daily loading of 30–40 tons and maintain a balance of traffic in each direction. They had to charge the company's published scale and were prohibited from allowing special rates and discounts, the commonest form of competition between the canal carriers. In return they received a 20 per cent discount on the monthly carriage account, out of which they had to meet their terminal costs, the supply of canvas sheets and ropes, liability for damage and find a profit. The agreement also provided for an interchange of trucks between Grand Junction and London & Birmingham rails, enabling goods to be conveyed undisturbed the entire distance between Liverpool and London.

The carriers suspected a trap, but decided to bite. They saw the company's offer as no more than a grudging concession, a disguise for its real motive, which was to discover the source of their traffic and then attack it. An agreement surrounded by thinly veiled mutual hostility had little chance of surviving for very long. Each side saw the threat of exploitation in the other's actions, and not surprisingly recriminations soon broke out.

The Grand Junction accused Pickfords of falsifying invoices, misstating the class of goods in order to have them conveyed at a lower rate. But it reserved its particular anger for the firm's practice of collecting small parcels, charged to customers at so much per parcel, packing them into hampers and then presenting them in that form to the railway company for conveyance at the much cheaper bulk tonnage rate. The company objected for two reasons. Pickfords pocketed a profit which the company wanted for itself and secondly small parcels, formerly carried by coach or van, were a category of business to which all railway companies specifically laid claim when promoting their Bills in Parliament. It regarded the firm's action as downright dishonest even if not technically illegal. Pickfords denied the charge and in turn replied with accusations of discrimination and poaching of traffic.

A situation already smouldering with discontent became even more tense. The Grand Junction decided on a general reduction of its freight rates and also that it could no longer trust the carriers to perform the loading and invoicing of their wagons honestly. It insisted that terminal services at Manchester should be undertaken by employees of the Liverpool & Manchester Railway Company and moreover that their cost should be charged against the 20 per cent discount allowed to the carriers. A collision between the two sides became inevitable. Pickfords' contract expired on 30 September 1840 and the Grand Junction decided not to renew it. The company's agency with Chaplin & Horne was working smoothly by then, so it was at last in a position to dispense with the carriers. Pickfords wanted to continue on Grand Junction rails, but charges of 2s 6d per day per wagon for permission to take Grand Junction wagons beyond Birmingham were, and were no doubt meant to be, prohibitive. There were other complaints also.[15] When the Grand Junction refused to concede to Pickfords the same terms and facilities it allowed to Chaplin & Horne, a protracted legal battle commenced.

Had Pickfords been totally dependent on the Grand Junction, its railway career would have been short indeed. That it was not was because the London & Birmingham Railway Company, which controlled the other half of the line to London, took quite the opposite view. Despite occasional hesitations, the London & Birmingham Company welcomed the carriers and kept its line open to them. At one point it even considered going so far as to contract out the whole of its carrying operations, to Pickfords. The proposal would have required Pickfords to divert all possible traffic from canal to rail, in return for 5 per cent of the net profit. The railway's benefit was seen to lie in the acquisition of an immediate flow of traffic without the trouble of finding experienced staff skilled in the complex business of organising goods traffic. However neither this nor a modified plan, which would still have left Pickfords in a favoured position, was implemented. According to Baxendale the change was made at one of the times when policy veered temporarily in favour of the railway company being its own carrier.[16] Perhaps the directors were also sensitive to the fact that Baxendale was at the time employed by the company as superintendent of the out-door department.

In the event the London & Birmingham did not escape a charge of favouritism to Pickfords.[17] The firm did in fact enjoy an initial privileged position on the company's line, although this was really a result of Baxendale's own foresight. Early in the summer of 1838 he anticipated a water shortage at Tring Summit on the Grand Junction canal, a notorious trouble spot, which, if it happened, would disrupt the canal trade. He therefore negotiated a special agreement with the London & Birmingham to transfer some of Pickfords' traffic to the railway if a drought occurred. It was explicitly an emergency, limited arrangement; the London & Birmingham then lacked the capacity to operate a full goods service. Consequently when trouble began in the September, the company had to refuse nearly all other applications for assistance. Pickfords invoked its agreement with the company but only two other firms, Bache & Co., and Golby & Co. of Banbury, were admitted, each allowed to send only a small quantity of traffic. Throughout the furore which followed, stoked, it seems, by the fact that the letters refusing accommodation to other firms rather tactlessly carried Baxendale's signature as the railway official responsible, both the London & Birmingham Company and Pickfords vigorously rejected the allegations of an attempted monopoly. The railway company insisted, and the company records confirm, that the deal with Pickfords was temporary and that as soon as the necessary warehouses, wagons and locomotive power were available the line would be thrown open to all carriers on equal terms.[18] This promise was fulfilled in April 1839, but not before a petition had reached Parliament protesting at the railway company's action.[19]

Pickfords' use of the London & Birmingham railway, therefore, commenced amidst conditions of confusion and continued against a background of uncertainty. Although the company did not change its policy in respect of goods traffic, there were whispers to the contrary from time to time. There must have been some strength of opinion which fostered the opposite view. Shareholders were told at the annual general meeting in February 1839 that when the line was open to all carriers the company would also undertake goods traffic in order to ensure fair rates were charged. Such a policy would have been the worst of all compromises since, as the Grand Junction had found, its interests would inevitably have conflicted with those of the carriers. A year or so later there was further doubt, and Baxendale found it necessary to ask the directors to dispel rumours that the company was considering whether it should commence carrying. He wished to be sure that before he proceeded with planned investment in railway premises his capital would not be destroyed by a change in the company's policy. 'Should the company contemplate becoming carriers', he wrote, 'it would be worse than folly for private individuals entering into competition.'[20]

The organisation and control of goods traffic was recognised as one of the most difficult aspects of railway management. Companies had to select between four possible choices – to contract out the goods traffic completely, to provide power but leave the organisation to the carriers, to admit the carriers but also compete with them, to reserve the traffic as an exclusive monopoly. It was not easy to decide which was better, the 'open' policy, which allowed access to the carriers, or the 'closed' policy, which shut them out.

Opinions expressed and decisions taken reveal the differences between and within railway boards of directors. Theodore Rathbone, deputy chairman of the North Union line, believed his company's open policy to be correct, whereas his co-director Hardman Earle, who, significantly, was also a member of the Grand Junction board, was convinced of the opposite view.[21] Decisions taken spread across the entire range of possibilities. In 1839, of the eight principal railway companies then in operation, the Liverpool & Manchester, Leeds &

Selby, and Newcastle & Carlisle Companies were exclusive carriers, the Bolton & Leigh was leased to the carrier John Hargreaves, the North Union followed the same policy as the London & Birmingham, and the Stockton & Darlington Company carried alongside other parties. The Grand Junction monopolised all traffic between London and Birmingham but admitted carriers to the London traffic. Companies progressively began to carry, exclusively or in conjunction with other carriers, but such important lines as the Manchester & Leeds, North Midland and Midland Counties, in addition to the London & Birmingham, continued the open policy five years later.[22]

PICKFORDS' RAILWAY OPERATIONS

It was against this background that Pickfords' railway operations were built up. Individual lines were adopted piecemeal, as the various lines were finished, and by 1839 sufficient of a network had been built for a complete system of railway carrying to be contemplated. By the autumn of that year Pickfords was undertaking daily rail services between London, Liverpool and Manchester, between Birmingham, Derby and Nottingham, and between Leeds and York. The gaps were bridged by canal and wagon links, but as railway construction progressed these were steadily reduced. In 1841 the rails of nine separate companies, the Liverpool & Manchester, Grand Junction, London & Birmingham, Manchester & Leeds, North Midland, York & North Midland, Midland Counties, Birmingham & Derby, and Birmingham & Gloucester, covered much of Pickforks' traditional area of operations and carried the bulk of the firm's railway business.

Elsewhere some railways were employed but not others. Lines through the eastern counties were largely ignored. Those to the west and south of London similarly received little attention, chiefly because the areas they served contained few centres of manufacturing and so were not expected to generate much merchandise traffic. The one exception, the firm's rapid build-up on the London & South Eastern railway in the early 1840s, is probably best explained by Baxendale's position as director and for a time chairman of that company. Warehouses were rented at Tonbridge, Staplehurst and Ashford and road links put on to Maidstone, Canterbury and Hastings before branch lines were built to them. Depots were opened at Dover, Folkestone, Hythe and Cranbrook, and a number of other places along the south coast. In 1844, however, Baxendale was ousted from the chairmanship during a prolonged absence abroad, where he was recuperating after a breakdown in his health. Pickfords lost its position and was obliged to return most of its warehouses to the company.[23]

The other main extension into new territory was northwards, to Scotland. Traffic for places beyond Lancashire and the West Riding had previously been handed on to other carriers. But as the east and west coast rail routes to Scotland were laid down, Pickfords' interests were drawn into that area. For a time its services across the border were a makeshift effort. In the early 1840s west coast traffic was forwarded from Fleetwood to Scotland. In the east, goods were taken by rail for as far as the line had been built and then on by wagon. The road haul through Durham, Northumberland and the borders was steadily reduced until only the uncompleted bridge at Berwick stood in the way of a continuous line of rails. The final stage came in 1847 when premises were taken in Edinburgh and Glasgow, a few months before the completion of the rail links with England. Pickfords could now proudly advertise a comprehensive carrying service by rail to all the major towns and cities of England and Scotland.[24]

It was in the early days of this programme that Baxendale talked to the directors of the London & Birmingham Company about his planned investment in railways. Pickfords' canal headquarters at City Road Basin could not cope with railway traffic and had to be replaced. Moreover Baxendale believed that the London & Birmingham's provision for goods traffic at its terminus in Camden Town seriously underestimated the likely growth of goods traffic. For both of these reasons he bought a plot of land in Camden, on the south bank of the Regent's canal and adjacent to the railway company's goods station, and built on it a new, railway, headquarters which combined administrative offices, warehousing accommodation and stables. Opened in December 1841, the scale and functional design of the building, specially suited to fit the needs of railway traffic, and the speed with which traffic could be processed, drew admiring comment. The total scheme incorporated a private dock and layby on the Regent's canal, in order to integrate canal and rail traffic (a special hoist loaded goods to and from barges drawn up directly below the railway warehouse), together with a private bridge over the canal which gave access to the London & Birmingham line. Extra rails and a turntable were added later, and then a sidings adjoining the railway company's own depot. The Camden building, which cost about £40,000, expressed Baxendale's conviction that the carrier's future lay with railways.[25]

The choice of Camden emphasised Pickfords' continued preoccupation with traffic between London, the midlands and the north.[26] Traffic passed constantly through the warehouse, its direction in or out determining how it was handled. 'Up' traffic, which arrived partly by day but chiefly by night, was unloaded from the railway trucks, sorted and arranged in order of the London delivery districts and reloaded on to road wagons ready for distribution. 'Down' traffic came in overnight from the London warehouses and had to be sorted and loaded by town of consignment, ready for the departure of the first goods train at 6.00 a.m. The two categories of traffic therefore fell into distinct phases of working and demanded quite different treatment. The depot was accordingly divided into two separate operating sections, each with its complement of porters and clerks. The rhythm of work depended on the timetable of goods trains, so that one side might be idle while the other worked at full stretch. Round-the-clock working required double relays of staff in both parts of the depot.

In dispatching goods from Camden the over-riding principle, as it had been on the canals, was to trunk traffic direct and undisturbed to its place of destination. Traffic which employed both canal and rail was trans-shipped at Camden, Rugby or Birmingham. Otherwise the objective was to send whole truck-loads to each town to which Pickfords carried by rail. Breaking bulk was not only inconvenient and costly, it added enormously to the risk of theft. Incomplete loads were put together and sent to Derby, where traffic from the west of England was assembled. Full loads could be guaranteed from Derby northwards. The procedure had the advantage that Pickfords was able to offer a regular, daily service to many towns which did not attract sufficient loading to fill a wagon. In order to provide this service the firm was willing to pay for each truck at a nominal loading of $3\frac{1}{2}$ tons, even if it carried only 30 hundredweight. It is not surprising, therefore, that Pickfords preferred the smaller standard-gauge trucks as more suited to its purposes than those employed on broad-gauge lines.

THE CARRYING QUESTION: PICKFORD & CO. *v.* THE GRAND JUNCTION RAILWAY COMPANY

The 'open' system of goods traffic operations was clearly preferable to the carriers, but it was wasteful. Consignments of 30 hundredweight in $3\frac{1}{2}$ ton trucks wasted wagon space and locomotive power, a loss which, like the multiplication of terminal facilities, increased with each additional carrier on the line. Disputes between carriers and railway companies compounded the waste. Traffic sent by circuitous routes incurred unnecessary wagon miles while resources lay idle on the line under boycott. Railways which acted as exclusive carriers had the opportunity to benefit from economies of scale by carrying in full wagon-loads and maximising, by way of full train-loads, the use of locomotive power. Although there are doubts as to whether they actually did so, that was the rationale on which the exclusion of the carriers was justified.[27] The latter denied the argument and moreover asserted that a small element of waste would in any case be preferable to the tyranny of a railway monopoly.

The appropriate balance between the railways and the established canal carriers became a matter of public and at times heated debate. Was a compromise between the two, to preserve scarce national resources invested in canals, either possible or even desirable? There were, it is true, a few ineffective calls for a balanced programme of railway and canal transport. But Parliament was not willing to undertake such a task nor delegate the necessary authority to a substitute body.[28] When the carrying question came to Parliament, therefore, it arrived not in the form of a grand debate, a forerunner of 'road versus rail' in the 1930s, but rather as a request for judgement whether powers exercised under its statutory authority were being abused and the rights of individuals trampled under foot. The main drama, in which Pickfords played the hero and the Grand Junction Railway Company the villain, occurred elsewhere, in the law courts. Its form and characterisation was shaped by the firm's particular dispute with the Grand Junction. But its substance pertained to the carrying trade in general. Could any carrier, however powerful, compete effectively with a railway company over its own rails? And by implication, were Parliament and the country happy to look the other way while the carriers were dispossessed? Both sides claimed to be protecting the public interest. Would Parliament decide?

When Pickfords pitted its resources against the Grand Junction in legal battle it was widely recognised that fundamental issues were at stake.[29] Pickfords was fighting for survival, and if it, the leading carrier, failed there could be no hope for any other, while the Grand Junction was equally determined to be master in its own house. The case was also acknowledged to be raising fundamental principles of law. Precedents were going to be set and hence the action was taken as a special case, before three judges instead of a jury. Their lordships were asked to decide whether, in certain specific matters, the railway had acted 'reasonably' and without 'undue preference' as its statutes required. The form of the questions was crucial. The court's function was of a negative kind, to decide only whether the railway company's behaviour infringed the statutes by which it was authorised, not to instruct it how to behave in order to observe them. The possibilities of manoeuvre turned the case into a litigant's paradise.

The pleadings were under two heads. The first concerned the appropriate charge for small parcels. Small parcels were lucrative business. They were charged at a special rate, considerably higher than the general rate on merchandise, and most Railway Acts gave a company the right to take all small parcels sent for conveyance by passenger train. Pickfords and other carriers tried to hold on to this traffic by packing parcels in hampers and presenting them for conveyance by goods trains, at the tonnage rate. The Grand Junction retaliated by levying a special high rate on such hampers. One consignment, submitted by Pickfords as a test case, would have been charged 9 shillings at the tonnage rate but the special rate demanded was £3 1s 6d. Pickfords refused to pay and asked the court to declare that such a charge was 'unreasonable' and therefore illegal. At issue, it was alleged, was the control of the trade between London and Lancashire. Freight rates had been so squeezed as to leave very little margin to the carrier on his ordinary rail business; only the revenue from parcels traffic allowed any serious competition to continue.

The second charge accused the Grand Junction Company of discriminating in favour of Chaplin & Horne. As agent to the Grand Junction, Chaplin & Horne received a rebate of 10 shillings per ton, in return for which it performed cartage and delivery services in London and acted for the company on London & Birmingham rails. The Grand Junction's refusal to allow Pickfords the same terms constituted the other charge, of 'undue preference'.

Legal argument was already developing nicely when the Commons' Select Committee on Railways was reappointed, in January 1840, under the chairmanship of Lord Seymour. This was the sign for a flow of petitions, eleven in all, during February and March, from carriers, merchants and traders in various parts of the midlands and north of England.[30] The House of Commons was asked to protect 'fair and free competition for the carriage of goods on railways'. One even hinted at a total ban on railways acting as carriers. Seymour's committee gave full consideration to the carrying question, and Pickfords' dispute with the Grand Junction figured prominently. The committee initially leaned towards the system on the Liverpool & Manchester railway whereby the company carried subject to maximum charges, but it finally reported in favour of the carriers. The clinching argument was seen to lie in the untrammelled clarity of the carrier's liability for goods in transit. A railway company might carry more efficiently and cheaply on its own line, but the prospective chaos if liability for through traffic became a pawn of inter-company disputes could not be tolerated. Fatefully for the carriers, however, no legislative action was recommended.[31]

Parliament's refusal positively to discriminate in favour of the carriers meant that their case was already as good as lost. The courts could only interpret the terms set by Parliament. So although Pickfords won a series of judgements against the Grand Junction Company it gained no significant advantage. Some concessions were made, but there were many subtle ways of negating an unfavourable verdict. Appeals were made to the Board of Trade but to no avail. And when Parliament looked at the matter again, in 1844, it showed even less desire to intervene.[32] The carriers departed but the basic issues remained. Undue preference, reasonable rates, terminal charges, as well as the problem of amalgamation and natural monopoly, all continued to trouble Parliament for years to come.

THE END OF THE AFFAIR

Pickfords' campaign against the Grand Junction was waged as vigorously outside as inside the courtroom. Its strength on canals helped. As far as possible, traffic passing from London to Liverpool was taken to Birmingham by rail and sent on from there by canal. Traffic which had to go by rail was subject to delay. The Grand Junction insisted on an additional charge for each truck taken beyond its line in order to enable through traffic to proceed undisturbed, but because Pickfords refused to pay the extra, it was obliged to break bulk at Birmingham. Goods had to be unloaded at the Grand Junction's Vauxhall Station, carted to that of the London & Birmingham Company and then reloaded into that company's wagons for the rest of the journey to London. The resulting delay caused Pickfords' traffic to arrive in London a day later than that of Chaplin & Horne.[33]

Sometimes it was possible to avoid the Grand Junction line entirely. Traffic could be sent to Rugby and then dispatched on a circuitous route through the midlands system, by way of Derby and Leeds, to Manchester, and finally to Liverpool. In spite of the long detour Pickfords was able to offer competitive rates and succeeded in holding traffic. During 1842–3 it paid the Manchester & Leeds Railway Company some £1,500 per month for traffic carried over its rails,[34] revenue which in other circumstances would have gone to the Grand Junction Company. Fierce inter-company rivalries, as trenchant as those notorious locomotive jousts suggest, helped the carrier's cause. Companies looking for weapons to aim at their rivals could be tempted by the offer of traffic withdrawn from an opponent.

The one line on which Pickfords was absolutely dependent was the London & Birmingham railway. It was the firm's lifeline for access to and from London, and to friendly systems in the midlands. Pickfords' railway aspirations were, therefore, tenable only so long as the London & Birmingham remained committed to its open policy. In the meantime the firm's services from Camden could develop and Pickfords soon became the largest single carrier of traffic on the London & Birmingham line. In 1846 traffic passing through Pickfords' Camden depot was estimated at 1,600 tons per week, or 85,000 tons per annum, possibly a tenth of the total of goods traffic on the line.[35] Hostile changes were, however, already on the way.

There is little doubt that the effective development of railway traffic in the early 1840s was severely hampered by the existence of so many small operating companies each vying vigorously with the rest. The emergence, by amalgamation, of larger operating units were, therefore, together with the creation of the Railway Clearing House, important steps forward.[36] The formation of the Midland Counties Railway Company gave the lead in 1844. The London & Birmingham and Grand Junction Companies then decided to sink past differences and to merge with the Liverpool & Manchester (already in fact absorbed by the Grand Junction) and the Manchester & Birmingham Companies in the new London & North Western Railway Company. Standard procedures and uniform policies could thereafter be applied over a large part of the railways system. The long-run benefit of these changes cannot be doubted, but there was a price to be paid, and it was the carriers who paid it. Standard practice on the London & North Western was to exclude carriers from the goods traffic.

Pickfords' lifeline had gone. From the summer of 1847 the London & North Western shut out the independent carriers. But just before the door slammed, the firm scrambled through to safety. If the London & North Western was to operate a complete goods service, including collection and delivery, it was going to need horses, stables, wagons, carts, town receiving offices, and so on. Chaplin & Horne, inherited from the Grand Junction, could provide some of these but not enough. To buy the services of one of the leading carriers was an obvious way of acquiring the rest. And as the London & North Western's main territory was the central belt between London and Lancashire it was equally obvious which carrying firm to choose. Baxendale's railway ambitions may have been brutally crushed but he remained, as ever, a realist. Survival was more important than sentiment. Pickfords joined Chaplin & Horne as co-agent to the new railway company.

REFERENCES: CHAPTER 6

1 Report of William Cubitt, February 1825, to the chairman and committee of the Liverpool and Manchester Railway Company, Baxendale papers.
2 The next two paragraphs follow the argument of M. C. Reed, *Investment in Railways in Britain, 1820–1844* (London: Oxford University Press, 1975), ch. 1.
3 The 1825 boom gave rise to much discussion on this head: *Quarterly Review*, March 1825; Mather, *After the Canal Duke*, ch. 2; Richards, *Leviathan of Wealth*, pp. 56 ff.
4 Reed, *Investment in Railways*, Fig. 1, p. 8, Fig. 2, p. 12; also H. G. Lewin, *Early British Railways, 1801–1844* (London: Locomotive Publishing Co., n.d., preface 1925), map 4 facing p. 124.
5 T. R. Gourvish, *Mark Huish and the London & North Western Railway, a Study of Management* (Leicester: Leicester University Press, 1972), is the indispensable study of railway management before 1860, and provides the relevant background for this and the next chapter.
6 Liverpool & Manchester Railway Company, board minutes, 19 October 1829, PRO/BTHR Rail 371/1.
7 Liverpool & Manchester Railway Company, board minutes, 9, 16 June 1828, 19 June 1829, PRO/BTHR Rail 371/1.
8 Liverpool & Manchester Railway Company, board minutes, 6, 16 November, 21 December 1829, 8 February 1830, PRO/BTHR Rail 371/1; G. L. Turnbull, 'A note on the supply of staff for the early railways', *Transport History*, vol. I (1968), pp. 3–9.

9 Liverpool & Manchester Railway Company, board minutes, 22 November 1830, PRO/BTHR Rail 371/2.

10 'The genesis of the container', *Railway Gazette*, 13 October 1933, p. 529; evidence of Bass and Hayward, *RC on the Gauge of Railways*, PP, 1846, vol. XVI.

11 Grand Junction Railway Company, board minutes, 21 September 1836, PRO/BTHR Rail 220/1.

12 Grand Junction Railway Company, board minutes, 16, 21 March 1838, PRO/BTHR Rail 220/2.

13 Grand Junction Railway Company, board minutes, 17, 21 November 1838, PRO/BTHR Rail 220/2; Pickfords' contract is reproduced in *SC on Railway Communication*, 1840, Q. 729; the following draws on the extensive evidence presented to this committee on the dealings between the Grand Junction railway and the carriers, and also on the railway press.

14 Grand Junction Railway Company, board minutes, 22 May 1839, PRO/BTHR Rail 220/2.

15 Grand Junction Railway Company, board minutes, 30 September 1840, and *passim* subsequent months, PRO/BTHR Rail 220/3.

16 'Heads of agreement between London & Birmingham Company with Mr. Baxendale', 24 November 1837, PRO/BTHR Rail 1008/105: the agreement was recommended for approval by the management committee, minutes, 6 December 1837, PRO/BTHR Rail 384/85: the revised scheme, 'Plan to be proposed for carrying on the railway business', also came from the management committee, PRO/BTHR Rail 1008/92: see also Baxendale's evidence, *SC on Railways*, Second Report, 1839, Q. 2422.

17 Much of the detail is in Baxendale's evidence, *SC on the London & Birmingham Railway Bill*, PP, 1839, vol. XIII, and the evidence of Baxendale, George Carr Glyn and Richard Creed, *SC on Railways*, 1839.

18 London & Birmingham Railway Company, minutes of management committee, 3 September 1838, PRO/BTHR Rail 384/85; board minutes, 5 October 1838, PRO/BTHR Rail 384/3, following the recommendation of the committee of administration, PRO/BTHR Rail 1008/92; joint circular between Pickfords and the London & Birmingham denying allegations of attempted monopoly, PRO/BTHR Rail 1008/111.

19 This petition, *Parliamentary Debates*, 3rd series, vol. 46, cols 1220–1, led to the appointment of the Select Committee on Railways that session; also, *The Times*, 27 March 1839, p. 5.

20 Baxendale to London & Birmingham directors, 5 February 1840, PRO/BTHR Rail 1133/149; London & Birmingham's AGM, PRO/BTHR Rail 1110/260, a reference I owe to Dr M. C. Reed.

21 See their evidence to *SC on Railways*, Second Report, 1839.

22 *SC on Railways*, Second Report, 1839; *SC on Railways*, Fifth Report, PP, 1844, vol. XI, appendix 2, p. 22.

23 London & South Eastern Railway Company, board minutes, 1843–5, especially 4 July 1843, 25 September 1844, PRO/BTHR Rail 635/17, 18; Diary of Joseph Hornby Baxendale, 1843, Pickfords Removals Ltd.

24 Maps of Pickfords' railway services, 1841, 1844, Pickford papers; *Glasgow Post Office Directory*, 1847–8, appendix, p. 139.

25 *Penny Magazine*, 8, 22 October 1842; *Railway Times*, 4 December 1841; for discussions with the Regent's Canal Company, board minutes, January–April 1839, 10 March 1841, 26 June 1844, 6 November 1846, 17 February 1847, PRO/BTHR Rail 860/36, 38, 40, and correspondence between Baxendale and the canal company, January to April 1839, PRO/BTHR Rail 1133/46; for the development of Camden, London & Birmingham Railway Company, board minutes, 22 November 1839, 18 December 1840, 8

October 1841, 12 July 1844, 13 March 1846, PRO/BTHR Rail 384/4, 5, 6, and *RC on Metropolitan Termini*, PP, 1846, vol. XVII, Baxendale's evidence.

26 This account of Pickfords' railway working is drawn from evidence presented to; *RC on the Gauge of Railways*, 1846, *RC on Metropolitan Termini*, 1846, *SC on the Oxford, Worcester & Wolverhampton and the Oxford & Rugby Railway Bill*, PP, 1845, vol. XI; Camden warehouse was described in the *Penny Magazine*, 8, 22 October 1842, and also in the *Quarterly Review*, vol. CLXVII (1848–9), pp. 23 ff., subsequently reproduced as F. B. Head, *Stokers and Pokers* (1849; Newton Abbott: David & Charles, 1968).

27 B. Poole, *Twenty Short Reasons for Railway Companies Being Themselves the Carriers of Goods* (Liverpool: 1844); and *A Dozen More Short Reasons . . .* (1844); Gourvish, *Mark Huish*, pp. 43, 131 ff.

28 James Morrison, MP, *Parliamentary Debates*, 3rd series, vol. 33, cols 980–1; Poulett Thomson, *Parliamentary Debates*, 3rd series, vol. 31, cols 684–5; Sir Harry Verney, *Parliamentary Debates*, 3rd series, vol. 31, cols 1113–4; *The Times*, 8 August 1836; H. Parris, *Government and the Railways in Nineteenth Century Britain* (London: Routledge & Kegan Paul, 1965).

29 For a fuller discussion, Jackman, *Development of Transportation*, appendix 14; *The English Reports*, vol. 152, Exchequer Division (1915), pp. 525–36; *Railway Times*, 1840–3; for the railway side, Gouvish, *Mark Huish*, pp. 79 ff.

30 *House of Commons Journal*, vol. XCV, pp. 64, 104, 114, 121, 136, 158, 171, 184, 198, 205, 261.

31 *SC on Railway Communication*, five reports and evidence, 1840.

32 Memorial of Pickford & Co. to the Board of Trade, February 1844, PRO/BTHR Rail 1133/147; another petition, signed by numerous traders, PRO/BT 6/281; *SC on Railways*, Fifth Report, 1844.

33 Grand Junction Railway Company, board minutes, 3, 7 October 1840 and subsequently, PRO/BTHR Rail 220/3; Mills's evidence, *RC on the Gauge of Railways*, 1846, QQ. 1954–2059.

34 S. Salt, *Statistics and Calculations Essentially Necessary to Persons Connected with Railways or Canals*, 2nd edn (London and Manchester: 1846), p. 77.

35 Mills's evidence, *RC on the Gauge of Railways*, 1846.

36 H. Pollins, *Britain's Railways: An Industrial History* (Newton Abbot: David & Charles, 1971); Gourvish, *Mark Huish*, pp. 103 ff.; P. S. Bagwell, *The Railway Clearing House in the British Economy, 1842–1922* (London: Allen & Unwin, 1968).

7

The Railway Agent,
1847–1900

About mid-century, Britain's economic and political history entered a quieter phase. For the next twenty to thirty years there were no equals to the dramas of parliamentary reform, chartism, free trade. While these battles were being fought out, the transformation of the British economy towards its modern, industrial form had been quietly proceeding in the background. On the basis of a more diverse range of economic activities, freed from the instabilities engendered by uncertain domestic food supplies and supported by strong overseas demand for its manufactures, Britain enjoyed two or three decades of more or less prosperous conditions. And if towards the end of the century the pace of economic growth slackened, at least the sharp contractions of the economy which had been so damaging in earlier years were avoided.

Generally sustained expansion of the economy meant greater and greater volumes of traffic to be conveyed, plenty of business for the new railway system.[1] Railways made rapid progress, receiving great stimulus and few checks from the general development of the economy. Vigorous demand for railway services made for healthy traffic and revenue returns, as rival modes of transport were swept aside. For other reasons, too, railway companies could feel more secure. Threats from rival promotions receded as higher construction costs raised the barriers to entry and the completion of the main network reduced the scope for major new lines. But if external pressures eased, fierce internal competition ensured that profits were hard won. There were no easy pickings. The strongest company faced keen rivalry from its territorial neighbours, and by the end of the century the dead hand of state regulation of railway rates had rendered those profits even less easy. Not unlike the economy, railways began the second half of the nineteenth century in conditions of apparent strength, but ended it on a hesitant note.

Railways reflected features characteristic of the economy at large in several ways, perhaps most conspicuously in the transforming role of fixed capital. Enterprises built on large quantities of fixed capital became quite different kinds of business units from earlier forms which had been largely the personal expressions of individuals, and which invariably perished with them.[2] On the railway, it was the rails, stations and rolling stock which expressed the company's personality, the house style, rather than the shareholders or general manager. Moreover, the bigger and more complex such organisations became, the more their administration and management could be standardised. Business was conducted according to strict rules to which all, customers as well as officers, had to conform. The personal touch was much reduced, but so was the interdependence between the business concern and individual, dominant personalities. The Huishs, Allports, Findlays, Watkins, left their mark,[3] but the railway companies they managed survived their departure. It had become much more difficult for large concerns which employed great quantities of capital to die than to survive.

For Pickfords, now a small firm in an ancillary trade to the railways, to tie up with one of these new giants obviously made a great deal of sense. But there were dangers. Clinging to the London & North Western's coat-tails promised salvation, but also the risk of being swallowed up entirely. To avoid this fate was not easy. After 1847 Pickfords' task was to acquire a dual, rather than a split, personality, to be loyal to its railway masters without losing its own identity, to be immediately recognised as both railway agent and independent haulier. To achieve the latter while preserving the former proved testing, but although there were fights along the way the job was done. The image of the canal barge dropped away, and Pickfords slipped into the new railway age. Within a few years it was impossible to think of railways without thinking also of Pickfords. When the young immigrant Scots William Hendrie and John Shedden decided to seek their fortunes in the railway cities of Toronto and Montreal, it was to the cartage of railway freight that they turned, setting out to become 'the Pickfords of Canada'.[4]

RAILWAYS: TRAFFIC, AGENTS AND CARTAGE

The belief that railways would eliminate the horse as a medium of transport was quickly dispelled. In fact, even more passengers and greater volumes of goods traffic began or completed their journey behind a horse. The reason was, of course, that although railways absorbed the longer-distance trade, they simultaneously created new demands for feeder services. Particularly was this so for freight. Passengers could take a cab or a horse bus to the station, or they could choose to walk, but goods and parcels had to be fetched. Railways were not the only stimulus to the extension of road haulage which, in the guise of urban cartage, marked the later nineteenth century, but they were by far the most important.

Freight traffic has received little attention in transport history.[5] Railway historians, for example, have preferred the colour of snorting passenger expresses and the drama of horrendous crashes to the dull routine of the tank engines, trundling up and down the line with merchandise, minerals and livestock. By so doing they miss out more than half the story, since it was the latter which paid the greater part of the annual dividend. Windfall passenger profits did not last long. From 1852, a familiar statistic, passenger revenue fell behind that earned by goods traffic on Britain's railways. By the end of the century, passenger services, except in the southern commuter belt, scarcely paid their way. The most successful railway companies were those, like the North Eastern, which had a solid base of goods traffic on which to draw.[6] And of course it was the goods traffic which was of most interest to cartage firms like Pickfords.

Actually it was one part of the goods traffic, general merchandise, which cartage firms would have their eye on. Minerals, the largest component, and livestock were handled by other agencies. So was some of the general merchandise. But the rest, especially that which required collection and delivery services, fell to the railway companies to deal with, which they frequently did by passing it on to cartage agents. The railway statistics usually quoted for this period do not make clear the importance of the merchandise trade to the railways. The figures in Table 7.1 are intended to correct this. They demonstrate that for all its less weight and greater trouble compared with minerals – it was not homogeneous, it was more difficult to load and required more expensive terminal facilities – merchandise traffic contributed a larger share of total income. Throughout the period, its value was of considerably greater importance than its volume. In the mid-1850s 40 per cent of the total goods tonnage contributed almost 75 per cent of the revenue from that source. These proportions slowly fell thereafter, but still remained at about 30 per cent and 55 per cent respectively in 1900.

In absolute terms railway merchandise traffic grew steadily rather than rapidly, by a factor of four between 1855 and 1900 in respect of receipts, and by a factor of five in respect of volume. And it was the latter, of course, which determined how much cartage was needed, how much a railway company would have to spend on horses and carts, or alternatively how much business it would hand over to its cartage agent. The volume growth of railway merchandise traffic is, therefore, the best available indicator of the likely trend of railway agency business. The railway cartage agent was, moreover, an integral part of a

Table 7.1   *The Growth of Railway Goods Traffic, England and Wales, 1850–1900*

	1850	1855	1860	1865	1870*	1875	1880	1885	1890	1895	1900
Total Traffic Receipts (£m.)	12·4	18·4	23·5	30·2	41·4	51·7	55·8	59·3	68·3	72·8	89·4
Freight receipts (£m.)	5·9	9·2	12·5	16·2	22·4	28·0	30·5	31·3	36·0	37·0	45·3
Freight receipts as share of total receipts	47·6%	50·0%	53·2%	53·6%	54·1%	54·2%	54·7%	52·8%	52·7%	50·8%	50·1%
Merchandise Traffic											
Receipts (£m.)		6·7	7·8	10·3	13·1	15·8	16·9	17·3	19·8	20·7	24·9
Share of total freight receipts		72·8%	62·4%	63·6%	58·5%	56·4%	55·4%	55·3%	55·0%	55·9%	55·0%
Tonnage (m. tons)		20·2	24·5	30·7	59·0	53·4†	59·4	62·5	74·3	80·0	102·6
Share of total freight tonnage		37·8%	33·0%	32·5%	42·0%	31·6%	29·6%	28·6%	28·7%	28·5%	28·5%

Source: Railway Returns.
Notes:
* Figures for 1871; the tonnage figures for 1870 are defective.
† The London & North Western, alone of all railway companies, did not separate minerals from merchandise tonnages in 1875. The share of merchandise in that year has been estimated from the return of 1880, when the two categories were next separated.

very sensitive area of railway business. It was essential for cartage services to be performed efficiently, so as not to lose valuable traffic, and cheaply, so as not to drain away hard-earned revenue. This was true whether or not a railway company provided its own cartage. And it also meant that even when it chose to employ an agent, it had to exercise strict control. The strains which arose between Pickfords and its major rail employer, the London & North Western, need to be considered in this light.

By joining forces with the London & North Western, Pickfords did more than secure a foothold in the rising railway industry; it became an ally of the most powerful railway company of the day. In mid-century the London & North Western was the dominant force in railway affairs. It controlled about an eighth of the entire railway mileage and a similar share of total railway capital. It accounted for about 20 per cent of total receipts, passenger and goods, and on its system was the stretch of rails, between London and Rugby, which carried the heaviest tonnage per track-mile of the whole railway network.[7] The weight of business transacted and the physical extent of the empire controlled from Euston, the headquarters of the London & North Western, laid the basis for the company's pre-eminence in railway politics. Pickfords could only have gained from the backing of such a weighty ally, and although the firm concluded agency agreements with several other railway companies[8] its position clearly rested ultimately on its special relationship with the London & North Western. However, more than its political clout, the company's traffic was particularly attractive, especially in the 1850s. At nearly half of its total receipts, revenue from goods traffic followed the norm, but the place of merchandise traffic, at 80 per cent of the company's freight receipts, was exceptional.[9] Since the London & North Western supplied little of its cartage requirements itself, this, together with a substantial parcels traffic, promised a sizeable chunk of business for a cartage agent.

Pickfords benefited from its railway business in several ways, all very real if not always easily measured, all conferring certain advantages over competing firms. It escaped, for example, the petty persecution which eventually persuaded Kenworthy & Co. to give up its railway business.[10] It enjoyed privileged access to the railway goods yard together with the concession, of material value in what became a highly competitive trade, of being able to fetch in goods an hour later than other firms. The London & North Western provided other, tangible accommodation at its stations, offices, stables, warehouse and storage space for vehicles and other equipment. In the 1880s, for example, Pickfords leased from the company large stable blocks at Camden, Broad Street and Haydon Square, together with space for a house, grain and chaff mills, farrier's shop and harness room. Similar provision, on a lesser scale, was made in the provinces.[11] With the agency, then, went the use of prime central sites, close to the sources of traffic and at rentals which if more than nominal were evidently some way below the full market rate. And since a parallel deal was concluded with the Midland railway in 1850, which lasted for a decade, these privileges were enjoyed over two major rail systems which together controlled a wide area of country stretching from London through the heartland of the industrial economy as far north as Newcastle in the east and Carlisle in the west.[12]

There were other elements of subsidy, apart from preferential rents. The contract was conducted on a break-even basis, the agent being reimbursed its costs at a rate set by the London & North Western. Terms were renegotiated as costs, especially provender costs, rose and fell, the purpose being to protect against a loss, definitely not to provide a profit. But the definition of costs was broadly drawn, to include all elements which contributed, without being restricted to the working of the contract, office rents, clerical salaries, the purchase and maintenance of stock as well as the direct costs of putting a horse and cart on the road. And although Pickfords might, and did, complain that a fuller reckoning of their costs should be taken account of, it enjoyed a distinct cross-subsidy every time staff and stock primarily recruited for and paid by the contract were employed, quite legitimately, in some other use. Again it is unlikely that fodder prepared on railway-owned premises and possibly conveyed by rail free of charge was fed only to horses employed in railway work. Contract work could be kept separate from the rest of the business in the accounts but not in actual operations, and what was intended to support the one must, to some extent, have spilled over into the other.

The benefits were not, however, all on one side. Pickfords made positive contributions to the London & North Western. The railway company had to have cartage services, both to provide collection and delivery of its own traffic and to meet the competition of other lines on the streets of London and elsewhere. The advertising value of a well-turned-out cartage fleet, apart from its functional worth, was quickly appreciated. The London & North Western's own cartage resources were, however, limited. It inherited the stock of the former Grand Junction railway at Liverpool, Manchester and Birmingham, together with that of Chaplin & Horne, the Grand Junction's agent in London. These were retained, but even together could not cope with the expanded area and volume of traffic controlled by the amalgamated company. Pickfords' strength and national spread of outlets provided the width and depth of coverage which the railway itself could not. The result was a hybrid system in which Pickfords and Chaplin & Horne were employed as joint agents, alongside the London & North Western's own services. In any particular place cartage would be supplied by one, two or all three of them.

Like other railway companies, the London & North Western employed its cartage services as a 'loss leader' in order to attract traffic on to its line. Premier railway or not, it did not escape vigorous competition. Initially this originated most forcibly from canal traders, both the thirty-odd carrying firms dispossessed when the railway abandoned the toll system and also canal companies, especially those which invoked the 1845 Act and erected carrying departments. At this stage most railway companies were still building up their locomotive and goods departments, and were not yet ready to attack the bulk, low-grade traffic which was in contention. In one sense the opposition was highly successful. Many canal companies carried their highest volumes of traffic ever during the late 1840s and early 1850s and some, such as the Bridgewater,[13] even managed to compel individual railway companies to sue for peace. The London & North Western felt the draught as, according to Huish, the general manager, traffic was diverted to the canals.[14] But the canals' crucial weakness was also revealed. They no longer possessed the merchandise trade which had long subsidised the general traffic. Revenue no longer covered costs, dividends fell and the canals were soon reduced to a parlous financial condition. From the early 1850s the pressure waned. Railways were by then fully equipped and had moreover discovered that infiltration of canal ownership, as the lemmings sold out, provided a more effective means of obstructionism and was less costly than price wars. In the meantime Pickfords was constrained by the London & North Western to bring all possible former canal traffic to the railway.

Inter-company rivalry within the railway industry was something quite different.[15] Although direct opposition soon gave way to traffic-sharing arrangements, some competition remained. Even pooling schemes were not free from the possibility of manipulation. Receipts were divided according to the origin of traffic and the route it took, and neither of these was beyond influence. Here the cartage agent could have a special part to play, enabling its employer to reach beyond its own system of rails. Pickfords, for example, gave the London & North Western a foothold in Derby, to which the company did not have a direct line.[16] As a result, instead of traffic for London & North Western stations being handed to the Midland railway, which could be expected to direct it over its own rails as far as possible, it could be picked up by Pickfords and consigned to the nearest point of the London & North Western system. In the 1850s the London & North Western's dominance of railway business slipped a little, especially as the Great Northern began to bite into traffic along its eastern frontier. The defensive schemes and alliances negotiated by Huish in an attempt to halt the slide must have been assisted by his control of the cartage agents' widespread services as a tactical weapon in the campaign.

Pickfords' contract with the London & North Western survived for over fifty years,[17] but it had its troubles. It got off to a difficult start, relations were rarely smooth for very long and at times drifted close to total breakdown. The birth pangs were particularly painful. The firm which had done more than any other to teach the railways the goods traffic business now had to defer to the strict discipline of its former pupil. And the fact that that discipline was administered by the likes of Huish, Poole and Eborall, Pickfords' chief adversaries on the Grand Junction railway and now managers of the London & North Western's goods traffic, did nothing to sweeten it. Again, former rivalry with Chaplin & Horne had to become harmonious co-operation. As in all mergers, it would be difficult, and take time.

Collaboration between Pickfords and Chaplin & Horne was an essential part of the London & North Western's strategy. The two firms were appointed as joint partners in what was conceived of as a single agency, to be operated on terms intended to bring the best out of both of them. They had different strengths and traded independently, but were paid according to the volume of traffic they *jointly* provided. If their income was made dependent on their collective efforts, they could be expected to concentrate their attention on securing the maximum volume of traffic for the railway and not waste time and energy fighting each other for a larger individual share.

The theory was impeccable, but could not stand the strain of the real world. In fact both agents found cause to criticise the other. Pickfords resented being excluded from the passenger parcels traffic which had been conceded to Chaplin & Horne, largely, it must be said, as a reward for converting its former coaching offices into parcels receiving offices for the London & North Western and for running horse buses to the company's stations. But Pickfords blamed its exclusion from this traffic for the difficulty it found in fulfilling its part of the contract. Assertions by the railway side that Chaplin & Horne provided a cheaper and more efficient service were attacked as symptomatic of the company's general bias against the firm. A long wrangle followed when the London & North Western deducted £1,000 from Pickfords' claimed allowances on the grounds that, by comparison with Chaplin & Horne's charges, they were excessive. The more fundamental point, however, and the reason for Chaplin & Horne's discontent, was that Pickfords failed to come up with the volume of traffic it ought to have done. The division of the proceeds of the joint agency had been agreed at 64:36 in favour of Pickfords, on the expected relative contribution of tonnage. However, for the first three and a half years of the contract, for which alone there are data, Pickfords fell well short of the target, at about 55 per cent of the whole. So when the contract came up for renewal in 1852, Chaplin & Horne, naturally enough, demanded a more realistic distribution. Pickfords resisted and trotted out all its grievances, but was forced to compromise at

60:40.[18] Both sides were aggrieved and drifted into open rivalry with each other. As David Stevenson, long-serving official of the London & North Western's goods department, later observed, the whole purpose of the joint agency had been nullified.

> Their implacable competition with one another, in seeking the trade, was a source of weakness to the company; for the agents would expend as much strength in getting customers from one another as in drawing them from . . . other competitive services . . . Mr Horne threw all his excitable and inexhaustible energy into the combat; while the three sons of Mr Baxendale took the management of Pickford & Co.'s department with increased personal feeling and angry opposition.[19]

The London & North Western put up with these skirmishes between the agents, but to its own authority it would brook no challenge. They were to be quite literally agents, deputed to undertake certain specified duties on behalf of the railway and to regard its interests as taking precedence over their own. Insubordination was promptly stamped on, as when Pickfords slipped in a few cargoes it should not have done with its remaining canal traffic and Huish threatened to scrap the contract if they were not immediately stopped. Decisions were handed down, to be accepted by the agents willy-nilly. The renewal of the contract in 1852 starkly illustrated the railway company's attitude. Instead of a guaranteed salary of £7,500 and no upper limit, it offered a minimum of £10,000 but a maximum of £11,000. Since Pickfords and Chaplin & Horne had in 1850 been netting about £16,000 between them, this represented a sharp cutback. Pickfords protested and tried to negotiate, but the railway side refused. It was told bluntly to accept the offer or break off the contract. It accepted.

How close Pickfords came to breaking its ties with the London & North Western in 1852 is not known; probably not very. For all the irksome frustrations of its reduced condition in life, it ultimately faced exactly the same choice as it had in 1847 and had in the meantime witnessed the demise of former colleagues on the canals who had been unable to find a niche in the railway world. Things could have been a lot worse. Much of the firm's organisation had been preserved, its resources redeployed rather than run down. Its railway business was coming along quite nicely, for other companies as well as for the London & North Western. At the Camden warehouse, now owned by the London & North Western but still worked by Pickfords, extra rails had to be laid down and access bridges to the main line widened.[20] There was still only one realistic choice, the London & North Western agency, warts and all. Moreover as time passed, some of the warts were dissolved. The railway's approach softened a little and in 1866 it even went so far as to concede the arbitration clause long sought by Pickfords but previously refused as 'not consistent with our relative positions'.

Although the London & North Western contract was not the only source of Pickfords' revenue, it did provide the main core of the firm's business during these years. It is a great pity, therefore, that very little is known about the conduct of it after the first few years. To have been able to detail its development would have cast valuable light on what remains a largely unexplored area of transport history. However useful it is to explain how cartage firms like Pickfords fitted into the railway scene in the Victorian age, it is frustrating not to be able to examine how things worked out. From what records remain, it is possible to pick out only the main ups and downs of the story.

Relations remained rather taut. One wrangle led to the railway company, in the early 1860s, taking over the supervision of both its agents' railway warehouses at Camden. In 1858 David Stevenson, an officer in the goods department, complained to Richard Moon, one of the directors and soon to be chairman of the London & North Western, that members of the public who had taken goods to Pickfords' depot at Camden were being sent on to King's Cross, the terminus of the Great Northern.[21] This was bound to touch a raw spot and invite retaliation as the Great Northern was nibbling into London & North Western traffic on the east coast route and had only a few months earlier won important concessions in respect of the division of traffic pooled between them. Chaplin & Horne was not specifically mentioned but as it was included in the proposed punishment, withdrawal of unsupervised working, it was evidently considered to be equally guilty. The punishment was exacted a few years later when Moon took over as chairman. B. W. Horne tried unsuccessfully to get an injunction to keep the railway out. Pickfords' riposte was to pull all its best men out of Camden.

Pickfords left Camden probably in 1864,[22] two years before the next renewal of the agency was due. Relations had apparently deteriorated quite badly, but discussions about a new contract provided the occasion for a fresh start. At least that is what the more conciliatory tone and content of it suggest. There was less stress on the agent's inferior status and, as already noted, the principle of arbitration was admitted. The ceiling on earnings was removed and replaced by a flat rate commission of 1 penny per ton. There was an extra 4 pence per ton commission on all additional traffic, agreement that all parcels of less than a hundredweight sent by the goods trains should be reckoned as if they were full weight, free carriage of stores and free travel passes for staff on agency business. Not all these concessions were new, but the total package appears to have been deliberately more favourable to the agents.

Some discord continued, but relations had achieved a sufficiently even tenor by the early 1890s for the principle of fixed term contracts to be replaced by an open-ended agreement subject only to six months' notice on either side. The anxiety which remained probably arose out of uncertainty about the London & North Western's own intentions. In the later years of the century it was extending its own cartage work and cutting down that which it gave to Pickfords. In 1877, as part of this programme, it absorbed the agency business of Chaplin & Horne and there was at one time talk of its buying Pickfords. No such move came off, and indeed the firm even profited from the demise of its erstwhile partner for it at last gained access to the passenger parcels traffic it had so long coveted. And with new business went new horizons. London was rapidly growing outwards beyond the area of free cartage and delivery into the mushrooming suburbs. Collection and delivery of suburban traffic the London & North Western readily agreed to forgo, and leave it all to its remaining cartage agent.

One of the lesser but none the less revealing complaints made against Pickfords in the early years by certain London & North Western directors was that the carts employed in agency work advertised the firm's name in lettering larger than that of the railway company's. Presumably Pickfords mended its ways and showed due deference for the future. The incident was trivial in itself but perhaps indicates the subtleties of balancing off loyalty to the railway against total sub-servience. No doubt by the end of the century long years of practice had made the posture easier to carry off, but Pickfords' own personality still came through. Almost as the century closed Frederick Harrison, then the general manager of the London & North Western, commenting on Pickfords' loyal service to the railway, remarked, as something of a curiosity, how 'many old-fashioned firms . . . to this day refuse to acknowledge any particular railway company, and look upon Pickford and Co. as their carrier. They have given their goods to Pickford & Co. during the last fifty or sixty years, dating back perhaps to the time when they were carried by road waggons, and to Pickford & Co. they would give them still, not caring what railways they are sent by.'[23]

NINETEENTH-CENTURY URBAN CARTAGE

Pickfords perhaps managed to preserve its separate identity with customers because although it was most prominent as cartage agent to the London & North Western, it was never confined exclusively to that role. It was not bound to the one railway company but developed ties with others, notably the Great Western and the south coast companies. Increasingly London based, the firm could handle any railway traffic passing to and from the capital. Customers paid to have all their cartage needs taken care of, preferring to deal with the one firm rather than a dozen different railway companies. The railway agent could be more than a mere instrument, adding a distinctive quality of service that was worth paying for. Nor was that service itself necessarily confined to railway work. If for the rest of the nineteenth century railway traffic formed the backbone of urban cartage, there were influences at work which enabled cartage firms to stretch their interests into areas of business in which the influence of railways was less obtrusive and occasionally entirely absent.

One of the most marked features of employment growth in the later nineteenth century was the large flow of men and boys into urban cartage. The general report of the 1901 census drew attention to the 'remarkable' increase which had taken place in this category of employment in the 1880s and 1890s.[24] It can, moreover, be seen from Table 7.2

Table 7.2   *The Growth of Road Goods Haulage,*
England and Wales, 1861–1901

	1861	1871	1881	1891	1901
Carmen, Carriers, Carters * Wagoners: England and Wales	67,651	77,177	125,342	170,256	272,960
Increase per decade		14%	62%	36%	61%
Carmen, Carriers, Carters *† Wagoners: London	14,700	20,700	32,000	43,801	60,519
Increase per decade		41%	55%	37%	38%
Commercial Road Vehicles:** Goods (GB)		286,000	388,000	500,000	702,000
Increase per decade			36%	29%	40%
Railway Merchandise (m. tons):†† England and Wales	25	59	59	74	103
Increase per decade		136%	0	23%	39%

Sources:
* Decennial Census, especially Tables 34 and 35 of the *General Report*, 1901. 'Wagoners' excludes those employed on farms.
† Decennial Census; C. Booth, *Life and Labour of the People of London*, Vol. VII, p. 287.
** F. M. L. Thompson, 'Nineteenth-century horse sense', *Economic History Review*, 2nd series, vol. XXIX (1976), p. 72.
†† *Railway Returns.*

that this rapid recruitment to the trade had been going on for a couple of decades before that. By the end of the century there were more persons employed in road haulage than in road passenger transport, and almost as many as in railway service. Why this rapid acceleration? Booth[25] linked the growth of urban cartage to the expansion of railway traffic and Table 7.2 shows that both employment in cartage and railway merchandise traffic, to which the demand for cartage would be most closely linked, about quadrupled during the four decades from 1860. However a closer look at the figures indicates that this cannot be a complete explanation. Much of the growth of railway merchandise traffic was concentrated in the 1860s and 1890s. Although London cartage also grew very quickly in the 1860s, its continued rate of increase from the 1870s, and that of employment in the trade as a whole, was running at a level much higher than the growth of railway business would explain, even if the argument is extended to include all railway traffic, not just the merchandise component. If the positive relationship between railway traffic and urban cartage is to be maintained, it has to be shown why, in the later nineteenth century, the additional railway traffic required a more than proportional increase in cartage resources to service it. Alternatively it might be that the relationship was breaking down and that the expansion of urban cartage is to be attributed to quite different causes.

The nature and organisation of railway goods traffic was in fact undergoing very considerable change. These were the years when traders began to complain bitterly about railway charges, while the railway companies equally complained about the decline in the average weight of consignments and the greater cost of working the goods traffic. It is not necessary to go in to the wider debate here,[26] but it is important to recognise that there was a significant change in the composition of railway traffic. Internal communications had been revolutionised, by the railway itself, by the penny post and the electric telegraph, and were to be further transformed by the telephone. As a result traders changed their pattern of ordering from infrequent but large consignments to frequent and small ones, relying on the regularity of railway services to maintain a steady flow of stocks. Traders thereby transferred the burden of stock holding elsewhere, either to the warehouses, in the form of higher administrative costs, or to the railways in the form of lower truck-loadings and more expensive terminal facilities. Pratt drew exactly this comparison, ascribing equally to railways the warehouseman's complaint that 'the net result . . . of this revolution in trading conditions is a large increase in labour and expenses, without any corresponding increase in receipts. The greater number of parcels is out of all proportion to the greater value of the business done.'[27]

These changes were concentrated in two main categories of traffic, shop goods, the daily orders of thousands of retailers from their central warehouses, and the mushrooming parcels traffic. Small parcels had long been a feature of Britain's commercial life. Speed of dispatch had always been of the essence, and what the stage-coach could achieve the railway passenger trains could excel. The trade was enormously stimulated by the advance in commerce and communications from mid-century, and as the Post Office's parcel service did not begin until 1883 and even then imposed an upper weight limit of 11 pounds, the bulk of the business was carried by the railway.[28] The dispatch by rail of thousands of these small parcels, each less than 28 pounds and packed in special hampers, became the normal means by which

London warehousemen and major stores, especially in the drapery trades, supplied their numerous retail outlets. In the 1870s the wholesale drapery house Bradbery Greatorex & Co. reckoned to send 200,000 bales and parcels in this way every year to the 12,000 retailers with whom it dealt. Other firms in other trades were sending off goods at a similar rate, Marshall & Snellgrove, wholesale and retail silk merchants, Maple & Co., furniture makers and upholsterers, and Mark Brown & Co., wholesale straw manufacturers.[29]

Shop goods and parcels had one other thing in common: both demanded maximum speed. The key word was 'express', and herein lies one of the clues to the expansion of cartage services. Traders expected to be able to send in their orders of an evening and receive their goods the next day. To hasten the passage of these goods through the termini, the railway companies had to put on additional collection and delivery services and were moreover pressed to extend them to all stations and to widen the area of free delivery. Carthorses could not be worked more intensively than three delivery rounds every two days. Two or three delivery rounds each morning, afternoon and evening, for collection and delivery went on until seven or eight o'clock at night, inevitably meant more horses, more carts, more men. To accommodate such traffic railway companies found themselves having to spend more on cartage resources which brought little financial return.

They had little option, however. The 1880s and 1890s were marked by the growth of 'trader power', demands above all for cheaper and better facilities for goods traffic, which led ultimately to the government intervening to freeze freight rates at their 1894 level.[30] The virtual elimination of any remaining flexibility of prices pushed the railways even more strongly towards the traditional mode of competition in transport, by qualities of service. Companies decided they had to get closer to their customers and in order to do that several pursued a deliberate policy of expanding their cartage fleet, or introducing them if they had previously done without. The Midland railway had adopted this tactic much earlier when, in 1860, it dispensed with Pickfords' services and set up its own establishment. Others followed suit, the Great Northern, the Caledonian, the Great Western, either by the purchase of previous agents or the creation of whole new departments. It was to the same purpose that the London & North Western had bought out Chaplin & Horne in the 1870s and had been steadily absorbing contract work from Pickfords. Even so it remained much more reliant on its cartage agent than other major companies. In the 1890s the London & North Western employed less than half the 1,350 horses owned by the Midland railway and only a hundred more than the London & South Western which, although the most important of the south coast lines, carried less than a quarter the amount of merchandise. Railway-owned horses, about 6,000 in all, together accounted for about a quarter of the total number employed in cartage work in London. The railway owned stud continued to increase, to over 26,000 by 1914, and so too did that of other carriers. The predictable result was the emergence of excess capacity in the London cartage trade and with it an even keener edge to the force of competition. And almost equally predictable were attempts to redress the balance, such as the merger in 1912 of the London cartage fleets of the Great Northern, the Great Central and the Great Eastern.[31]

Parcels traffic gave rise to specialised services. Parcels receiving offices, supplemented by numerous shops which acted as auxiliary offices, were opened throughout the business districts of London and other major cities. Railway companies organised frequent collections from these offices, and also from individual firms which regularly dispatched large quantities of parcels. A number of private firms supplied the services, some of them, Globe Parcels Express Co. and Fosters Parcels Express Co., created specifically for this purpose, others, most notably Carter Paterson & Co., adding to its existing range of railway linked cartage services. They collected parcels, packed them in hampers, took them to the station in London and arranged for their final delivery either by one of their provincial branches or through a local agent.[32] Their services were highly competitive, with an emphasis on speed, as the 'Express' in their titles was meant to imply. Parcels traffic took off in London in the 1860s and explains some of the marked expansion in that decade in the number of carmen employed in the capital. Parcels was a similarly expanding traffic in the provinces. A survey of the London & North Western's parcels business in Birmingham, Manchester, Liverpool and Nottingham in the early 1880s indicated a substantial and growing volume of traffic. Almost $1\frac{1}{2}$ million parcels were passing annually through Manchester, the largest of the four.[33]

Pickfords took advantage of the new opportunities offered. By the late 1870s it had adopted the title of 'town carrier', an indication that it had moved into the parcels business. In 1880 it was one of six parcels firms in London, other than the railway companies. If the number of receiving offices indicates the relative size of the firms, Pickfords with sixteen and Carter Paterson & Co. with fourteen were already dominant. Admission to the London & North Western's parcels traffic on the demise of Chaplin & Horne in 1877 must have boosted Pickfords' position considerably, even if the railway company was careful to reserve the best business, contracts with a number of government departments, for itself. Similar services were developed in Birmingham in the 1880s, and presumably in other provincial centres.[34]

Conveyance to and from railway stations, for parcels, merchandise traffic, and so on, formed the bread and butter business of urban cartage. But there were also two other strands, one linked to the railways, the other, to become of major consequence in the years ahead, largely distinct from them. The first comprised a group of functions where railway handed over to road or was in some way deficient. Pickfords, for example, provided regular cartage for the War Office in the 1860s, dealing with consignments of munitions to Portsmouth and Devonport. These would normally have gone by the South Eastern, the nearest railway to the factories, but the company declined to guarantee next-day delivery on the argument that it could not so bind the London & South Western railway to which it would have to pass them. Instead the munitions were carted across London to the London & South Western's goods yard at Nine Elms and thence consigned throughout by the one company, which could provide the necessary guarantee.[35] There must have been other interstices to be filled.

Elsewhere there were railhead deliveries to be made, meat carted from Liverpool Street and Broad Street stations to Smithfield, a trade in which Pickfords was prominent in the 1890s.[36] And there were imported provisions to be distributed to the new retail grocery chains, Lipton's and Home & Colonial. Instead of relying on the railways, some of these firms contracted with cartage firms for the regular delivery of their goods and had the vehicles so employed turned out in their own livery. This was the origin of contract hire. By the end of the century Pickfords had contracts of this kind with Peek Frean & Co., Home & Colonial and Maypole in London and with Lewis's in Birmingham. These are the known examples; there must have been others.

There were close links between railway traffic and the docks, cartage to and from them, and the provision of shipping and forwarding services. Pickfords had been Custom House agents in London since the 1830s and by the 1880s its advertised services included the clearance of goods for shipping and the payment of duty on bonded goods at several other ports, Liverpool, Southampton, Dublin, Bristol, Portsmouth and West Hartlepool. Forwarding agents were employed all over the world. It had also become cartage agent to the East and West India Docks Companies.[37] Moreover, there was a more direct interest in shipping. In 1897 the firm bought the lease of Phoenix wharf, Clink Street, in Southwark, and renamed it Pickfords' wharf.[38] To it were brought the imported provisions distributed by the firm on behalf of the retail grocery chains it serviced. There were also shipping services to the Isle of Wight. Pickfords began carrying to the island from Portsmouth and Southampton by sailing boat in 1862, an extension no doubt of its cartage work for the south coast railways. A fleet of four steam vessels was introduced in the 1880s and the Isle of Wight service gained a special place in the firm's activities.

The other main strand in the development of urban cartage had nothing directly to do with railways; indeed, it announced the commencement of road transport's competition against them. London, from the 1860s, and provincial cities later, were marked by a rapid and continuous acceleration in suburban living. London above all grew to a size at which it generated a large and purely internal demand for road transport, for goods as well as passengers, the carman's horse and cart as much as the horse bus and the horse tram.[39] Parcels again figured prominently, the delivery of shoppers' purchases from London stores or the regular orders of suburban retailers from central warehousemen. An important segment of the growing parcels business was confined within the urban area of London, and at no point touched the railway. By the end of the century such traffic could be delivered over a distance of 10–15 miles so much more swiftly and economically by road that the railway just could not compete.[40] 'Road versus Rail' had been notified for a future agenda.

Suburban growth also influenced Pickfords' development. The counterpart of the London & North Western's promise to channel goods for delivery in London's suburban districts in Pickfords' direction is to be found in the firm's commitment of resources in those areas. In the 1880s leases were acquired of properties in Chalk Farm, Deptford, Penge and Stratford, and in the 1890s premises were bought, probably often the freehold of sites already leased, in Balham, Brixton, Finsbury Park, Fulham and Pimlico and also in the outer suburbs of Brentford, Caterham, Croydon, Edmonton, Kingston, Lee and Walthamstow.[41] Each suburban centre served a number of local collection and delivery districts, and all were linked together by a couple of central depots. Each night traffic was brought into the central depots from the suburban offices, and the railway stations, sorted into its appropriate districts and reconsigned to the various suburban offices in time for the morning delivery. The central depots were the hub of a road transport system, the spokes of which radiated to all parts of London.

In many ways, therefore, Pickfords enjoyed the best of both worlds. By its contract with the London & North Western it retained a prominent place in the railway transport system. It chafed at the bond a little sometimes, and indeed soon determined to break it, but to the end of the nineteenth century there was no viable alternative. Moreover it had achieved a delicate balancing act. It was a full part of the railway world without being confined to it. It had developed other interests, in town cartage, in shipping and forwarding, in contract hire, and in household removals which, in the 1880s, grew out of general cartage into a specialised business. Above all it had survived and with the full range of its national framework of operations preserved, a factor of inestimable advantage when, in the next century, road transport again came to the fore.

THE BUSINESS

Having outlined the main developments in road haulage in the second half of the nineteenth century, it remains to consider how Pickfords itself fared during those years. Alliance with the railways ensured survival. Did it also guarantee prosperity? It appears to have done so although, because of the extreme thinness of the evidence, it is possible to make the case in only very general terms.

It is not known how much traffic Pickfords handled either for railways or independently, but its volume presumably determined the number of horses employed. The firm's horse strength is known. A stud of 880 horses in 1850 had doubled by about 1870 and doubled again by the early 1890s, indicating roughly a fourfold increase in the scale of operations over the half-century, an expansion broadly in line with the growth of railway merchandise traffic. The local concentration of horse strength is also known, and serves as a broad guide to the relative importance of the various towns from which the business was conducted. Numbers edged up everywhere, but the increasing concentration on London was emphatic. In the first decade of the railway agency the London stud grew threefold and thereafter more than half of the firm's horses were employed in the capital. Long the principal centre of the business, London now became dominant. Outside London, too, the balance of strengths changed. Leicester ceased to have any special significance in the firm's organisation; Manchester gave way to Birmingham as the leading provincial centre of the business. Other places, such as Leeds, Liverpool, Sheffield and Wolverhampton, retained their relative positions while substantial strength was built up in the south and south-west of England, especially in Bristol, Exeter, Plymouth, Portsmouth and Reading, an area which had previously been little explored.[42] More ambitiously, a Paris office was briefly considered but not pursued.

Visitors to Pickfords' main establishments in London in mid-century were impressed by a distinctive scale and complexity of operations, a solidity which marked the firm off from others. Dickens, for example, reporting in the 1860s on various forms of horse transport in London, was 'at once struck with an air of substantiality which is different to anything we have yet seen during the tour' when he looked over Pickfords' railway warehouse at Camden. Mayhew wrote in a similar vein. His tour of Pickfords' premises left him with a strong impression of bustle and large-scale activity. The firm's headquarters in Wood Street appeared as 'an enormous mercantile establishment with a huge staff of busy clerks, messengers and porters'. He was 'amazed' and 'bewildered' by the scenes he witnessed at the railway warehouses at Haydon Square and Camden. Years later, in the 1890s, Gordon, after a similar tour, remarked on Pickfords' enormous business.[43]

The scurry and the bustle suggests good business. Did it also mean good profits? Mayhew commented on 'an air of substantial sedentary wealth', but were appearances reliable? The estimated profit figures already referred to (and see Appendix 1.1) which run to 1870, suggest they probably were. Profits were generally a good deal higher, in money value, than they had been before the railway agency had commenced. The previous peak profit of £48,000 in 1838 was not surpassed, but there were a number of particularly good years, and no catastrophes, not even in 1867 when, for example, the London General Omnibus Company, in the sister branch of road transport, crashed into deficit.[44] Annual fluctuations in Pickfords' estimated profits in the period bear little relationship to the trend of railway traffic, and are more probably to be explained by movements in the cost of fodder and bedding. Not until the 1870s did provender costs both fall substantially and stabilise, as firms switched over to feeding cheaper, imported grains. A comparison of Pickfords' estimated profits with those of the London General suggest a further benefit arising from the firm's agency with the London & North Western. Pickfords' profits were smaller, over comparable years, but a lot less volatile, an indication perhaps that the obligation to supply cartage at cost, although disliked, in fact served to protect the firm by passing a share of the effective burden to the railway company.

There are no further usable figures until the 1890s, when profits averaged £59,000, for the two years 1896-7, and £33,000 in 1898-9.[45] What of the intervening years from 1870? It is likely that they were generally prosperous. The market for horse-operated road services was growing rapidly in London and although so too was the supply it appears that at least the bigger firms in the trade did well. On the passenger side both the London General and the London Road Car Company, apart from occasional setbacks, returned steady dividends. In haulage, Carter Paterson enjoyed mixed success between 1888 and 1892, but then profits rose strongly to a peak in 1897. There is no reason to believe Pickfords' experience was markedly different. Indeed during the 1890s the firm was able to invest £130,000 in the purchase of a number of freehold properties, and as there is no sign of any mortgages or other loan instruments, they were presumably financed out of revenue.[46]

Throughout this half-century Pickfords remained in the hands of the Baxendale family and for much of the period under the distant but watchful eye of Joseph Baxendale himself. He could not bring himself to continue in the day-to-day management of the business following the deal with the railways and handed over control to three of his sons, with whom, in fact, that agreement was formally concluded. It was not an easy inheritance. Baxendale might no longer sit in the counting-house, but his shadow lingered on. He remained a partner in the business and carefully scrutinised the accounts to make sure his capital was being properly applied. Although he kept to the sidelines, Pickfords was still in a very real sense 'his' firm. In his young manhood he had battled strenuously to save it from collapse, committing all his resources of energy and finance. And these battles remained vivid to him, indeed returning to haunt him in old age when, in his view, he saw the business sliding once more.

Baxendale reacted sharply to the drop in profits in the mid-1860s. His advice was probably not sought, but that did not deter him from providing it. It was contained in a number of crisp letters to his sons, which tend to suggest a state of rather prickly relationships. Baxendale was clearly disappointed in his successors, and told them roundly that they lacked application and enterprise. He trenchantly advised his eldest son, Joseph Hornby, to spend less time on his steam yacht and get back to the business. Joseph Hornby admitted he and his brothers lacked their father's dedication, but then 'we have hardly had the same stimulus'. He insisted, however, that the business was sound, but he had been sufficiently provoked to protest, surely a very revealing remark, 'I think you sometimes forget that I am fifty years old'.[47] Talk of selling out to the London & North Western in 1870 must have further saddened him and he again wrote, to his second son Lloyd, about the strains of the early years. He concluded, disappointed but resigned, 'In closing the accounts for the year that has now passed, I will look with great attention. If those for whom the business has been kept together will not think it worth-while to give the necessary attention to the affairs, this will be an important question in looking for an arrangement with the London & North Western Railway whilst I am still with you.'[48]

Whatever his feelings about the fate of the business, Baxendale left his family well provided for. When he died in 1872, at the age of 84, he bequeathed to them a personal estate of some £700,000. He had spent carefully and saved regularly throughout his life and the just reward for such thrift was, in true Smilesian style, the accumulation of a portfolio of bonds, stocks and properties which at his death was yielding an annual income of £30,000. By any definition Baxendale had become a wealthy man, a privilege his sons enjoyed in turn.

Joseph Baxendale's death initiated a period of change in Pickfords' ownership and management. The three sons, Joseph Hornby, Lloyd and Robert Birley, had been running the business since 1847, but what they contributed to the management of the firm cannot really be said. They seem to have relied on senior clerks, in their father's view to an undue extent since he more than once complained of the business being left to take care of itself. As it happened none of them survived their father for very long, all three dying between 1878 and 1886. Their place was accordingly taken by the next generation. Joseph

William Baxendale, Joseph Hornby's son, joined the firm in 1871 and became a partner in 1879. Lloyd's two sons followed, Lloyd Harry in 1879, Francis Hugh in 1884, as the junior partners. When the partnership was re-formed in 1894, Joseph William received eight shares, and his two cousins six and three respectively. The only further significant change occurred in 1901 when the three decided to secure the benefits of incorporation and converted the firm into a private limited company.[49]

The century ended, then, with Pickfords well entrenched in urban cartage, still firmly tied, if a little restively, to the London & North Western. It was now an old established firm, perhaps a little set in its ways. It was, however, approaching another critical phase in its history. Not only did competition press unabated, especially from vigorous newcomers like Carter Paterson, but a major new break in technology, motorised road transport, was at hand. Could the third generation of Baxendales meet the challenge and avoid the fate which had befallen their precursors in the Pickford family nearly a hundred years before?

REFERENCES: CHAPTER 7

1 G. R. Hawke, *Railways and Economic Growth in England* (Oxford: Clarendon Press, 1970), ch. III; Pollins, *Britain's Railways*.
2 B. Supple, 'The great capitalist man-hunt', *Business History*, vol. VI (1963–4), esp. p. 55; S. G. Checkland's review of Coleman's *'Courtaulds'*, *Economic History Review*, vol. XXIII (1970), pp. 556–60.
3 T. R. Gourvish, 'A British business elite: the chief general managers of the railway industry, 1850–1922', *Business History Review*, vol. XLVII (1973), pp. 289–316.
4 Pennington, *Railways and Other Ways*, p. 104.
5 None of the standard company histories has much to say about this side of railway business.
6 R. J. Irving, *The North Eastern Railway Company, 1870–1914: An Economic History* (Leicester: Leicester University Press, 1976); also 'Profitability and performance of British railways, 1870–1914', *Economic History Review*, 2nd series, vol. XXXI (1978), pp. 46–66.
7 Gourvish, *Mark Huish*, p. 141, and tables 12, 21, 47, 53 and 59; the ton/mileage is from D. Lardner, *Railway Economy* (London: 1850; Newton Abbot: David & Charles, 1968), p. 190.
8 The Midland, South Eastern, Caledonian and others, duplicate contracts, PRO/BTHR Rail 1133/39–43.
9 Gourvish, op. cit., Table 59.
10 *SC on Railway and Canal Bills*, PP, 1852/3, vol. XXXL, evidence of J. S. Pixton.
11 Duplicate contract, 1 February 1887, PRO/BTHR Rail 1133/37.
12 Minutes of the general locomotive and general merchandise committee, 14 May 1847, PRO/BTHR Rail 410/221.
13 F. C. Mather, 'The Duke of Bridgewater's trustees and the coming of the railways', *Transactions of the Royal Historical Society*, 5th series, vol. 14 (1964), pp. 131–54.

14 Confidential report . . . upon the working of the merchandise traffic, PRO/ BTHR Rail 1008/93; Gourvish, *Mark Huish*, pp. 139–40.

15 Gourvish, op. cit., chs 6, 7.

16 *RC on Railways*, PP, 1867, vol. XXXVIII, pts I and II, James Allport, Q. 12484.

17 The main sources used for the relations between the two are, minutes of the general locomotive and general merchandise committee, 1846–51, PRO/BTHR Rail 410/221; minutes of the cartage arrangements committee, 1877–84, PRO/BTHR Rail 410/574; minutes of the cartage and agency committee, 1884–91, PRO/BTHR Rail 410/575; minutes of the goods committee, from 1892, PRO/BTHR Rail 410/199; minutes of the goods traffic committee, 1898–1901, PRO/BTHR Rail 410/201; duplicate contract, 1 January 1847, PRO/BTHR Rail 410/776, and subsequent renewals PRO/BTHR Rail 1133/28–37.

18 Memoranda and correspondence concerning the renewal contract, 1852, PRO/BTHR Rail 1133/38.

19 Stevenson, *Fifty Years*, p. 21.

20 Duplicate conveyance of Camden warehouse, Pickfords to the London & North Western, September 1847, PRO/BTHR Rail 1133/27; minutes of the general locomotive and merchandise committee, 10 September 1847, 20 November, 15 December 1848, PRO/BTHR Rail 410/221.

21 Stevenson, op. cit., pp. 33 ff.; Stevenson to Moon, 4, 9 October 1858, PRO/BTHR Rail 1008/112.

22 Joseph Hornby Baxendale's Diary for that year refers to Pickfords 'entirely altering the terms and conditions' on which it conducted the contract. Pickfords Removals Ltd.

23 *The Railway Magazine*, vol. 1 (1897), p. 194.

24 *Census of Population*, 1901, General Report (Cd 2174), PP, 1904, vol. CVIII, p. 99.

25 C. Booth, *Life and Labour of the People of London*, Vol. VII (London: Macmillan, 1896), pp. 323 ff.

26 G. Alderman, *The Railway Interest* (Leicester: Leicester University Press, 1973), chs 6, 7, 9; P. J. Cain, 'Railway combination and government, 1900–1914', *Economic History Review*, 2nd series, vol. XXV (1972), pp. 623–41, and 'Railways versus traders: the genesis of the Railway and Canal Traffic Act of 1894', *Journal of Transport History*, new series, vol. II (1973), pp. 65–84.

27 E. A. Pratt, *Railways and Their Rates* (London: John Murray, 1906), p. 92.

28 R. Hill and G. B. Hill, *The Life of Sir Rowland Hill* (London: De La Rue, 1880), Vol. 2, p. 336; C. E. R. Sherrington, *A Hundred Years of Inland Transport* (London: Duckworth, 1934), p. 228.

29 HLRO, minutes of evidence, HC, 1879, vol. 18, SC on the London and North Western Railway (Additional Powers) Bill and the Midland Railway (Additional Powers) Bill; also 'memorial of railway agents, carmen, carriers and contractors protection association' against the Bills, PP, 1878–9, vol. LXIII, p. 319; and *SC on Railways*, PP, 1881, vols XIII, XIV, evidence of George Findlay, Q. 14,090 ff.

30 Cain, 'Railways versus traders'.

31 F. S. Williams, *The Midland Railway: Its Rise and Progress* (London: Strahan, 1876), pp. 323–4, 633 ff.; W. J. Gordon, *The Horse World of London* (London: Leisure Hour, 1893; Newton Abbot: David & Charles, 1971), ch. III; J. P. Wallace, 'A history and survey of the road transport operations of the British railways' (unpublished MA thesis, Cardiff, 1947), ch. 3.

32 The location of these offices in London and the traffic generated by parcels and normal goods vehicles in the early twentieth century is noted in *RC on London Traffic*, PP, 1906, vol. XLVI, Plan 7 and Tables 1 and 2.

33 Minutes, cartage arrangements committee, 10 August 1882, PRO/BTHR Rail 410/574.

34 C. Dickens (younger), *Dickens' Dictionary of London* (London: Charles Dickens, 1880), p. 208; supplementary agreement, 31 December 1877, PRO/BTHR Rail 1133/33; minutes, cartage arrangements committee, 15 June 1882, PRO/BTHR Rail 410/574.

35 *RC on Railways*, 1867, evidence of Capt. H. W. Gordon, Q. 13,559 ff.; also appendix CO.

36 *RC on Labour*, PP, 1893, vol. XXXIII, evidence of E. Bellard, secretary of the London carmen's trade union. He picked out Pickfords in the meat trade and contract hire. He provides a useful glimpse of London cartage in the 1890s.

37 *London Post Office Directory*, 1881 (Traders and Court), conveyance directory, p. 2478.

38 Register of London premises, PRO/BTHR Rail 1133/135.

39 H. J. Dyos, *Victorian Suburb. A Study of the Growth of Camberwell* (Leicester: Leicester University Press, 1961), pp. 19 ff., 60 ff.

40 *RC on London Traffic*, PP, 1905, vol. II, evidence of J. F. S. Gooday, Q. 18,552 ff.; T. C. Barker and M. Robbins, *A History of London Transport, Vol. I, The Nineteenth Century* (London: Allen & Unwin, 1963), p. 202.

41 Register of London premises, PRO/BTHR Rail 1133/135.

42 'Horses returned for assessed taxes, 1822 to 1866', PRO/BTHR Rail 1133/147; *SC on Horses*, PP, 1873, vol. XIV, Banks's evidence, Q. 3,631; information from Mr Keith Chivers; Gordon, *Horse World of London*, pp. 60–1.

43 *All The Year Round*, 25 July 1863, pp. 522–4; H. Mayhew (ed.), *The Shops and Companies of London* (London: 1865), pp. 49–51; Gordon, op. cit., pp. 60–1.

44 Barker and Robbins, *London Transport*, Vol. I, p. 175.

45 Draft scheme for amalgamation between Pickfords and Carter Paterson & Co., 1901, PRO/BTHR Rail 1130/76.

46 Carter Paterson & Co., minutes of meetings of proprietors and board of directors, 1887–1900, PRO/BTHR Rail 1130/1; register of London premises, PRO/BTHR Rail 1133/135.

47 Several letters, July 1866 to April 1868, Baxendale papers.

48 Joseph Baxendale to Lloyd Baxendale, 11 May 1870, Baxendale papers.

49 Articles of partnership, 31 August 1894, PRO/BTHR Rail 1133/53; notice of Pickfords' conversion into a private limited company, PRO/BTHR Rail 1133/125.

8

Rail, Road and Reconstruction, 1900–33

By the turn of the century, the road transport industry was already beginning to display symptoms of overcapacity. In London, with which Pickfords had now become closely identified and where the train of events can be most easily observed, keen price competition, reduced profit margins and long hours of work for the men were the background to the first stirrings of a movement towards larger-scale organisation on both the goods and passenger sides of the industry. The rise of motor transport, which together with the progressive intrusion of the state into the formulation of transport policy has been the dominant feature of the transport industry in the twentieth century, added a greater sense of urgency and a new dimension as its immense productivity began to bite deeply into the hitherto impregnable territory of the railways. New capital threatened old and insistent demands were raised that the national interest required a compromise between the two. 'Road versus Rail' was to be resolved, not in the classic nineteenth-century manner, in which rail simply eliminated its rivals, but in a new, collectivist way in which each transport mode would be allocated its appropriate share of the market. The state was to be the means by which this objective was to be achieved, regrouping the railways in 1921 and setting up the London Passenger Transport Board in 1933, eventually, in the belief that such conflicting interests could not be reconciled unless all lay under one authority, to assume ownership and control of the entire industry. Several White Papers and Transport Acts later, the nirvana of inland transport, a fully rational, co-ordinated transport system, has yet to arrive.

Although for much of the period the pressure towards larger-scale organisation was rather less on the goods side and concentration reached much lower levels than in road passenger transport, Pickfords was not exempt from these general influences. It began the new century still tied to the London & North Western and although it was about to break loose from that particular relationship, railways remained the backdrop against which the business was conducted and, indeed, again became, in the 1930s, a dominant influence on the firm. And the attempt to break loose, combined with the need to come to terms with motor transport, so weakened the firm as to compel it to seek alliances with its major competitors and to become part of larger trading organisations until it, too, was absorbed into the state machinery of nationalisation.

RAIL

In January 1901, Pickfords informed the London & North Western that it had decided to end its long association with the railway company. Six months' notice was given of its intention to withdraw from the agency contract. No specific reason was forthcoming, but from various comments in the press, when the news got out, it is not too difficult to see what lay behind it.[1] Although apparently muted in recent years, the firm had still not lost its old sense of grievance, that the London & North Western did not pay a fair price for its services and that it was not given a fair chance to develop its railway business. Pickfords was, for example, prohibited from encroaching on the London & North Western's goods traffic whereas canvassers for the railway company's own cartage services could freely approach any of Pickfords' customers. For years it had bowed to necessity, unable to make an effective protest, but at last it saw the chance of escape. In 1899 the renamed Great Central railway had opened a new station in London, St Pancras, and a way of breaking out of the London & North Western's stranglehold on traffic to the north. Pickfords, banking on its customers remaining loyal, envisaged a new balance of power in which rival railway companies jostled for its traffic and with which the firm negotiated freely, as an equal. It was a serious miscalculation.

Indeed it may be doubted whether there was any calculation at all, for it appears to have been more in the way of a gamble pushed through by the two junior directors, L. H. Baxendale and F. H. Baxendale, against the views of their cousin and chairman, J. W. Baxendale, and those of the senior staff.[2] Since the London & North Western agency represented about half of Pickfords' total railway business they were certainly taking a large risk, one which proved to be disastrous. Pickfords became cartage agent to the Great Central[3] but, even buttressed by a similar deal with the Lancashire & Yorkshire railway, the new arrangement failed miserably. The Great Central line was poorly situated, largely failed to draw traffic from others and was quite unable to dent the London & North Western's position. And, of course, the London & North Western took steps to defend itself. At first it had tried to negotiate a compromise with Pickfords, not with much hope of success since it recognised that the firm's purpose was not better terms but freedom. When these efforts failed, the railway company moved swiftly to protect its goods traffic. It instituted a vigorous canvass of all of Pickfords' customers, acquired an additional 500 horses and 200 wagons and successfully held the bulk of its traffic. Pickfords lost heavily. In 1900, the last full year of the contract, Pickfords' tonnage account with the London & North Western had totalled about £178,000; in 1902 it fell by about a half and had soon dropped to less than a quarter of its former level. Contract work for the Great Central and the Lancashire & Yorkshire lines so failed, by a long way, to make up the balance that the firm's total railway business was cut by about a half. Apart from the loss of revenue, the 'fringe benefits' of the former contract had also to be given up, as a result of which several northern offices, which had depended on London & North Western traffic, incurred trading losses and had to be closed.

In an effort to halt the slide, Pickfords took to the courts once more.[4] Following an earlier, successful application by the firm to the Railway and Canal Commission, the London & North Western had been ordered to distinguish its cartage and delivery charge from the cost of conveyance between stations and to quote both separately. Pickfords' case in 1907 was that the rate quoted by the London & North Western for cartage and delivery was more than it would allow as a rebate to those, including firms like Pickfords, who undertook their own cartage and that it was on account of this illegal discrimination that the firm's earnings had fallen away so badly. The verdict was lost, after an appeal, and Pickfords' use of the London & North Western declined even further. Eventually old differences were patched up and a new agency contract begun in 1911, but it brought only a modest recovery. Railways continued to hold a prominent place in Pickfords' operations for many years to come, but during that pre-1914 decade its attention was being increasingly drawn to a new mode of transport: motorised road haulage.

ROAD

The main lines of the growth of motorised transport in the present century are well known, and will not be rehearsed here, except to point out that yet again most attention has been devoted to the passenger side of the industry. The development of the private motor car has been extensively written about and the motor bus has received its share of attention. The commercial goods vehicle and the road haulage industry built upon it have, in contrast, been largely neglected. Studies of 'the motor industry' have appeared in which the commercial goods vehicle, for some time now one of the industry's most successful components, scarcely gets a mention.[5]

The commercial motor, the bus as well as the goods vehicle, was held back longer than the private car by the restrictive highway legislation of the nineteenth century. The Locomotives and Highways Acts of 1896 removed some of the constraints by raising the speed limit for light locomotives from 4 to 12 miles per hour, thereby creating the basis for the British motor manufacturing industry. The private motor car was further boosted by the Motor Car Act of 1903 which distinguished the 'motor car' from the 'light locomotive' and raised its speed limit further, to 20 miles per hour. The commercial motor had to wait a little longer, until the Heavy Motor Car Order of 1904 which increased the permitted tare weight from 3 tons, the definition of a 'light locomotive', to 5 tons. The Order came into force in March 1905, and with it the real beginnings of commercial motor transport.[6]

There had, of course, been experiments with motors before then, but none had been particularly successful, and these failures contributed to the lifting of the weight limit in 1904. A purpose-built goods vehicle was required rather than the prevailing efforts to adapt horse vehicles and to stretch the lighter private motor by building a van body on to a motor-car chassis. It took a long time for a reliable vehicle to be produced and a great deal of experimentation with the three main forms of propulsion available, the steam, petrol and petrol-electric engines. The haulage equivalent of the London & General Omnibus Company's 'B' type bus, the first to be put into successful operation, was perhaps the Leyland XT, a 35 horsepower 3-tonner which Carter Paterson adopted in large numbers in 1908,[7] although not enough is known about the manufacturing side of commercial motors to be in any way sure. In any case there was still a long way to go before vehicles spent more time on the road than in the repair shop. Pickfords' records recount a long series of broken gear levers and drive chains, broken crankshafts and faulty parts. Steamers were easier than petrol vehicles to drive, having fewer moving parts and simpler gear changes, but drivers' negligence, by failing to get steam up properly or replenishing the water supply from duck ponds or horse troughs thereby picking up small debris which blocked the inlet pipes, caused similar breakdowns. For firms which employed motors in large numbers, a skilled mechanic on the staff and its own repair shops were a necessity.

For all that, the introduction of motor vehicles in road haulage went ahead steadily; 4,000 goods vehicles in use in 1904 had become 40,000 by 1911, but although the number had doubled again by 1914 the annual rate of increase, less than 20,000 vehicles, was still only modest.[8] The penetration of motors in road haulage proceeded much more slowly, at least in London, than in road passenger transport. In 1913, whereas only 6 per cent of passenger vehicles in London were still drawn by horses, the proportion for goods vehicles was 88 per cent.[9]

There are several reasons why the adoption of goods vehicles was so much slower. Their technical development, especially the heavier vehicles, was much less rapid. Although by about 1912 reasonably efficient machines were available, it was not until after the First World War that all doubts were removed. Moreover the pattern of ownership was different; the majority of horse buses and trams belonged to a handful of concerns whose scale of operations was large enough to make the employment of the more productive motor vehicle worthwhile, whereas most goods vehicles were employed by small traders and small haulage contractors whose needs were still adequately met by the horse. Large employers of goods vehicles did switch, department stores like Harrods, for whom a light delivery van sufficed, and the major haulage fleet owners, like Pickfords and Carter Paterson, but even together these represented a relatively small proportion of the total number of vehicles on the road. In addition, horse and motor had, for haulage purposes, quite different strengths which did not easily combine. The horse was supreme for regular, concentrated deliveries where the total distance to be travelled was small; Carter Paterson, for example, still had 800 cartage and delivery districts in central London in 1914, each of which was only half a mile square. Operational arrangements built around the working capacity of the horse did not suit the comparative qualities of the motor, its ability to carry greater weights at faster speeds and over greater distances. Motors were best employed where these advantages could be most exploited, in part substituting for horses, rather more in developing new areas of business, over longer distances, from which horse transport had been excluded. They required, therefore, quite a different framework of operations, ultimately the wholesale scrapping of the horse-based organisation. Inevitably it took time, and money, for the appropriate restyling to be carried out.

In the background lay the usual management decision in the face of any major technological advance – how far and at what rate to take it up and what effect it would have on the rest of the organisation. Pickfords, like the London bus companies, proceeded fairly cautiously; it was soon convinced that the future lay with motor transport, but whether powered by steam or petrol engine it was less certain, and in any case did not rush to get rid of its horses. The possible use of motors was first discussed by Pickfords in 1902, a service between London and Birmingham to be worked by steam traction engines. Thorneycrofts was consulted and estimates made of the likely cost and potential traffic, but it was eventually decided that with the existing speed limit the scheme was impracticable. In September 1903, however, two light traction engines were ordered from Wallis & Stevens of Basingstoke, followed by an order for twenty more two months later. They were a new type of vehicle, a scaled-down traction engine specially developed by that firm to meet the statutory weight limits for 'light locomotives', which could haul a trailer carrying from 5 to 8 tons. At this stage orders were put out to tender and, as in the London motor bus trade, restrictive conditions were attached to them in an attempt to keep ahead of competitors. Pickfords' order stipulated that Wallis & Stevens should not supply the same vehicles to any of the firm's competitors for at least eighteen months. The system of tendering also had another practical use; manufacturers willing to buy back obsolete vehicles in part exchange were likely to win a repeat order.

Motors had a higher work rate and higher earnings rate than horses but they were also a lot more expensive and made economic sense only where they could be kept fully employed. Regular, bulk traffic movements were ideal and these were found in some of Pickfords' contract cartage, the first vehicle apparently being introduced on a laundry contract for St Bartholomew's Hospital, but predominantly in the transfer of large consignments of parcels between the firm's central and district sorting depots in London. A motor could perform two round trips per day, replacing two teams of horses, six or eight in all. By the end of 1904 motors were being used for transfer work between the central depot at City Basin and Brentford, Fulham and Kingston. After initial teething troubles, the motors performed satisfactorily and were progressively extended to other districts. By 1906 motor transport was firmly established and it was decided to establish a small limited company, 'The Motor Cartage and Carrying Company', in anticipation of future needs. A little later, in 1908, a motor firm which had gone into liquidation, 'The Motor Delivery Company', was acquired. It was retained as a separate company until 1910 when all Pickfords' motor business was merged into a single motor department. At this time, too, a garage was opened at Hackford Road, Brixton, to service the motor fleet.

Motors were also tried for delivery work in some of the London suburbs. Here delivery districts, varying from 1 to $9\frac{1}{2}$ square miles, were bigger than in the central area and were often at some distance from the suburban depot, features conducive to the substitution of motors. In 1912 an experiment was conducted with two petrol motors, one working from Poplar to the Woolwich and Plumstead districts, the other from Walthamstow to Loughton, Woodford and Chigwell, and both replacing several horses. The results were interesting. The Poplar motor coped satisfactorily but that at Walthamstow did not and had to be assisted by the restoration of a horse van. In neither case, however, were operating costs significantly reduced, indeed at Walthamstow, although a higher volume of business was transacted, average operating costs per parcel actually went up.[10]

Motors had a useful promotional value but there was no blind belief in their superiority. They made sense where they could take over the work of several horses at the same price level, since the pressure of competition prevented the introduction of a swifter motorised service being used as an excuse to increase rates, and perform it more cheaply. One, unfortunately isolated, set of figures, for June 1908, indicated that steam vehicles could perform transfer work 15 shillings a day cheaper than horses, not a large margin in itself but a substantial saving in the aggregate when recouped on many routes over many months.[11] Costs were carefully watched and if a motor did not pay its way it was withdrawn, unless there were other, compelling reasons to prevent it. A case in point was the introduction of an experimental petrol motor instead of horses at Brighton to deal with holiday luggage traffic. Its running costs were twice its earnings, but because Carter Paterson was also making a similar, unsuccessful experiment, it was allowed, for prestige reasons, to continue. When both firms saw sense and restored horses, the volume of traffic handled dropped, but so did costs, and a profit was earned.

Although the main decision lay between horses and motors, it is important to emphasise that there was also a real choice between kinds of motor, petrol or steam. Steam had much in its favour, especially in the form of the steam lorry which could tow a trailer as well as carry a load itself. Steam vehicles were cheaper than petrol motors to buy and run, easier to drive and maintain, and suppliers, with a long tradition of steam engineering to draw on, quickly came up with a reliable product. Their drawback was that they were slower than petrol motors. Choice between the two depended on the purpose for which they were required, or, as Pickfords advertised, 'petrol for speed: steam for heavy haulage'. Only in exceptional circumstances could petrol compete with steam for heavy loads, as in Sheffield, for example, where the superior climbing ability of a 5-ton Commer petrol lorry enabled it to cope more easily than a steamer with the city's steep hills and led Pickfords to employ it for some heavy contract work there.

The speed advantage of petrol vehicles was, however, reduced when rubber tyres were fitted to steam lorries, and the balance tilted even further when petrol was discovered to be a fruitful source of government revenue. In 1911 one of the leading motor journals, *Commercial Motor*, ran a long series of articles showing how even at the $3\frac{1}{2}$-ton weight the rubber-tyred steamer could hold its own against petrol. Twelve months later the journal was explaining how, despite increased fuel prices, petrol could still compete with steam. When petrol was rationed during the war, the steamer received a further boost. Pickfords' bias was towards the side of steam. Unlike Carter Paterson, which in 1911 switched entirely to petrol even for transfer work between sorting depots, Pickfords took the view that 'with regard to motors for depot services at present there is apparently no useful alternative to steam'.[12]

Although the firm did not ignore petrol motors and indeed seriously considered buying a fleet of a hundred of them a year later, its traffic tended to be of a heavier variety than Carter Paterson's, and so it needed the greater haulage power of steam. In 1919 two-thirds of its fleet of forty-six motors were steamers.

An experimental motor service between London and Luton was abandoned in April 1909, but it was precisely in this sort of context, where its advantages of speed and distance could be exploited, that the future contribution of the motor vehicle really lay. There was as yet no further significant breach of railway traffic, but the motor's operational range was steadily pushed out to distances of 30 and 40 miles. Several experiments were undertaken, by other firms as well as Pickfords, with services from London to places like Margate, Maidstone and Brighton. However the most immediate result, again paralleling the development of buses, was the provision of motorised services to outer suburbs of London like Watford, Romford, Woking and Staines. Carter Paterson led the way with its 'Home Counties Express' in 1911 and Pickfords followed with its own, less well-named, 'Outer Area Service' a year later. These were highly promising areas of business, convincingly demonstrating the unique qualities of motor transport, but they had to be cut back during the war and only really got into their stride when peace returned.

RECONSTRUCTION

The introduction of motors sharpened even further the keen edge of competition between the London haulage firms. In 1906 Pickfords and Carter Paterson were seen to be 'running a neck and neck race . . . for, while we see the Express Motor delivery vans of the one company running in all directions, we see displayed on every van belonging to the other company particulars of the large number of motors they are now using'.[13] Although that same year Carter Paterson registered two small subsidiary companies, 'The London & Provincial Motor Despatch Company Ltd.' and 'The London Motor Parcels Express Ltd.', for the purpose of checking 'the enterprising spirit displayed by the promotors of motor traction',[14] its shareholders were warned the following year that intense competition continued unabated, forcing rates and revenue yet further down.

Pickfords could have been no less anxious to see the fierce competition in the London haulage trade brought under control. As happened with the buses, the introduction of motors aggravated the current over-supply of cartage services, driving rates down and further squeezing profit margins. All firms in road transport, bus companies as well as haulage concerns, felt the draught at some time or other during the years 1900-1, 1907-10 and 1912, when either profits fell sharply or actual trading losses were incurred.[15] Profits generally recovered from these setbacks, broadly in line with the trade cycle, but for horse-based transport, as Barker and Robbins remark, 'the halcyon days were clearly past'.[16] And as it was against this weaker financial background that large sums had to be laid out on expensive and uncertain new forms of capital investment, it is not surprising to find those having to grapple with the problem looking for ways to defend their interests. In both passenger and goods road transport in London each financial setback prompted renewed efforts to reduce the damaging effects of excess competition.

Pickfords was particularly vulnerable. Its profits dropped more sharply than others and also, more critically still, failed to recover. The financial data for these years are patchy so the real picture is not fully known. A single profit figure of £8,600 in 1905 suggests a small rally,[17] but it fell a long way behind Carter Paterson's achievements. It seems that Pickfords was becoming financially enfeebled; the costs of its break with the London & North Western were striking hard. Dividends due in 1900 were not fully paid until the middle of 1906 and no dividend was paid on ordinary shares between 1906 and March 1910. Various efforts were made to boost revenue, sales of poster space on the firm's delivery vans, the sale on commission of railway and steamships tickets (the origin of the firm's travel department), and the cartage to and from London termini of railway passengers' luggage in advance and railway traffic to the south coast generally, but none of them could generate revenue of the scale that was urgently needed. Unable to pay its way out of current revenue, Pickfords was sliding into increasing reliance on overdraft and mortgage.[18]

At a time when its investment needs were large, Pickfords was in fact being drained of capital. Not only was the motor programme expensive, and the rate of depreciation costly because of the high degree of obsolescence of the early models, the firm had to absorb the cost of scrapping a large number of its horse vans previously employed on the London & North Western contract. More serious still was a quarrel between the directors and the retirement from the firm of J. W. Baxendale, the chairman and major shareholder. He had opposed the break with the London & North Western and, disillusioned with the outcome, he decided to quit the business and withdraw his capital. The remaining directors could not afford to buy out his £220,000 holding of preference and ordinary shares and instead he agreed to accept £166,000 worth of 4 per cent debenture stock, a heavy future interest charge on the business. The nominal share capital was slashed from £457,000 to £105,900 and further borrowings were required to finance the necessary liquidation and reconstruction of the company. Any scheme, therefore, which would help to ease the pressure could not fail to be of interest.

Pickfords and Carter Paterson, the two dominant firms in the London road haulage trade, had long been playing cat and mouse with each other, the one sneaking in an earlier delivery or later collection in order to be one jump ahead of the other. From now on their activities were to be closely bound together, passing from vigorous opposition to mutual co-operation and eventually to complete amalgamation. Talk of a merger between the two dated back to 1899 and terms of a possible agreement were actually drafted in 1901,[19] in the same year and for the same reason, a sharp fall in profits, that the London bus companies first discussed the same objective. Although nothing materialised on that occasion, the continuing pressure on rates and revenue and Pickfords' weakening financial condition made some form of agreement a matter of urgency. Firms sought to steal others' traffic by tendering cut-price rates, and traffic losses to McNamara's, Beans Express, Suttons and Globe Parcels Express were being reported to Pickfords' directors with increasing frequency. When competitors were quoting prices cut by up to 25 per cent, decisions to hold traffic at any cost were becoming ruinously expensive. Something had to be done.

Pickfords' first step, in 1905, was to invite the Globe Parcels Express to join it in a working arrangement, but to no avail. Two years later, with trade slackening as economic activity turned down, the firm entered upon a limited agreement with Carter Paterson and Beans Express. Initially a profit pooling scheme was projected, but something much less than that was finally implemented, no more than a system for fixing agreed rates. A three-man council was set up, one member from each company, delegated to draw up a schedule of rates to which all would adhere, especially when asked by a firm to tender for a contract presently held by one of the others. Breach of the agreed rates was penalised by a heavy fine, three times the annual value of a contract so acquired, payable to the aggrieved party. The signatories pledged mutual assistance 'in the event of fire, strike, lock-out or labour combination', but otherwise insisted on its limited function: 'It is not a partnership.'[20]

This agreement had some effect beyond the fixing of agreed rates in that the three firms began to exchange traffic with each other in places outside London. Pickfords consigned traffic to the others at places where it had no establishment and they did likewise. However, in its key purpose of stabilising rates, it failed. It could not control non-member firms, like Suttons and Globe Parcels Express, and even the three member firms, borne down by the pressure on rates, could not resist the temptation to underquote each other. The scheme cracked under the strain and collapsed; from April 1911 the three-man council ceased to meet. It was obvious that if such pressures were to be overcome, nothing short of a full amalgamation would do.

Indeed, just as the rates agreement was breaking up rumours began to appear in the press of an impending merger between several of the leading parcels companies in London. Denials were put out, but steps towards an eventual amalgamation, extended to include the London Parcels Delivery Company, were, in fact, even then being taken. Carter Paterson already owned a small number of shares in the London Parcels Delivery Company and from May 1911 it began deliberately to extend its holding. A few months later the firm's managing director, J. J. Paterson, was authorised to attend a conference of other carriers in order to effect an amalgamation. By September 1912, the year the London Traffic Combine, for passenger business, came into existence, terms had been agreed between the four companies, Pickfords, Carter Paterson, Beans Express and the London Parcels Delivery Company, but to avoid a hostile reaction it was decided to 'keep the new arrangement as reasonably quiet as possible'.[21]

The amalgamation was carried through by Carter Paterson absorbing the other three, its share capital being increased from £250,000 to £775,000. Beans Express and the London Parcels Delivery Company were bought out completely. In a complex financial arrangement, whereby Pickfords' share capital was transferred to the new concern and former Pickford shareholders received Carter Paterson shares in exchange, Pickfords passed into the ownership and control of Carter Paterson. It never again functioned as an independent concern. The firm's position further emphasises the decline in Pickfords' fortunes which had occurred since the turn of the century. Had the scheme projected in 1901 gone through, Pickfords, contributing 60 per cent of the capital, would have dominated the proposed joint company: in the scheme actually implemented in 1912, Carter Paterson was dominant. Although face was saved to some extent by Pickfords' chairman, L. H. Baxendale, becoming chairman of the joint board, the real power lay with the Patersons.

The purpose of the amalgamation was to bring under the control of a single organisation a larger share of the London cartage trade, to reduce operating costs by eliminating overlap, hopefully to ease rates upwards again and ultimately to gain a larger profit from the revenue earned by the joint concerns. To achieve this end by welding into a single, cohesive unit four companies which had long fiercely opposed each other was a formidable task. So much of the effectiveness of the cartage companies, especially in the important parcels trade, depended on the quality of their carters, the loyalty of them to their own firms and their ability to sniff out business on the street. For a Carter Paterson man to accept a Pickford man as a colleague, to exchange traffic with him instead of cutting in on him, to use a Pickfords' vehicle or deliver to a Pickfords' office as readily as to his own, required a reversal of habit which only time could achieve. Since to ensure the full benefits of the merger extensive reorganisation of this kind was required and since it was essential that the staff should co-operate actively with the changes, it was wisely decided to proceed slowly and cautiously.

A start was made by rationalising central services, such as the provision of fodder and veterinary services and the use of repair shops and bodywork construction yards, in which both Pickfords and Carter Paterson had been largely self-sufficient. The best-placed or best-equipped premises now served the whole group and the surplus was disposed of. When a new scheme of management for the joint businesses was introduced in January 1915, the provision of horses and fodder, finance, property and audit were all brought under the direct control of the joint board.

Substantial economies were also achieved on the operating side, by a similar rationalisation of cartage services and associated offices, depots, staff and stock. The group's parcels business in London, from which the pressure to amalgamate had primarily arisen, was tackled first. Duplication was eliminated by concentrating the group's future structure of services on the former Carter Paterson parcels network. As part of the reorganisation Beans Express became a collecting agency only and Pickfords ultimately withdrew from parcels traffic in London and its outer suburbs altogether. Rationalisation of the group's provincial parcels traffic, however, worked to Pickfords' advantage since it had the largest number of provincial branches and was therefore best placed to undertake that section of the joint business. And that was as far as the rationalisation programme got, the outbreak of war in 1914 putting an end to plans to integrate the other components of the business. Heavy cartage, shipping, travel and household removals, in which the other three companies had much less interests, were as a result largely left to Pickfords, a separate domain within the wider group.

There was one further reason why, apart from the war, reorganisation had proceeded rather less completely than intended. Before the amalgamation had really got into its stride it was hit full force, a cruel irony, by the sudden appearance of a totally new and extremely powerful competitor, the firm of W. & G. Express Carriers. This was the creation of W. & G. du Cros, pioneers of motor cabs in London and backed by a family fortune deriving from the exploitation of the Dunlop process of making pneumatic rubber bicycle tyres.[22] Announced in February 1913, the new firm built up rapidly; by September it had 100 light motor delivery vans on the road and plans for another 250. It mounted a vigorous attack on the group's parcels business in London and the home counties, and rebuffed an approach to discuss rates. The joint board was driven to desperate measures to fight off the challenge, a price war and a hurried programme of spending on additional motor vehicles, exactly the opposite of what the amalgamation was intended to achieve. Failing to drive off the upstart, the board tried to buy it off. Terms for an amalgamation had been successfully negotiated when war came and the deal was dropped. From that point, however, W. & G.'s opposition slackened. It turned to war work for the government and in order to concentrate on that decided, in the summer of 1915, to dispose of its parcels business. Carter Paterson bought it and promptly closed it down.

THE WAR AND AFTER

Some of the effects of the war were felt equally by all sections of the Carter Paterson group. Immediately war was declared, horses and vehicles were claimed under the War Office registration scheme – a small annual subsidy in return for their release, if required, for the army's autumn manoeuvres and, of course, in the event of war – and others simply commandeered. By 1918 some 2,500 men, 1,800 horses and 85 motors had been lost to the war effort.[23] Women replaced men, even as carters, but substitute vehicles became almost unobtainable as the output of commercial motor manufacturers was also pre-empted for the army. Indeed, so critical was the shortage of motors that some small firms seem to have been bought not for the sake of the business but for the vehicles they possessed! In addition fuel became scarce and expensive; petrol was rationed and the supply of hay and straw, which were brought under the control of the War Office in order to ensure supplies to the army, became a nightmare. Steam motors, which used domestic coal, were revived and horses brought back.

Otherwise it was the parcels business, and therefore the Carter Paterson side of the group, that was most severely hit. As firms moved out of London and reduced their volume of trading, the parcels trade collapsed; the group's traffic fell from 28 million parcels in 1914 to only 10 million in 1918. 'Carman' could not be claimed as an essential, skilled occupation, and all the best were eventually lost to conscription. The extent as well as the quality of the parcels service declined. Many services in London and the provinces were abandoned, revenue fell, but costs declined much more slowly because of the wartime inflation. Heavy losses were made in 1916 and 1917 and morale slumped badly.

Pickfords' side of the group did rather better. Although travel and provincial traffic tailed off, other activities were stimulated. Movement out of London and other towns provided business for the firm's household removals section. More storage space for furniture was also needed and extra warehouses, not yet purpose-built depositories, were acquired for the purpose. Pickfords' wharf also did well, but the major beneficiary was the firm's motor department. Having given up light parcels traffic, Pickfords' motor fleet was predominantly composed of heavy vehicles, well suited to transport aircraft frames and other war material. Much of the fleet was contracted out to the Ministry of Munitions and because of that connection exemption badges were allocated for fitters and drivers, and privileged supplies of motors and petrol obtained. When in 1916 and 1917 the group as a whole was sliding into deficit, Pickfords' operations showed a useful profit.[24]

The group ended the war on a more positive note. Pickfords' profits advanced strongly and the parcels business was restored to profitability by a hefty increase in rates, a step previously shied away from for fear it would depress a declining volume of business even further. In September 1919 the shareholders were informed that the backlog of deficits and interest payments had been cleared and that for the first time since 1914 a dividend could be paid on the ordinary shares. Plans were laid for the future, cautiously but with some optimism. There was some concern whether the government's wartime subsidy of railway freight rates would be continued, and possibly even be extended to the GPO's parcels service, and representations were made to those officials at the Board of Trade from whom the new Ministry of Transport was being formed urging that such a policy would mean the end of private transport firms like Carter Paterson and Pickfords.[25] Provided that doubt could be dispelled, however, there was every reason for optimism. Motor vehicles, especially petrol motors, had proved their worth during the war and it was obvious that the return of normal conditions would see a major extension of motor transport. Orders were placed for large numbers of new vehicles, at first chiefly for the parcels service, which was revived in 1920 with the intention of delivering up to 70 miles and more from London, well beyond the pre-war limit, but ultimately for all other areas of the business as well. The future was to lie with motor transport.

Pickfords, however, did not participate in this particular development programme. While these plans were being discussed, a bid was received from Hay's Wharf Cartage Company for Pickfords' section of the joint business, all the non-parcels interests which had not been fully integrated before the war and were therefore easily detachable. Hay's Wharf Cartage Company was a subsidiary of the Proprietors of Hay's Wharf, an old established concern which had extensive dockland interests. It controlled several wharfs and also had, through another subsidiary, Humphery & Grey (Lighterage) Ltd, a share in the river traffic. Dockside work included heavy cartage, to provide which the Hay's Wharf Cartage Company, originally formed as Cliffords Ltd, was set up in 1912. Hay's Wharf specialised in the handling and cartage of imported meat and during the 1920s it acquired other wharfs, cold stores and meat cartage firms, including, in 1923, Robert Hall Ltd, the next largest cartage firm to itself, in a bid to strengthen its position in the trade.[26] Although Hay's Wharf's bid included all of Pickfords' operations, it was its sizeable meat traffic from the docks which had attracted attention.

The Carter Paterson group tried to interest Hay's Wharf in a merger or the joint flotation of a new public company, but the latter would not be drawn. A deal was therefore struck for the sale of Pickfords to Hay's Wharf, and share capitals and directorates were adjusted. L. H. Baxendale resigned as chairman of Pickfords in favour of Major O. C. Magniac of Hay's Wharf, but he and James Paterson remained as directors and also joined the board of Hay's Wharf Cartage Company. Although Pickfords and Carter Paterson now formally parted company, relations between them remained very close. Their premises were often physically very close, sometimes next door to each other, and some which had notionally been transferred during the rationalisation pro-gramme but legally still belonged to Pickfords were retained by Carter Paterson. Having eliminated the element of competition between them in the London parcels trade, in which in any case Pickfords' traffic had always tended to be of the heavier variety, quoted per ton rather than per parcel as with Carter Paterson, their interests were largely complementary and efforts were made to keep things that way. They tried to agree on rates and areas of influence, they exchanged traffic with each other, Carter Paterson acting for Pickfords in London, for example, and Pickfords for Carter Paterson in Birmingham, they notified each other when one bought a stake in another firm and even bought businesses jointly. In 1933 they bought a group of small parcels firms in Liverpool, merged them as the Karrier Parcels Delivery Service, and then operated it as a joint subsidiary. Not all was sweetness and light, however, especially when in 1932 Pickfords' London suburban service was revived in competition with Carter Paterson's Home Counties Express. By the early 1930s, indeed, as pressure in the road haulage industry built up once more, there were signs of further friction between the two and the threat of a return to the bitter conflict which had existed before 1912.

In the decade or so during which Pickfords belonged to Hay's Wharf, motor transport made very substantial progress. The number of road goods vehicles in use leaped from 41,000 in 1918 to 128,000 only three years later, a rate of expansion which was maintained for the rest of the 1920s.[27] The petrol engine triumphed over steam as important technical advances in engine efficiency and vehicle con-struction, combined with the adoption of pneumatic tyres, resulted in improved power/weight ratios. Petrol motors were able to carry heavier loads over greater distances at less cost, rendering conflict with the railways increasingly likely, although for much of the interwar years this was confined to particular traffics for which road transport provided a superior quality of service. The extent of Pickfords' conversion to motor transport can be illustrated by comparing the stock transferred to Hay's Wharf with that handed over to the railways, the firm's next owners, in 1933. Compared with the 1,580 horses, 1,900 horse vehicles and 46 motors, predominantly of the heavier range, passed on to Hay's Wharf in 1919, the railways received only 509 horses and 866 horse vehicles, but 628 motors.[28] The firm would be expected to have more than made up for wartime losses of motors during the intervening years, but what was most significant was the changed balance between horse and motor transport. The whole organisational structure of the business was altering rapidly, as petrol, garages and engineers replaced fodder, stables and vets. By the end of the 1930s, the old horse world of London, where the changes can be most closely observed, was fading rapidly.

Pickfords' development during the period of ownership by Hay's Wharf can be sketched only in outline as scarcely any records for these years have survived. However, a chart of Pickfords' organisation in the mid-1930s,[29] Figure 7, provides several good clues as to what had been happening. The chart is useful for two reasons; it specifies

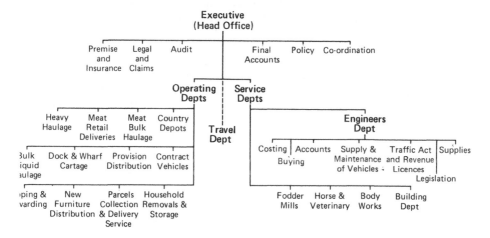

Fig. 7   *Pickfords' organisation in the mid-1930s*

in a way which is not possible previously the full range of Pickfords' operations and also, by emphasising the central role of the engineers' department in servicing the operating sections, it makes plain the extent to which motor transport had come to dominate the business. Even so it is important not to exaggerate the place of motor transport. Provincial traffic still relied extensively on the railways; dock and wharf cartage, retail meat deliveries, provision distribution and collection and delivery of small parcels all employed a mixture of horse and motor transport. So, too, did contract hire. But the business of bulk meat and liquids haulage, heavy haulage and household removals were transformed or created by motor transport.

Behind the motorisation of these traffics lay a great deal of technical progress in vehicle design. Meat was perhaps the easiest since once the refrigerated lorry had been developed distance was no obstacle. Meat was trunked by Pickfords from Aberdeen to London by road, and moved in bulk around the country from depots in London and Liverpool, the two main ports of entry for imported meat. The bulk transport of meat was one of the first traffics won from the railways by road haulage. The solution of similar technical problems in relation to bulk liquids, chiefly mineral and vegetable oils, together with changes in the pattern of demand, gained another branch of traffic for road haulage. The conveyance of petrol in bulk tankers, commenced by Pickfords in 1921 by the purchase of a small tanker business, B. T. Norris of Tooting, was aided both by the greater volume in which it was consumed and the switch from cans to pumps and roadside service stations as the means by which it was supplied to the public. Pickfords soon had several contracts which required fleets of a dozen or more 1,000-gallon petrol tankers.[30] By the mid-1930s some tankers carried as much as 3,600 gallons. Vegetable oils posed different problems; they required special steels for the tanks, temperature control to maintain the contents in a liquid form, an important advance this because previously oils had solidified in transit and had had to be reheated in order to be pumped out, and a means of cleansing the tanks between cargoes, which was performed by injecting steam into them.[31] This provided another useful line of business, including a long-running contract with Unilever.

The activity with which Pickfords is today most readily associated, household removals and storage, came strongly to the fore after 1920, largely as a result of the adoption of motor transport. Pneumatic-tyred petrol vehicles were introduced in 1924, eliminating the grime of steamers, to be followed in the early 1930s by the first lightweight Bedford vans, then with a capacity of 1,000 cubic feet. Removals by road became so much easier and swifter than by rail. Families could travel with the van and next-day deliveries were guaranteed up to a distance of 100 miles or so. Steps were taken to put household removals on to a secure footing. Several small local businesses were bought and the firm's wide spread of provincial branches was used to maximum advantage. It was at this time that the firm's 'back-loads' system of operations was established in order to keep rates down and so match the cut-price, fly-by-night operators employing ex-army lorries. The outward movement of all vehicles was carefully monitored from head office and arrangements were made as far as possible for a reverse removal to be undertaken on their return. In this way Pickfords could operate a highly competitive, nationwide removals service, while economising on vehicles and empty mileage. And further economies were achieved by combining the sale of removals with the sale of travel. Pickfords' travel service, which blossomed greatly in the inter-war years, coach tours of the Swiss lakes being its speciality, subsidised the removals side by paying the rent of the firm's high street offices and the salaries of clerks who also dealt with removals. Within Pickfords the economics of travel and removals have remained to this day closely interlocked.

Finally motor transport transformed the business of heavy haulage, the movement of abnormal, indivisible loads. Several technical advances were again important, the development of the more powerful diesel engine in particular, and also the introduction of low-loading platform trailers, pneumatic tyres and mobile petrol–electric cranes for the manipulation of heavy machinery. As with tank haulage, a small business, London Traction Haulage, was acquired to provide a more substantial base for the firm's existing heavy haulage activities and to be the springboard for their further development. Until 1930 Pickfords' heavy haulage interests were confined to London, but the purchase by Hay's Wharf in that year of Norman E. Box Ltd, then profitably employed in transporting heavy electrical equipment for the construction of the National Grid, supplied additional outlets in Birmingham and Manchester.

During the 1920s and 1930s, Pickfords, like Carter Paterson, became more and more closely identified with motorised road haulage. They were, moreover, by far the two largest firms in the industry. It is not surprising, therefore, that when the four main-line railway companies, having eventually been authorised to own and operate road vehicles, looked round for means to counteract the loss of prime goods traffic to road haulage, their attention was soon directed to Carter Paterson and Pickfords.

REFERENCES: CHAPTER 8

1 Cuttings from various journals, PRO/BTHR Rail 1133/147; London & North Western Railway Company, minutes, goods traffic committee, January–August 1901, PRO/BTHR Rail 410/201, 202; this chapter is based chiefly on the minutes of the board and directors' committee meetings of Pickfords, Carter Paterson and Hay's Wharf Cartage Company. Further references to these sources have been kept to a minimum.
2 This was the explanation given to me by the late Capt. G. Baxendale, the son of F. H. Baxendale, and himself subsequently a director of Pickfords.
3 Passenger train parcels agreement, goods cartage agreement with the Great Central Railway Company, Pickfords Removals Ltd, files 119, 138.
4 Evidence and judgement, Pickfords Ltd v. The London & North Western Railway Company, 1907, PRO/BTHR Rail 1133/137.

5 Most recently, K. Richardson, *The British Motor Industry 1896–1939* (London: Macmillan, 1977); for the general background, S. B. Saul, 'The motor industry in Britain to 1914', *Business History*, Vol. 5 (1962–3), pp. 22–44; E. L. Cornwell, *Commercial Vehicles* (London: Ian Allan, 1963).

6 Marked by the first publication, 16 March 1905, of *The Commercial Motor*.

7 'The Carter Paterson Story', *Modern Transport*, 11, 25 June, 16 July 1960.

8 British Road Federation, *Basic Road Statistics* (London: BRF, 1969), p. 3.

9 Barker and Robbins, *History of London Transport*, Vol. II, p. 190; chs 6–8 of this volume describe the emergence of the London Traffic Combine in the years before 1914, a trend which is almost exactly paralleled in timing and causality in the London haulage trade. References below to developments in the London bus trade are drawn from these chapters.

10 Minutes, directors' committee, 3 April 1912 to 22 January 1913, PRO/BTHR Rail 1133/17.

11 Minutes, directors' committee, 24 June, 1 July 1908, PRO/BTHR Rail 1133/14.

12 Minutes, directors' committee, 27 March 1912, PRO/BTHR Rail 1133/17.

13 *The World's Carriers and Contractors Review*, vol. 2 (1905–6), p. 149.

14 Carter Paterson directors' report to the annual general meeting, PRO/BTHR Rail 1130/2.

15 For Pickfords and Carter Paterson, see Appendix 1.2; for the bus companies, Barker and Robbins, *History of London Transport*, Vol. II, chs 6–8, *passim*.

16 Barker and Robbins, op. cit., p. 124.

17 The comment was made that heavy depreciation charges had required the year's profit figure to be written down to this level.

18 Pickfords' bankers, Glyn Mills & Co., were becoming increasingly anxious about the firm's financial condition. I must thank Dr P. L. Cottrell for extracts from the bank's advances, engagements books B/3 10, B/3 12, B/3 13.

19 Draft proposals, PRO/BTHR Rail 1130/76.

20 Working agreement, 24 October 1907, PRO/BTHR Rail 1130/35.

21 Minutes of Carter Paterson board, 28 October 1912, PRO/BTHR Rail 1130/3; various drafts, correspondence and memoranda concerning the amalgamation are at PRO/BTHR Rail 1133/140, and Rail 1130/35, 45.

22 *The Commercial Motor*, vol. 17 (1913), p. 152; *The World's Carriers . . .*, vol. 10 (1913–14), p. 27; A. du Cros, *Wheels of Fortune* (London: Chapman & Hall, 1938); C. H. Wilson and W. J. Reader, *Men and Machines: A History of D. Napier & Son* (London: Weidenfeld & Nicolson, 1958), pp. 71, 94.

23 Memorandum on Carter Paterson & Co.'s business, 11 April 1919, PRO/BTHR Rail 1130/82.

24 See Appendix 1.3.

25 Memorandum on Carter Paterson & Co.'s business, 11 April 1919.

26 A. Ellis, *Three Hundred Years on London River: The Hay's Wharf Story* (London: Bodley Head, 1952); for other companies acquired, see the list of Hay's Wharf's subsidiaries in 1933, Appendix 2. To service its inflated cartage fleet, Hay's Wharf also, in 1920, bought out Hazeldine's, the long established horse-van construction and maintenance business, but disposed of it a few years later, Pickfords Removals Ltd, box file, purchases of companies.

27 British Road Federation, *Basic Road Statistics*, p. 3; (PEP), *Motor Vehicles* (London: Political and Economic Planning, 1950), pp. 68–72.

28 Papers concerning the sale to Hay's Wharf, 1919, and preliminary survey of Pickfords business, August 1933, Pickfords Removals Ltd.

29 *Railway Gazette*, 12 March 1937, p. 487; some of the details in the following

section are from Anon., *Transport Saga* (London: printed privately, 1947), but mainly from surveys, and associated papers, of the Carter Paterson and Pickfords businesses, August and September 1933, Pickfords Removals Ltd, railway files, negotiations with Pickfords and Carter Paterson, G1/72256 (19).

30 Richardson, *British Motor Industry*, ch. 8; Pickfords Removals Ltd, bundle of vehicle hire contracts.

31 *Railway Gazette*, 8 May 1936.

9

From Railway Ownership to Nationalisation

The granting of road powers to Britain's railway companies was the subject of heated debate and several government inquiries during the 1920s and 1930s.[1] No one denied the railway companies the right to undertake road services which were complementary to their railway operations and several of them, the Great Western in particular, had been running such services since before the war. The test, broadly speaking, was whether traffic commenced or terminated its journey by rail. For such traffic reasonable feeder and delivery road services, which might extend to operations ranging widely from central railheads, were accepted as lying within the companies' statutory powers. Opinions differed sharply, however, as to whether the railway companies already possessed, or should receive, the right to convey traffic which at no stage passed over their rails. The railway companies maintained that to deny them road powers was discriminatory and effectively prevented them from earning a fair return on their capital: road transport interests insisted that the railway companies should confine themselves to railway operations and that the railway companies' purpose was not to build up road transport, as they had done, to the great benefit of the economy and society, but to shackle, if not destroy it, and thereby preserve, indirectly, a control of passenger and goods traffic which they had failed to maintain by open competition.

The various strands of the 'road versus rail' debate of these years have been sufficiently rehearsed elsewhere and need only be summarised briefly.[2] The railway companies' case was that road transport's power of competition rested largely on the subsidy it received, in respect of track costs, from the rest of the community. It thus enjoyed a privileged position in respect of goods traffic and was, moreover, exempt from the statutory limitations which so constrained the railway companies' own commercial freedom of action. In response to the charge that it did not pay its way, the road transport side pointed to the large contributions it made to the Exchequer in the form of road fund taxes and the petrol duty and the fact that these exceeded by a fair margin what was currently being spent on highway development. In the background lay debates about the national interest, especially whether the country could afford to let the large capital invested in railway working, £1,000m. by 1930, be destroyed by unbridled competition from road transport.

Following earlier abortive attempts to obtain road powers, the four main-line railway companies submitted to Parliament, in February 1928, identical Bills requesting permission to own and operate road vehicles.[3] The Bill was vigorously contested in the House of Commons but after exhaustive inquiry at the committee stage, a joint committee of both Houses sitting for thirty-seven days through the months of May and June, the Second Reading was carried by a surprisingly large majority. The railway companies were quite certain why they wanted road powers, in order to protect railway traffic and revenue, less sure how that objective might be best achieved. Ford, the chief goods manager at Paddington, laid great stress, in a policy statement concerned with merchandise and mineral traffic which he circulated to his department in the August, on using the new powers to improve the quality of the railway's own services, in respect of which much more was achieved than is often appreciated,[4] and also, at a lower order of priority, to negotiate working arrangements with road operators or to purchase appropriate road haulage concerns.[5] This last option, for the railway companies to acquire a financial stake in existing road transport undertakings and to exert their influence discreetly from the board room, out of the public eye, in order to harmonise road and rail interests, became the common mode of procedure for both the passenger and goods sides of road transport.

The passenger side was quickly attended to. Outside London, which passed under the control of the London Passenger Transport Board in 1933,[6] the majority of road passenger services had already come under the control of a handful of dominant groups and to acquire a substantial financial interest in them, up to but not exceeding 50 per cent in accordance with the undertaking given to Parliament as a concession to get the Road Powers Bill through,[7] was a matter of relatively straightforward, if testing, negotiations.[8] Within a couple of years, almost £8m. had been spent in this way by the railways and eventually about £9.5m. altogether.[9] Negotiations for a similar deal with road haulage interests were more protracted, partly because the organisation of the industry, predominantly composed of very small firms, did not lend itself to an equally neat solution, partly because the railways took a longer time to decide what to do. The trend was set, however, in 1930 when the LNER acquired Currie & Co. of Newcastle, for some years past the cartage agent to the former North Eastern

Railway Company; two years later the LMS bought a half-share of Wordie & Co., its Scottish agent, and also took over the business of Joseph Nall & Co. Ltd, its agent in Manchester.[10]

These were small firms, geographically confined and therefore not conflicting with the requirement imposed on the four main-line railway companies by the 1921 Act to maintain healthy competition but without invading each other's territory. Because Carter Paterson's and Pickfords' operations covered the whole country, no one company could enter into a deal with either of them, although the LMS toyed with the idea for a time, without infringing the statute. So when discussions got round to an arrangement with the two cartage firms, the negotiations had to be conducted in terms of a joint agreement with all four companies. The protracted negotiations between the two sides reveal that the united front presented to the public, in parliamentary inquiries and elsewhere, by the general managers of the four main-line railway companies was not always preserved behind the scenes.

The earliest evidence relates to a private discussion between the LMS and Pickfords.[11] Before the print was dry on that company's Act, the firm was in touch, inquiring how the LMS proposed to implement its new powers. The goods officers of the LMS were debating the same point. One proposal was for the creation of a subsidiary operating company, perhaps built on Pickfords as the nucleus. To meet the objection that an arrangement with Pickfords would infringe the 1921 Act, it was suggested that the scheme would do no more than restore to Pickfords its former agency agreement with the London & North Western, the chief constituent company of the LMS. Special pleading did not impress the company's legal officers, who insisted that the proposal was *ultra vires*. A more ingenious scheme was floated next. By then the LMS was supposed to be negotiating on behalf of all four companies with the Proprietors of Hay's Wharf for a half-share, to be subscribed equally between them, in Hay's Wharf Cartage Company and in Pickfords. But while doing so, it was simultaneously pursuing a separate deal for itself whereby the LMS would purchase a stake in the Proprietors of Hay's Wharf and so by virtue of its place in the holding company gain a more advantageous position in respect of the operating companies. The others, when they learnt about it, were not amused, especially as all through these proceedings Stamp, the chairman of the LMS, was assuring Milne, general manager of the GWR, that he was being kept fully in the picture! It is not surprising that negotiations proceeded cautiously between companies already sufficiently suspicious of each other for a traffic-sharing scheme proposed at one stage of the proceedings to be abandoned because no company could trust the others to abide by any agreement. And not without reason, since the LMS had already been temporarily tempted by a proposal from Pickfords that the firm might raid the other companies' territories by means of road deliveries from railheads within the company's own area, thereby circumventing the spirit, but not the letter, of the 1921 Act.

Ford, at Paddington, was also considering how the railways' new road powers should be exercised. In February 1929 he suggested to Ballantyne, his counterpart at Euston, that the main-line companies might with equal profit follow the example of the London bus and underground combine and devise a similar scheme for parcels and merchandise traffic. He proposed that the four companies should pool their cartage resources in London, take in a couple of the leading carriers and establish a powerful group which would provide a single and comprehensive service for the whole area. Later other road companies could be absorbed and the scheme extended to all major provincial centres. From such a position of strength they could expect to 'obtain or retain a much greater control of the traffic passing than we shall if we continue our present policy of fighting the Road Carriers for individual traffics'. Ballantyne's response was shrewdly cautious. He saw positive advantages in a pooling scheme, in association with Pickfords or Carter Paterson, especially since, as he saw it, the railway companies were by their present policies in many cases actually financing their direct competitors. The long-distance road services of many haulage firms were, he believed, in practice subsidised out of revenue they earned by performing local cartage services for the railways. To deny them such earnings would strike a sound blow at the opposition. But he also saw two major drawbacks. One affected all four companies: customers could well argue that because the railway companies controlled the road firm making a collection or delivery for them, it really made very little difference whether the traffic was directed by rail or by that firm's road services, with the result that even less traffic might go by rail. The second drawback arose from the special position of the LMS. It carried more merchandise than the other companies and was better located to effect collection and delivery in London. The LNER was more concerned with coal, while the GWR cartage services entailed a long and expensive haul from Paddington to central London and the City. The LMS, therefore, stood to lose most and gain least: in return for giving up the whole of its cartage revenue to a pool, it would receive only a quarter of any profit. Ballantyne's was in part a sectional view, but he could also see the wider perspective. Other railway officers could see only the losses. The majority of goods managers and cartage officers who met in the early months of 1930 to discuss the possibility of a working arrangement with Pickfords and Carter Paterson, with whom separate negotiations were being conducted, largely by Milne from Paddington, could find little merit in the proposal. They foresaw no economies emerging but only further delays to deliveries already under pressure for swifter dispatch. Co-operation would be preferable to competition, but they would not commit themselves further.

The operational staff were clearly unwilling to give up their cartage activities to the sort of pool envisaged by Ford. Equally there is no evidence of enthusiasm for a more limited arrangement with Carter Paterson or Pickfords. Much of the impetus behind the negotiations seems to have depended on the personal interest and initiative of Stamp and Milne and as each at times had different, even conflicting, views of what was being negotiated, and Milne tended to take offence on occasions at what he regarded as imperious behaviour by Stamp, their private relations were perhaps not conducive to rapid progress. Not, indeed, until the beginning of 1931 was a formal offer made for a half-share in the cartage interests of Pickfords and the Hay's Wharf Cartage Company, at this stage, that is, excluding travel and other activities from the deal. The same terms were offered to Carter Paterson. The intended scheme was for the two sides to float a joint holding company which would control four regional operating companies.[12] The new combine would convey short-distance traffic by road and receive the cartage work currently passed to outside firms, while in return it would endeavour to restore to rail the maximum possible long-distance traffic. Carter Paterson agreed but after some months' delay, while the Port of London Authority unsuccessfully promoted a Bill by which it would have acquired some of the firm's wharfs, the Proprietors of Hay's Wharf declined the offer. Pickfords was an integral component of the scheme, so negotiations were dropped.

It was a further eighteen months before a deal was finally concluded. In the interval the railway companies could observe with some satisfaction the trend of official pronouncements concerning the future development of road haulage. Both the Royal Commission on Transport and the Salter Report opted for the control of road transport, by a mixture of heavier duties on motor goods vehicles and a system of licences for their operators, and the substance of their recommendations was embodied in the Road and Rail Traffic Bill which was presented to Parliament in the spring of 1933. The resulting Act promised some relief to the railway companies, by causing road transport costs to rise, but also to the large haulage firms which had equally complained about the hit-and-run tactics of the shoe-string end of the industry. They, too, could plan more securely for the future and it was this turn of events which, together with a change of attitude within Hay's Wharf, seems to have given the final push to completion. Rumours spread that some of the leading road firms, including Tilling, Rudd, Sutton, as well as Pickfords and Carter Paterson, were planning a road transport pool in London. Certainly it was following a meeting in July 1932 between Heaton, chairman of Tilling, and Milne, who was now handling the negotiations in place of Stamp, at which such possibilities were discussed that the railway companies revived their bid and raised the stakes to the 100 per cent purchase of both Carter Paterson and Pickfords. Even so another twelve months passed before the deal was closed, following dark hints that Pickfords might be lost to a rival and possibly hostile bidder.

The Hay's Wharf Cartage Company, Pickfords, including all of its operations, and Carter Paterson became the joint property of the four main-line railway companies from 1 July 1933 and subject to their management control from the October. Hay's Wharf Cartage Company became a holding company only, initially as the means through which the two operating companies, Pickfords (with which to all practical purpose the cartage interests of Hay's Wharf had long been merged) and Carter Paterson, were supervised, and ultimately as the agency through which the rail companies' road haulage empire was erected and overseen. Each of the railway companies contributed a quarter of the purchase price and each therefore participated in the management of the haulage firms. The four general managers joined all three boards, Stamp as chairman of Hay's Wharf Cartage Company and of Pickfords, Milne as chairman of Carter Paterson. James Paterson was reappointed managing director of Carter Paterson and W. J. Elliott was promoted to become general manager of the other two companies. In December 1933, L. H. Baxendale resigned from Pickfords' board, thereby ending the family's link with the business which had lasted for almost 120 years. Various joint management committees were also appointed, not to oversee day-to-day affairs but to co-ordinate traffic activities and other matters. There was no attempt to impose strict terms of operations through the railway directors. The general managers were left with considerable freedom and Elliott certainly used it, combined with his own skill and energy, to take Pickfords forward on a major phase of expansion.[13]

The same ambivalence which characterised the railway companies' approach to the purchase of Pickfords and Carter Paterson was continued in their subsequent dealings with the two firms. Their overriding interest was their rail traffic, to protect what they had and to win back as much as possible of that which had been lost to road transport. The railway companies were uncomfortable, possibly unwilling participants in the world of road transport and their prevailing outlook led to a dilemma which could never be satisfactorily resolved. To the railways the purpose of Pickfords' and Carter Paterson's road operations was to draw the teeth of competing, independent hauliers: it was not to draw traffic from the railway and nothing was to be done which would in any way jeopardise the remaining railway traffic. The two propositions were, of course, incompatible: road services which were sufficiently successful to beat off competitors could not fail to attract traffic from the railway; conversely, as long as these competitors flourished the railways' traffic was at risk. Instead of following the logic of the argument, the railways expected the haulage companies to be 'railway minded', to put their own interests second and divert all possible, especially long-distance, traffic to the railway. Given the conflict in logic, it is not surprising that the two sides were soon at loggerheads in the joint management committees concerning appropriate roles and traffics.[14]

The railway companies had a substantial interest in long-distance household removals and looked forward to an increase in rail removals as a result of the new arrangement with Pickfords. The plan was for Pickfords to perform local services, packing and conveyance to the station, and when asked for a through road rate to supply the road/rail rate in addition. But hopes were not fulfilled; Pickfords' road removals increased while those of the railways stagnated. Harsh words were exchanged. Pickfords was accused of not being 'rail minded', and the railways tried to insist that all removals over 50 miles should be conducted by rail unless customers expressly stipulated, in writing, conveyance by road. Pickfords replied that customers preferred the superior speed and convenience of removal by road and, of no less importance, insisted that to comply with the railways' requirement would destroy its 'back-loads' principle, which had successfully frustrated an attempt by the Furniture Warehousemen and Removers Association to set up a clearing house scheme on the equivalent basis, and ultimately ruin its entire removals business. And if Pickfords fell the railways would still not benefit, as customers would simply employ another road firm. When requested deliberately to overquote in cases where both the firm and the railways were asked to tender for a job, Pickfords flatly refused.

Meat and chilled produce was another traffic into which road operators, Pickfords as much as any other, had bitten deeply, and was another source of dissension. To protect their own dwindling meat traffic, the railways, in 1936, bought the firm of Garlick, Burrell & Edwards. One of this firm's principal activities was the supply of contract road vehicles for the conveyance of meat and other chilled produce for the Union Cold Storage Company. One purpose was to acquire the road contract for the subsidiary companies, another was to transfer the maximum proportion of long-distance traffic to the railways. The purchase was made subject to an agreement[15] that all meat transported from London to places lying to the north and west of a broad arc stretching roughly from Exeter through Swansea and then eastwards through Nottingham to King's Lynn would be consigned by rail. And to ensure that the conditions of the sale were fulfilled, detailed consignment schedules were extracted in Liverpool and London, for each year from 1933 to 1939 and for each firm in the Union Cold Storage group, despite the very heavy clerical expenses incurred. The railways seemed satisfied that they received all the traffic they should have done, but whether the cost was worth it might be doubted.

A test case of the rail companies' attitude to long-distance road haulage and their willingness to tackle realistically the rival operations of the Bouts–Tillotson group, which carried between London and Lancashire and the West Riding, and similar groups, about which great fears were expressed, was an experimental trunk haulage service between London and Manchester. After several months of vacillation, wondering whether a road/rail container service at concessionary rates might not after all be sufficient, it was eventually decided to go ahead. The trunk was performed by Pickfords, with Carter Paterson and one of its subsidiaries undertaking collection and delivery in London and Manchester respectively. The service began in February 1934 but although instructed to take less than economic rates if necessary in an effort to strike at the opposition it was so hedged around with restrictions as to be doomed to failure before it started. Pickfords insisted that the trunk haul required at least nine new, modern diesels capable of hauling a 10-ton pay-load, but the railway companies refused to sanction the requisite expenditure. Instead the firm had to make do with two smaller vehicles taken off another service and one spare. Neither the new service nor the rates to be charged were to be publicised – even within the railway system it was to remain a secret to anyone lower than district officer. Only a 'discreet' and highly selective canvass for traffic was permitted and railway customers who also sent some traffic by road were not to be approached for that traffic in case they switched the remainder from the railway. Not surprisingly the service ran at a continual loss and was abandoned after fifteen months. Only the LNER was willing to consider an aggressive, fully resourced road service, recognising that although some rail traffic would inevitably be diverted, that was going to be lost in any case and at least the service would be under railway control. But the rest could not be persuaded that this would be a profitable use of railway capital. Meanwhile the Traffic Commissioners issued more and more vehicle licences for the trunk routes, explicitly refusing to concede, in the Bouts–Tillotson appeal case,[16] the railways' claim that long distance traffic was adequately provided for by themselves.

The principle that railway interests came first was reiterated in respect of parcels traffic. This was highly rated by the railways, on the traditional policy, preserved in the revised tariff schedules introduced in 1928, that traffic was charged according to its intrinsic value, 'what the traffic will bear', and fell an easy prey to road transport's 'cost plus profit' formula in which, where there was no exceptional risk, cost was determined by ease of stowage and handling. In order to assist railway competition with road transport, the Road and Rail Traffic Act introduced the principle of 'agreed charges' whereby a special low rate approximating to that by road was conceded to firms which contracted to dispatch all their traffic by rail.[17] The railways collected some useful business in this way, but their gain was their subsidiaries' loss. Suttons, purchased by the railways in 1935, specialised in packed parcels and suffered the loss of several thousand pounds' worth of revenue as a result of the railways' actions. Suttons' board minutes for these years crackle with thinly veiled anger at the railways' behaviour, complaining bitterly of 'Railway Aggression' and demanding stridently, 'Are we partners or rivals ?'[18]

As well as trying to sort out relationships with their subsidiary companies, the railways were also worried about what the proper relationship ought to be between them and independent road operators. Both Pickfords and Carter Paterson, for example, provided services to the arch-enemy, the Bouts–Tillotson group, and also received services in return. To continue them smacked of fostering the opposition, yet to withdraw them might provoke their rivals to go all out for a fully independent service. The whole approach was again totally negative, even though Pickfords and Carter Paterson earned a fair net revenue from the exchange of services. The decision eventually taken was to retain existing links, chiefly in order to be in a position to influence the activities of mushrooming clearing houses and incipient schemes of nationwide organisation in the industry. This suspicion of non-associated firms was inevitably transmitted to them. To the rest of the road haulage industry Pickfords and Carter Paterson were railway controlled, serving a different interest and not easily accepted. Some doubts were cleared when both firms joined the National Conference of Express Carriers in 1938[19] and subsequently played a leading role in it, but even after the war a legacy of distrust remained.

Clearly the railway companies' excursion into road haulage could not reverse their decaying financial condition. Their problems were too deep-rooted for that and lay as much, if not more, in the depressed condition of the economy which denied the railways the heavy mineral traffic, especially coal, which had underpinned their prosperity in the past, together with the statutory constraints imposed upon them, as in the intrusion of road transport. And even in the road haulage industry itself, in which it built up a considerable empire, it never achieved a position of dominance from which to impose its will. As late as 1938, the combined motor fleet of the railway companies and their road haulage subsidiaries totalled at the most 15,000 vehicles, only about 18 per cent of the professional haulage fleet, vehicles awarded an 'A' category licence under the 1933 Act, and less than 3 per cent of the total number of vehicles on the road. The vast majority were traders' own-user vehicles, qualifying for 'C' category licences, which together conveyed between 70 and 80 per cent of aggregate road traffic. The bulk of road traffic was, therefore, beyond the railways' grasp no matter how many haulage firms they bought up. And in an industry populated by a large number of very small operators, the average fleet size among professional hauliers being less than three in 1938 and there being only twenty-two fleets of 100 vehicles or more, the chances of attaining a dominant share of the remaining 20–30 per cent of road traffic were indeed remote.[20]

This is not to say, however, that the railway companies' move was an error of judgement, a diversion of resources which might have been employed elsewhere more effectively, in electrification schemes, for example, as the Royal Commission on Transport suggested and historians have agreed. That particular counter-factual can not be pursued here, but, to pose another one, it is difficult to believe that the actual level of railway goods' traffic would have been no different, at least as far as diversions to road haulage were concerned, had Pickfords and Carter Paterson, the only two major firms in the industry, not been acquired. What margin of difference they made could only be a matter of speculation. But one thing is clear, the road haulage subsidiaries more than paid their way and made a useful contribution, which could have been more had they been given their head, to the railways' revenue account. The railway companies claimed to look for a return of 6–7 per cent on their road transport investments,[21] in line with rates of return claimed for motorised road transport generally,[22] and by and large they received it. By 1938 some £14m. had been invested in road transport on which an average yield, embracing both share and loan capital, of about 9 per cent was earned, but only about 5 per cent on that part of it, £4·5m., employed in road haulage. Within this latter category, Pickfords was the clear leader: in 1934 its rate of return on share capital was 3½ per cent, rising to 10½ per cent in 1938, when the average return inclusive of loan capital reached 7 per cent, and almost 12 per cent in 1939.[23] It remained a profitable enterprise throughout the period of railway ownership. To suggest, therefore, that the 'road transport undertakings of the railways brought in little additional revenue' is well wide of the mark.[24]

Whatever the verdict on the success or otherwise of the railways' investment in road haulage, there is no doubt that the benefit to Pickfords was enormous. The railways' great stock of property could be drawn on, at favourable rents, for furniture depositories and office developments. Guarantee bonds against stocks of rail tickets were no longer required and Pickfords also received advertisement space at railway stations. The movement of heavy loads by road over railway bridges was eased. All of these smoothed operations but were insignificant when compared with the flow of capital which the railway companies pumped into their subsidiaries. In December 1933 the LMS minuted the opinion that all possible road haulage concerns of substance should be bought, preferably through the agency of the Hay's Wharf

Cartage Company. In the years which followed a recognisable version of this policy was implemented as H. Bentley & Co. (Bradford) Ltd, Chaplins Ltd, Coulson & Co. Ltd, Crouchers Ltd, Express Transport Service (Wellingborough) Ltd, Garlick, Burrell & Edwards Ltd, Shepard Bros Ltd, Swift Parcel Delivery Ltd, Sutton & Co. Ltd, Sutton & Co. (Manchester) Ltd, Venn & McPherson Ltd, and a host of smaller fry were gathered into the net. The majority of these concerns were attached to Pickfords, which thus enjoyed the heady experience of company accumulation and rapid business growth. Property was modernised, notably a new mechanised parcels depot at Willow Walk and a new wharf at Cowes for the expanded Isle of Wight trade, and the motor fleet was extensively overhauled and expanded. The rest of the 1930s were not depression years for Pickfords.

The outbreak of war in 1939 brought a return to the traumatic conditions of twenty-five years before. Vehicles and staff were lost to the war effort and petrol and rubber were again in short supply. Apart from special removals, like the transfer of the BBC to Bristol, Pickfords again secured government contract work and contributed its quota of vehicles to the national meat pool.[25] The total business remained profitable, but the parcels side slumped badly. Sutton's board minutes recount a sad tale of collapsing traffic, disruption due to air-raid damage and trading losses in the years 1940–3, compared with a profit of £32,000 in the last year of peace.[26] The Carter Paterson organisation, to which Suttons was attached, also came under severe pressure. During the 1930s that firm's services had been extended, especially in the provinces, and although the intention was to avoid overlap with Pickfords there was nevertheless considerable duplication. Such luxury could no longer be afforded.

By 1943 several of Carter Paterson's subsidiary operating companies had been suspended and in the November measures were introduced for the complete merger of both Pickfords' and Carter Paterson's parcels services in the London area under the management of W. J. Elliott. Receipts were to be pooled and to facilitate the arrangement the ownership of Carter Paterson was transferred from the railways to the Hay's Wharf Cartage Company. The details of the rearrangement are not available but it evidently took the form of a ruthless economy drive, whatever was necessary to restore the parcels business to profitability. James Paterson, who for several years had been managing director of Carter Paterson, promptly resigned because of what he regarded as a total abnegation of the principles on which that firm had been built up. He explained to the board:

Carter Paterson has always been a business of character. It places 'service to the public' first, trusting that reward would follow. In many years of peace it followed but, – in addition, the character brought a unique fame. The public policy, arising out of modern tendency and accelerated by the war imposes changes. This makes it necessary for me to modify my hope which has been to hand on the torch to a much younger man who would understand that character, preserve it, and enhance the fame. In the future I hope that this character may be so strong as to prevail over any policy which puts money profit first. Such a change would have an adverse psychological effect on the whole of those who are preserving the character of Carter Paterson. Such a policy would be retrograde because I believe that the tendency of public utility services will be towards emphasis on service, efficient service, but not based on private profit.[27]

The reorganisation of the London parcels business into a joint service was introduced on 1 March 1944, and then progressively extended to the rest of the country. The following year it was expanded to include the home counties and, with the return of peace, a full national road parcels service, again under Elliott's management, was launched on 1 January 1946 as the 'Carter Paterson and Pickfords Joint Parcels Service'. Based on the Carter Paterson organisation, it incorporated all the various parcels delivery firms which had been acquired since 1933.[28] Trunk services linked the sixty-six regional depots with London and with each other. When introduced, the joint parcels service employed a fleet of 1,150 motors, 300 horse vans and a staff of 4,500.

By the end of the war, the Hay's Wharf Cartage group, in which Pickfords was the dominant element, had developed into a powerful trading concern.[29] Its range and scale of transport services were unrivalled, it promoted travel and also possessed a high degree of self-sufficiency. In addition to parcels, its haulage services included household removals, heavy haulage, tank haulage, contract hire and special contracts like that servicing multiple retail grocery chains. The transport of meat still remained under government control. The servicing of the motor fleet and horse vans was undertaken internally, by the Express Motor & Body Works Ltd at Enfield, a subsidiary of Carter Paterson, and the Benefit Tyre Company Ltd, which belonged to Pickfords. Travel had become big business; during the war the railway companies had agreed to buy Thos Cook & Son Ltd, which they did through the agency of Hay's Wharf Cartage Company. The group's travel business was now concentrated on Cooks, and Pickfords' travel service reverted to a commission role, although its alliance with removals was preserved. Shipping and forwarding overseas, including air freight, was undertaken through other subsidiaries, England's & Perrott's Ltd and Hernu, Peron & Stockwell Ltd, again businesses acquired since 1933.

In 1946, therefore, the Hay's Wharf Cartage group stood poised, well placed to challenge the postwar transport world. But events took a different course. Already a new Transport Bill was being discussed in Parliament, designed to achieve compulsorily through the agency of the state that integration of transport, especially between road and rail, which voluntary measures had so far failed to produce. The Transport Act of 1947 took the railways into public ownership, and with them their vast array of subsidiary activities. Ironically enough, had Pickfords not belonged to the railways it could have escaped nationalisation as the majority of its operations fell outside the main range of road services to be taken over. As it was, it was swept into the net along with the rest. The following year Pickfords came under the authority of the Road Transport Executive of the British Transport Commission and from 1 January 1949 it entered a new and continuing career as a part of the public sector of the economy.

During the thirty years since nationalisation Pickfords has undergone many dramatic changes, which can be briefly recorded.[30] Travel has retained a minor role, preference being given to Cooks, but since that firm's return to private enterprise Pickfords' own travel service has come back strongly. Parcels, contract hire and meat were, however, all lost, sooner or later, to other parts of the public road haulage sector. British Road Services was organised into eight divisions and Pickfords became the nucleus of the eighth, Special Traffics Division, concerned with household removals, tank haulage and heavy haulage. Several other firms dealing with Special Traffics were merged with it so that Pickfords' own operations cannot, from the available public record, be separately identified. So matters remained until denationalisation, following the Transport Act of 1953, resulted in the creation of a number of public operating companies, including BRS (Pickfords) Ltd to conduct the former business of the Special Traffics Division. The dismantling of the British Transport Commission took Pickfords, in 1963, into the control of the Transport Holding Company, from which, in 1969, it was transferred to and remains a part of the National Freight Corporation.

   Internal reorganisation has accompanied changes in external control. In 1964 the firm resumed the title of Pickfords Ltd and in the late 1960s its three main branches of activity, household removals, tank haulage and heavy haulage, were converted into separate operating companies, controlled by Pickfords Ltd. Since 1970 the firm has been dismembered. Pickfords Heavy Haulage Ltd and Pickfords Tank Haulage Ltd have been hived off completely, transferred to separate functional divisions of the National Freight Corporation. Pickfords Removals Ltd, with its ancillary Pickfords Travel Service Ltd, now survives as the legal heir of the Pickfords of Poynton.

REFERENCES: CHAPTER 9

1 The major inquiries were *SC on Transport*, Second Report and Evidence, PP, 1918, vol. IV; *SC on Transport* (*Metropolitan Area*), PP, 1919, vol. VII; Ministry of Transport, *Report of the Committee on Road Conveyance of Goods by Railway Companies* (Cmd 1228), PP, 1921, vol. XVII; *RC on Transport*, which produced two interim reports and evidence (Cmd 3365) (Cmd 3416), PP, 1929–30, vol. XVII, and a final report, *The Co-ordination and Development of Transport* (Cmd 3751), PP, vol. XVII; and Ministry of Transport, *Report of the Conference on Rail and Road Transport* (Salter Report), 1932.

2 The best account is still G. Walker, *Road and Rail* (London: Allen & Unwin, 1942); for more recent summaries, H. J. Dyos and D. H. Aldcroft, *British Transport* (Leicester: Leicester University Press, 1969; Harmondsworth: Penguin Books Ltd, 1974), chs 11, 12, and Barker and Savage, *Economic History of Transport*, chs 6–8; K. G. Fenelon, *Transport Co-ordination* (London: King, 1929), is a useful contemporary view. Here and in *The Economics of Road Transport* (London: Allen & Unwin, 1925), Fenelon tends to the 'road interest' stance whereas C. E. R. Sherrington, *The Economics of Rail Transport in Britain* (London: Edward Arnold, 1928), Vol. II, pp. 286–300, adopts wholeheartedly the railway companies' position, a not surprising posture from the secretary of the Railway Research Service. There are useful files containing propaganda of both sides at PRO/BTHR Rail 258/383, Rail 424/27. It has to be emphasised that only that part of the debate which concerned road haulage and therefore has a bearing on the history of Pickfords is treated here.

3 F. J. C. Pole, *His Book* (printed privately, 1968), chs 17, 18; for the parliamentary proceedings on the Bills, *Parliamentary Debates*, 5th series, 1928, vol. 214, cols 301–59, 507–71, and vol. 219, cols 2543–626.

4 Wallace, 'Road transport operations of the British Railways . . ., chs 9–13.

5 Memo from Ford, 8 August 1928, PRO/BTHR Rail 258/383, pt 3.

6 H. Morrison, *Socialisation and Transport* (London: Constable, 1933).

7 Pole, *His Book*, p. 97.

8 J. Hibbs, *The History of British Bus Services* (Newton Abbot: David & Charles, 1968), pp. 99 ff.; for a summary of the road passenger groupings, *The Transport World*, 19 April 1934, pp. 203–9.

9 Ministry of Transport, *Railway Returns*, appendix 5, 1929–33, appendix 6, 1934–8.

10 ibid.; and successive issues, from 1933, of the *Universal Directory of Railway Officials and Railway Year Book* (London: Directory Publishing Co.).

11 The following is based on files belonging to Pickfords and the LMS, PRO/BTHR Rail 1133/141, 425/11, 425/12, 425/14, 431/15, 431/46, and files belonging to James Milne, general manager of the GWR, G1/72256 (19), Pickfords Removals Ltd.

12 This was the device employed when the LMS took a half-share in its Scottish agent, Wordie & Co., PRO/BTHR Rail 425/14.

13 The rest of this chapter draws generally on the board minutes, 1933–47, of the Hay's Wharf Cartage Company, Pickfords and Carter Paterson, Pickfords Removals Ltd.

14 Minutes of the joint management committee meetings, 1933–45, at the Railway Clearing House, PRO/BTHR Rail 1080/614–16. This attitude was not, of course, confined to road haulage, and was pursued in other, similar circumstances, notably in respect of air services, see J. King, 'Railway involvement in air transport in the British Isles, 1929–39', paper read to the

Transport History Conference, September 1977, and more generally Dyos and Aldcroft, *British Transport*, ch. 13.

15 Milne's file concerning Garlick, Burrell & Edwards, G1/84766, Pickfords Removals Ltd.

16 *Railway Gazette*, 19 February 1937.

17 The principle of agreed charges was introduced in section II of the Act; it did not stipulate the condition that a firm had to contract to send all its traffic by rail for the special rate to apply, but this seems to have been the way in which the railways implemented it.

18 Suttons' board minutes, 1935–9, with an especially vitriolic minute 26 June 1936, Pickford Removals Ltd.

19 C. S. Dunbar, 'Express Carriers. How private enterprise formed a national network', paper read to the midlands section of the Institute of Transport, 3 October 1967.

20 Walker, *Road and Rail; Fourth Annual Report of the Licensing Authorities, 1937–8* (London: HMSO), pp. 141–3.

21 See the various railway files concerned with the purchase of road haulage companies, PRO/BTHR Rail 425/11, 431/46, and for particular companies, Carter Paterson Rail 425/12, Chaplins Rail 390/1004, Hay's Wharf Cartage Company Rail 431/15, Suttons Rail 390/1014, Wordie & Co. Rail 425/14.

22 J. L. Grumbridge, 'The co-ordination of inland transport in Great Britain' (unpublished PhD thesis, University of London, 1939), p. 52, citing the *Motor Transport Year Book*.

23 Calculated from *Railway Returns*, appendix 6, 1934–8; the 1939 figure is from the *Railway Gazette*, 3 May 1940.

24 Dyos and Aldcroft, *British Transport*, p. 336. The statement there that in 1936, 'road transport operations carried out by the railways made a net profit of only £122,000', supporting an argument that capital invested in road transport would have been better spent in electrification, is strictly true as quoted, but it relates only to the railways' *own direct* road operations and excludes the £967,662 receipts from dividends and interest earned by their investments in road transport undertakings. See *Railway Returns*, 1938, Table A.1 – Summary table of financial statements, miscellaneous receipts, interest and dividends from investments in other undertakings, which, from the figures, cannot include interest on loan capital, and *Railway Returns*, 1936, appendix 6, from which the figure quoted above is calculated.

25 C. I. Savage, *Inland Transport* (London: HMSO; Longman, Green, 1957).

26 Suttons' board minutes, Pickfords Removals Ltd.

27 Carter Paterson board minutes, 29 November 1943, Pickfords Removals Ltd.

28 Appendix 2.3; also *Motor Transport*, 22 March, 19 April, 10 May 1947.

29 Appendix 2.4 for the constituent members of the group, excluding Cooks.

30 This summary is based on the published reports and accounts of the British Transport Commission, 1948–62, the Transport Holding Company, 1963–73, and the National Freight Corporation since 1969. Nationalisation and after in road haulage will have an interesting history, but one which will have to wait until the passage of time releases the relevant material from the thirty-year rule.

10

Conclusion

The decades of Pickfords' history which have now been surveyed witnessed a series of sharp breaks in the technology of inland transport. Turnpikes raised the quality of road transport services without distorting their organisation, but the canal, railway and motor vehicle all led to a substantial restructuring of the transport industry. The elements of continuity are few: many former turnpike roads are now replaced by motorways and bypasses; dreams of reviving canal transport still remain largely dreams; the railway is cut back and many of its parts reduced to car parks, nature trails or plain dereliction. Among the shades of transport past, Pickfords stands out as a living reality.

Yet in one branch of transport, road haulage, which might be considered to have been transformed more than any other, there is a striking similarity between the modern and the former shape of the industry. In the eighteenth century, road haulage divided into three groups of operators, London carriers, inter-provincial carriers and local carriers, categories which fit broadly the threefold distinction recognised by the 'A', 'B' and 'C' licence classifications of the 1933 Road and Rail Traffic Act. The 'C' classification was confined, of course, to own-use traders, but their operations were essentially local and to that extent compare with the local carriers of the pre-railway industry. The London carriers of the eighteenth century do, however, relate fairly closely to the 'A' licensees, public hauliers operating large fleets and specialising in the long-distance trade. The London carrier specialised in long-distance freight, his loadings were heavier than others', his wagons larger and the distances they travelled greater. He accounted for a much larger share of aggregate ton/mileage than the relatively small number of such operators would at first suggest. The same has been true of the 'A' licence operators. Although their vehicles represented, in 1958, only 10 per cent of the national haulage fleet, they were the most intensively used, were predominant among the heavier vehicles and contributed a more than proportionate share of total ton/mileage.

And the parallel extends further, to typical traffic movements. As
in the eighteenth century, the movement of goods has remained predominantly local. In the 1960s, 70 per cent of all road tonnage travelled
less than 25 miles, a radius of movement strikingly close to the typical
distance travelled by the eighteenth-century carrier.[1]

The predominant feature, however, has been that of change and
for a firm to surmount the changes, as Pickfords has done, has required
an ability to refashion its external form while preserving its inner
identity. The Manchester-to-London road haulage firm of the later
eighteenth century had become by the 1830s the country's premier
canal carrier. A few years later and there was a new personality, that
of railway agent, a transformation soon so complete that some contemporaries could imagine no other. Yet that, too, did not last. The
arrival of the motor vehicle enabled Pickfords to return to its original
sphere of road-based operations to become in the 1930s, when railway-
owned, the 'gentle giant' of motorised haulage. Each new mode of
conveyance was absorbed, so far as possible, and the firm's identity
substantially preserved. Even the long association with the London &
North Western did not result in the firm becoming submerged in it;
clients still consigned 'per Pickford' rather than by any particular
railway company. Its name remained a valuable trading asset.

Because Pickfords managed to retain a prominent position in the
transport industry, it has been able to meet periods of disruption from
a position of relative strength. Railways destroyed the traditional
carrying trade, but Pickfords gained a niche in the railway age. Nationalisation was no less a threat a century later, yet instead of being merged
into the anonymous operations of British Road Services, the Special
Traffics Division was erected around it. While Carter Paterson and
other historic firms were suppressed, Pickfords again survived, with
its name and much of its structure intact, ready to re-emerge, after
denationalisation, as a separate entity. At the times of crucial decision
Pickfords had been in the right shape to come through them, more or
less intact if not unscathed. Although fortune has played its part, so
has the human effort which kept the firm in its position of prominence.
It is in both these conditions that the reasons for Pickfords' long and
successful career are to be found.

Pickfords' history could be written, without undue distortion,
around the careers of three men: Matthew Pickford, Joseph Baxendale
and William Elliott. Each of them played an important part, guiding
the firm through challenging times to new levels of achievement.
Matthew Pickford recognised the opportunity presented by canal
conveyance and exploited it successfully; Joseph Baxendale enabled
Pickfords to negotiate the destructive attack of railways; and William
Elliott, a master of motor transport, supervised the vigorous expansion
after 1933 on which Pickfords' strength rested on the eve of nationali-

sation. In one way or another, potential death blows were averted.

Continuity was sufficiently uncommon in the eighteenth-century carrying trade, as in other spheres of business, for Pickfords to be an exceptional firm even before that century was complete. James Pickford had tried to sell in 1757 but there had been no further alarms. Son followed father, although Matthew Pickford did more than preserve the family business. The firm he handed on to his heirs had been transformed from a traditional London carrier into a 'modern' enterprise, embracing canal as well as road transport, with an extended framework of operations, multiple centres of control and in consequence an increasingly testing task of organisation and supervision. Growth owed something to the favourable economic climate but it was not automatic and probably depended more on Matthew Pickford's own abilities. Again it is important not to stretch the evidence, but he certainly displayed a range of activities not matched by other carriers. By the time of his death Pickfords was one of only two firms in the Manchester-to-London carrying trade to have survived from his father's days, and the only one to have adopted canal conveyance. The firm he passed on was largely his own creation.

Pickfords reflected the contemporary pattern in which businesses were intimately linked with the personality of the owner or a dominant partner. The more successful and exceptional the enterprise, the closer the identification and the less likely it was to survive his death. Individuals rather than institutions determined continuity but a business temperament was not necessarily handed on from father to son. So although after Matthew Pickford's death it is almost instinctive to view the efforts of his successors as deficient, history suggests a more lenient view. They were likely to have to struggle for survival, and the fact that the business was at least preserved was something to their credit. However else they might be judged, in the moment of crisis they selected partners who proved to have the depth of financial and emotional resources which the business required.

The business also required a man of unusual ability. Although Joseph Baxendale would not be placed in the front rank of contemporary entrepreneurs, he was not far behind them. He enjoyed considerable respect and was without doubt the dominant figure in his industry. To his own men he became a legend and his record confirms that they were not in error. Baxendale became Pickfords. His energy and drive restored the firm's flagging fortunes, as he took it to new heights in the canal trade. He was also alive to railways and prompt to adopt the new mode of conveyance. But railways were a technology of the kind which overwhelms rather than extends new opportunities. No matter how well prepared, Pickfords could not have resisted the onslaught of railway competition. On the other hand had it been less well prepared it would doubtless have shared the fate of most other canal carrying firms.

Moreover when it was time to make terms with the railways, Pickfords was, thanks to Baxendale, not empty-handed in the negotiations. Once railway companies had decided to undertake their own goods traffic, there was no possibility of Pickfords mounting any serious competition. It might have had a certain nuisance value but no more. However much the deal with the London & North Western was a compromise, it also had a more positive basis. The London & North Western was itself subject to strong pressure from rival lines and Pickfords could contribute towards meeting that competition. The firm brought traffic and skilled personnel and also, through its national scale of operations, access to parts of the country to which the railway company itself could not penetrate.

To Baxendale, the failure to preserve Pickfords' independence was a defeat. He retired from active management and, having already lost the chairmanship of the London & South Eastern railway, he withdrew to private life. There is no doubt, however, that in the long term the deal with the London & North Western was Pickfords' salvation. While other firms decayed, Pickfords became part of the railway industry. It enjoyed a privileged position, its railway agency work was guaranteed by the London & North Western, and as long as the railway connection persisted Pickfords was more likely to live than to die. The business could be left to take care of itself, as Joseph Baxendale complained in the 1860s, without coming to serious harm. Provided neither side terminated the agency contract, the future was secure. There was some talk of the Baxendales selling out to the London & North Western in 1870 but nothing came of it. For its part the London & North Western, while reducing Pickfords' agency work from time to time, showed no inclination to end the relationship and even in 1901, when Pickfords was set on breaking away, tried to preserve it.

The railway link was also important to Pickfords in another way. Apart from residual canal traffic, the long-distance movement of freight was accomplished by the railways. It was they, not the carrying firms like Pickfords, who provided a nationwide framework of transport services. Large volumes of local traffic remained, railway feeder traffic, rail collections and deliveries and purely urban freight, but for this small local firms would suffice. New transport firms like Carter Paterson and the parcels express companies which grew up after 1850 opened few branches outside London, handling provincial deliveries by way of local agents. One of Pickfords' attractions to the London & North Western had been its spread of local branches and the railway contract preserved a role for them into the twentieth century. Since many branches depended on railway work, they proved something of a burden in the short run when the London & North Western's patronage ceased, but when, in the longer term, road transport revived, Pickfords was the only firm which possessed a fully national organisation.

The value of the protection conferred by the London & North Western agency was only too clearly revealed when in the early years of the twentieth century Pickfords' directors chose to remove it. In view of the progress soon to be made by motor transport it is possible that the agency might not have lasted very much longer anyway, but the actual consequences were dramatic. An already crumbling financial condition received further heavy blows as revenue and profits slumped and a large slice of the firm's capital was withdrawn. In the early 1900s Pickfords came close to foundering, as it had done a century earlier. Again, however, a solution was found, on this occasion a negotiated takeover by its major rival. Although further shocks followed, from the effects of world war and the hardening of motorised competition, it was another forty years before the firm's survival was again at risk.

The revival of road transport resulted from the development of the motor vehicle. A new technology had to be mastered and modes of operation adjusted to it. Neither of these was easy to accomplish, even when not hindered by emotional attachment to horses. The motor engineer was the symbol of the new transport era and Pickfords again had the good fortune to find in one of this breed, W. J. Elliott, a man who could lead the firm into the motor age.

Elliott had been apprenticed to S. Hindley & Son, locomotive engineers, and joined Pickfords in 1905 when the firm bought a number of Hindley steam lorries. Beginning in the motor repair section, he commenced a career with Pickfords which ended in the boardroom. He learnt the business from the bottom, rising steadily through the motor haulage section. For not only was he an excellent engineer, he also proved to be a first-rate business man. His potential was noted in 1920, when he was manager of the motor department, at the time of the sale to Hay's Wharf. He was described to the new owners as more than a very capable steam and petrol engineer, 'a good combination of an engineer and an energetic, shrewd commercial man'.[2]

Technical mastery plus business acumen were the necessary qualities for success in motor haulage, and these Elliott possessed. His commercial responsibilities increased under Hay's Wharf and came to fulfilment from 1933 when he was appointed general manager of Pickfords and the Hay's Wharf Cartage Company by the railway directors. Railway capital and Elliott's drive took Pickfords forward on a new wave of expansion. Although he had left the workbench Elliott retained the common touch and enjoyed the confidence of his staff. In the 1930s and 1940s Pickfords was marked by the stamp of Elliott's personality as decisively as it had been by that of Joseph Baxendale. Elliott was also respected outside the firm. His work for the government during the Second World War earned him some influence in official circles; when the terms for nationalisation were being thrashed out in 1947, Pickfords was not without political weight.

During its long history Pickfords has experienced both success and decline. The transport system has been revolutionised several times, on occasions in a way destructive of even the strongest will to survive. Moreover since transport prospers and stagnates with the rise and fall of the economy, firms engaged in the supply of transport services can only expect shifting fortunes. But within the constraints of market forces and technological change, scope remains for individual qualities of entrepreneurship to be expressed. Fortune has played its part in Pickfords' survival, but the efforts of Matthew Pickford, Joseph Baxendale and William Elliott ensured that the firm could capitalise on it.

REFERENCES: CHAPTER 10

1 *The Transport of Goods by Road* (London: HMSO, 1959); *Survey of the Transport of Goods by Road 1967–1968* (London: Department of the Environment, 1971).
2 Memoranda concerning the sale of Pickfords to the Hay's Wharf Cartage Company, Pickfords Removals Ltd.

Appendix 1

The Financial Record

1.1 AN ESTIMATE OF PICKFORDS' DISTRIBUTED PROFITS, 1817/18 TO 1869/70

The figures which follow have been extracted from two items in Joseph Baxendale's personal papers. One, from which the figures in column 3 are taken, is an annual itemised statement, for the years 1817/18 to 1866/7, of his profit and salary from Pickfords, the value of his investments and other property, interest and dividends thereon, and household and other expenses. The second document is entitled 'Summary of Stock Account from 1st April 1817 to 1st April 1867, with memoranda relative to the commencement of the partnership'. The figures in columns 1 and 2 are recorded in this document as 'Credit of Stock Account', to which is added the note 'Interest not included, placed to the credit of each partner half-yearly'. This suggests that an annual financial balance was struck, recorded in the document only in five-year periods, but nothing is known, beyond the note just quoted, of the accounting practices employed. Even though profits had, by the terms of the partnership agreement, to be reinvested, at least some notional distribution would be required for the charging of interest and the determination of shares on the withdrawal or death of a partner. The figures in columns 1 and 2 therefore appear to be a crude guide to the profit performance of the business during those years.

To test this proposition Baxendale's annual statement of profit from Pickfords, column 3, has been multiplied by his known share in the partnership. The result, column 4, has been aggregated into five-year periods and annual averages, columns 5 and 6. For some periods, those ending 1821/2, 1831/2, 1841/2, 1846/7 and the years 1862/3, 1864/5, 1866/7, the two sets of data fit either exactly or almost so. Others fit less well, and the difference is quite large for the period ending 1826/7 and the year 1865/6, but on the whole they match up quite well. It seems reasonable to conclude that the two sets of independent data support each other sufficiently strongly to justify the tentative use made of them in the text. The figures demonstrate no relationship with any of the available price indices and are presented in current prices.

| | Credit of stock account (£) | | | Estimated distributed profits (£) | | |
| | 1 | 2 | 3 | 4 | 5 | 6 |
Year (1 April–31 March)	Total per five-year period	Annual average	Baxendale's share	Per annum	Annual average	Total per five-year period
1817/18			2,631 (×6)	15,786		
1818/19			2,271	13,626		
1819/20			1,463 (×5)	7,315		
1820/21			2,693	13,465		
1821/22	56,837	11,367	1,326	6,630	11,364	56,822
1822/23			741	3,705		
1823/24			1,487	7,435		
1824/25			2,326	11,630		
1825/26			243	1,215		
1826/27	47,671	9,534	3,355	16,775	8,152	40,760
1827/28			3,185	15,925		
1828/29			2,108	10,540		
1829/30			1,307	6,535		
1830/31			2,647	13,235		
1831/32	57,292	11,458	2,210	11,050	11,457	57,285
1832/33			3,549	17,745		
1833/34			6,035	30,175		
1834/35			4,763 (×4)	19,052		
1835/36			7,157	28,628		
1836/37	104,749	20,949	3,545	14,180	21,956	109,780
1837/38			12,000	48,000		
1838/39			15,096 (×2)	30,192		
1839/40			6,430	12,860		
1840/41			9,577	19,154		
1841/42	123,508	24,701	5,937	11,874	24,416	122,080
1842/43			10,232	20,464		
1843/44			10,316	20,632		
1844/45			5,000	10,000		
1845/46			13,105	26,210		
1846/47	105,864	21,172	14,278	28,556	21,172	105,862
1847/48			6,985	13,970		
1848/49			14,066	28,132		
1849/50			18,868	37,736		
1850/51			16,856	33,712		
1851/52	127,517	25,503	11,086	22,172	27,144	135,722
1852/53			11,979	23,958		
1853/54			8,476	16,952		
1854/55			11,090	22,180		
1855/56			8,102	16,204		
1856/57	126,004	25,200	15,238	30,476	21,954	109,770
1857/58			9,346	18,692		
1858/59			21,924	43,848		
1859/60			15,008	30,016		
1860/61			17,500	35,000		
1861/62	178,599	35,719	12,170	24,340	30,379	151,896

	(Total per annum)		
1862/63	20,011	5,003 (×4)	20,012
1863/64	25,023	4,506	18,024
1864/65	18,624	4,656	18,624
1865/66	20,245	2,411	9,644
1866/67	16,908	4,237	16,948
1867/68	25,310		
1868/69	28,216		
1869/70	41,809		

1.2 STATEMENTS OF NET PROFIT, CARTER PATERSON & CO. AND PICKFORD & CO., 1888–1912

Year (end 30 June)	Carter Paterson & Co. (£)	Pickford & Co. (£)
1888	6,763	
1889	11,743	
1890	—	
1891	6,064	
1892	6,304	
1893	14,598	
1894	16,905	
1895	30,259	
1896	29,742	59,265
1897	28,600	59,225
1898	19,837	32,622
1899	20,345	33,159
1900	15,992	5,073
1901	8,920	
1902	13,948	
1903	28,632	
1904	31,714	
1905	27,693	8,602
1906	24,741	
1907	16,831	
1908	20,542	
1909	31,849	−279
1910	35,986	16,278
1911	38,526	15,435
1912	18,005	

The Carter Paterson figures are taken from the draft accounts supplied to the board and subsequently reported to the annual general meeting, PRO/BTHR Rail 1130/1–3. The returned net profit figure was defined in 1902 as 'after provision for depreciation and payment of interest on loans and debentures'. The firm pursued a very cautious dividend policy, and rapidly built up a large reserve fund.

The Pickford figures are from several sources: those for 1896–1901 are from the draft scheme for amalgamation PRO/BTHR Rail 1130/76; that for 1905 from the year's annual general meeting, PRO/BTHR Rail 1133/1; and those from 1909 from the half-yearly balance sheets and profit and loss accounts PRO/BTHR Rail 1133/144,150. They seem to have conformed to the same principles as those used by Carter Paterson.

1.3 STATEMENTS OF NET PROFIT FOR THE CARTER PATERSON GROUP, 1913–19

Year (end 30 June)	Carter Paterson side (£)	Pickford side (£)
1913	40,581	15,116
1914	24,645	15,944
1915	17,712	10,167
1916	−18,171	7,214
1917	−12,484	8,585
1918	33,497	23,802
1919	82,781	47,570

The Carter Paterson figures are from the draft accounts presented to the joint board and subsequently to the annual general meeting, PRO/BTHR Rail 1130/4–7. The same source contains most of the Pickford figures, which can be checked against a statement of net profits 1912–18, supplied to the Hay's Wharf Cartage Company in 1919, Pickfords Removals Ltd.

1.4 NO USABLE PROFIT FIGURES ARE AVAILABLE FOR 1920–33, WHEN PICKFORDS WAS OWNED BY THE PROPRIETORS OF HAY'S WHARF

1.5 STATEMENTS OF NET REVENUE, HAY'S WHARF CARTAGE/PICKFORDS LTD, 1934–48

Year (end 30 June)	£
1934	20,314
1935	25,491
1936	33,918
1937	47,087
1938	87,533
1939	101,470
1940	191,632
1941	261,169
1942	353,149
1943	479,702
1944	618,573
1945	543,452
1946	644,350
1947	533,430
1948	464,044

These figures are extracted from the draft accounts presented to the Hay's Wharf board; from 1940 onwards they include the profits of the subsidiary companies, Pickfords Removals Ltd.

Appendix 2

Company Groupings

2.1 THE PROPRIETORS OF HAY'S WHARF GROUP, 1933

The Proprietors of Hay's Wharf

Wharfs: Chamberlain's; Cotton's Cold Store; Fenning's; Hay's Wharf & Dock; Mark Brown's and Davis'; New Hibernia & Old Hibernia Cold Stores; Stanton's; Pickford's & Hay's; Wilson Cold Stores & Wine Vaults; Greenbank.

Subsidiaries: Hay's Wharf Cartage Company Ltd; Humphery & Grey (Lighterage) Ltd; John Trapp & Son (Hay's Wharf) Ltd; The London Wharf Co.

Hay's Wharf Cartage Company subsidiaries

Pickfords Ltd; Pickford's & Hay's Wharf Shipping & Forwarding Company; Société Anonyme Pickford's; Pickford's Colonial Inc.; Pickford's (South Africa) Ltd; John Smithers & Son Ltd; Williams Cartage Ltd; Thos Norton & Son Ltd; Robert Hall Ltd; Continental Express Ltd; Norman E. Box Ltd.

Pickford's subsidiaries

London Traction Haulage; J. & H. Lindsay Ltd; James Hardaker Ltd; E. Brier & Sons Ltd; Karrier Parcels Ltd (with Carter Paterson).

2.2 CARTER PATERSON SUBSIDIARIES, 1933

Beans Express Ltd; City & Suburban Carriers Ltd; South Coast Carriers Ltd (which owned Bognor Coal & Transport Company Ltd); Leicester & County Carriers Ltd; Karrier Parcels Ltd (with Pickfords).

2.3 CARTER PATERSON AND PICKFORDS JOINT PARCELS SERVICE: ASSOCIATED COMPANIES

Pickfords Ltd
Chaplins Ltd
Crouchers Ltd
Shepard Bros Ltd
Venn & McPherson Ltd
Express Transport Services (Wellingborough) Ltd
Exeter Express Carriers
A. J. Hewitt & Co. Ltd
Swift Parcel Delivery Service Ltd

Carter Paterson & Co. Ltd
Carter Paterson (Midland) Ltd
Carter Paterson (Southern) Ltd
Carter Paterson (North-Western) Ltd
City & Suburban Carriers Ltd
Herd & Gerner Ltd

2.4 THE HAY'S WHARF GROUP IN 1947

The Hay's Wharf Cartage Company Ltd

Pickfords Ltd   Norman E. Box
Arthur Batty Ltd
Benefit Tyre Company Ltd
H. Bentley & Co. (Bradford) Ltd
Chaplins Ltd
Coulson & Co. Ltd
Crouchers Ltd
Express Transport Service (Wellingborough) Ltd
Garlick, Burrell & Edwards Ltd
A. J. Hewett Ltd
Hughes Bros Ltd
Removals & Storage Ltd
Shepard Bros Ltd
Swift Parcel Delivery Service Ltd
Venn & McPherson Ltd
Southport Engineering Co. Ltd

Carter Paterson & Co.
Beans Express Ltd
England's & Perrott's Ltd
Express Motor & Body Works Ltd
Herd & Gerner Ltd
Tersons
Hernu, Peron & Stockwell Ltd

Bibliographical Note

My borrowings from and my leanings on the work of fellow transport historians will have been apparent through the text and it is hoped that the end of chapter references make adequate acknowledgement of my debt.

The bulk of the primary material on which the study rests is part of the collection of British Transport Historical Records, now housed at the Public Record Office, Kew, London. Most of the Pickford and Carter Paterson records are located there. Other parts of that collection employed are the records of the various canal and railway companies referred to in the text.

Very few records remain with Pickfords itself; those still held relate chiefly to the years 1933–47 and comprise the board minutes of Hay's Wharf Cartage, Pickfords, Carter Paterson, Chaplins and Suttons, together with dealings with the four main-line railway companies. There are some duplicates at Kew. These records are housed at the Head Office, Pickfords Removals Ltd, Great Cambridge Road, Enfield.

I was also kindly allowed to use three collections of private papers. The Baxendale papers, the personal records of Joseph Baxendale, were made available by the late Capt. Guy Baxendale, of Uckfield, Sussex. Mr C. H. Pickford lent me his collection of family papers and the late Hon. Dorothy Pickford lent me the notes, which Mr Pickford now holds, compiled by her sister, the late Hon. Mary Pickford; both are cited as the Pickford papers. And Mr E. Halfpenny allowed me to consult his collection of family papers which relate to the Pickfords' bankruptcy in 1820.

Apart from small manuscript collections, cited in the references, the other main primary source is the parliamentary committee proceedings on railway and other private Bills in the House of Lords Record Office.

I would like to thank the various archivists and keepers of records for their assistance and for permission to consult and quote from the documents in their charge.

Index

Main themes and subjects

Printed and bound by CPI Group (UK) Ltd, Croydon, CR0 4YY

01/05/2025

01858389-0001